PREFACE.

"CAPTAIN, why don't you write a book?"

This question has been often asked me when relating some tale of adventure or humorous anecdote of my sea life.

"For the reason that I know nothing of book writing," I have replied. "A school experience of seventy years ago, cut short at the age of twelve years, was not likely to leave a boy, however bright, with a high order of literary attainment."

But, as years rolled on, after giving up the sea as a profession, I concluded to jot down from memory my quarter-century's sea experience.

The characters are from life, the scenes and incidents as they appeared to me at the time, in a story of a New England boy's career from the age of twelve to thirty-seven.

An orphan at five, on shipboard at twelve, exposed to temptation in every port, subjected to the rough usage and strict discipline of our merchant marine of sixty years ago, serving apprenticeship as boy, ordinary, and able seaman in the forecastle, graduating to third, second, and first officer with quarters in the land of knives and forks, *i. e.* the ship's cabin, and the sacred precincts of the quarter-deck, ending with the command and part ownership of a fine craft; in all that time his feet clear of a ship's plank but twelve months.

There certainly should be something interesting in such an experience.

The old-time sailing ships, with all the incidents connected with them, the captains who commanded and sailed them, the old-time sailors—jolly old sea-dogs—who manned them, are all of the past, and with them departed the glamour and the romance of the sea, never to return.

The march of progress never halts. Steamers have supplanted the old-time sailing ships in a great degree, canvas has given way to machinery and steam, steel and iron have been substituted for wood, sailors are superseded by engineers with their assistants, while the captain and officers of to-day must be proficient in the knowledge of steam and machinery, ere they can hope for a command.

The young men of the present generation know but little of the old-time shipping, or the old sailing-ship days, and in these pages to a certain extent the writer has endeavored to reproduce them.

Nearly all the veteran shipmasters, graduates of the old school, so many of whom I well knew, have furled their sails and dropped anchor, let us hope, in a safe, restful harbor, life's troubled voyage ended.

Some few yet remain, and to all such I give hearty greeting, trusting they will derive much pleasure from a perusal of these pages, which may be to them a reminder of their former lives.

The writer has long since given up the sea as a profession, but the salt sea breeze is still more grateful than the scent of roses, and on the waters of old ocean his happiest days were spent.

Thanking my many friends for their words of encouragement, trusting the work will meet with favor from the public, and be accorded

Ocean Life in the Old Sailing-Ship Days
By Captain John Whidden

TO

CAPTAIN JOSEPH W. CLAPP OF NANTUCKET

DEAR OLD BOY: Although nearly fourscore years have silvered your head, you yet retain your mirth and sense of humor, as evidenced by your frequent letters, which have been to me a source of inspiration. To you, then, in memory of the many pleasant days passed in genial companionship in old Montevideo, S. A., upwards of forty years ago, this work is affectionately dedicated by

THE AUTHOR.

BOSTON, 1908.

a hearty welcome in memory of the bygone days of the old sailing ships, I remain,

Heartily yours,

JOHN D. WHIDDEN.

OCEAN LIFE IN THE OLD SAILING SHIP DAYS

CHAPTER I.
1832-1845

IN THE FORECASTLE.—THE HALF CLIPPER "ARIEL"

I WAS born on High Street in Boston, Mass., in the year 1832, and lost my parents when I was but five years of age. My mother died at Mobile, Alabama, where my father was engaged in business, and my father died in Savannah, Georgia, the year after. Upon their decease, my grandparents having taken charge of my sister and myself, we were brought up in their family at Marblehead, Mass., and I attended the public schools until I attained the age of twelve years.

At this time I was called a very fair scholar, well up in reading, writing, and geography, fair in arithmetic, and intensely interested in books of travel and adventure, while all works treating of the sea, tales of travel in foreign lands, shipwrecks and everything pertaining to the ocean, had a very great fascination for me.

Marblehead being a seaport town, my time, when not in school or employed around the house doing chores, was spent with my companions about the wharves, swimming or climbing about the vessels at the docks, rowing around the harbor in the small boats, or dories, that we would borrow from the various captains or skippers of the fishing craft,—mostly schooners from fifty to ninety tons burthen, engaged in the Grand Banks fisheries, of which at this time there was a fleet of nearly a hundred sail, all hailing from and owned in Marblehead.

What a treat for us boys when a square rigger—as we designated all barks, ships, and brigs—came sailing into the harbor, perhaps from Cadiz, Spain, laden with salt for the fishing fleet to take to the Grand Banks of Newfoundland for their spring fares, and when she hauled into the wharf to discharge her cargo into the salt sheds, how we youngsters swarmed on board, exploring every nook and cranny of her, climbing over her rigging, daring each other to mount higher and higher, until with a feeling of triumph I at last placed my cap upon the main royal truck, the highest point, and looking down saw the admiring, though envious, gaze of my young companions!

Then, again, to sit around the fo'c'sle after the work for the day was over, to see the sailors at their meals, and hear them spin their yarns, was happiness indeed.

To go to sea, become a sailor, visit foreign lands, and in due time become the captain of a fine ship, this was the goal to be looked forward to, the great aim of our lives. It certainly was of mine, and I judge of all, or nearly all, of my playmates.

My grandparents were not in favor of my adopting a sailor's life, wishing me to learn a trade, but to this I was opposed, and rang the changes upon the advantages of a seafaring life, until they gave way and consented.

Shortly after this decision, on my return from school one day I was ushered into the parlor, where sat a gentleman in conversation with my grandmother, to whom I was introduced. He was Captain James King, of Salem, Mass., and I learned for the first time that I was to join the ship he commanded in two weeks, the ship being the fine new half clipper named the "Ariel," just launched, and lying at Newburyport, bound round to New York to load flour for Liverpool, England, from thence to China, she having been built for a Canton trader.

This was joyful news indeed, and I went out from the parlor, after making my best bow and answering all his questions in a satisfactory manner, the happiest boy in the old town.

During our conversation, my grandmother touched upon my good qualities, and said to Captain King that she did not see how she could part with me, I was so useful and willing to do anything about the house, such a help to her, etc., etc., to all of which I listened in considerable astonishment, for, while my grandmother was one of the best of souls and very fond of me, yet I was constantly getting into trouble, and received more scoldings, no doubt richly deserved, than pettings. In fact, at this time I had fallen into disgrace, and I afterward thought it the predisposing cause of her consent being obtained to my going to sea.

The facts were as follows: At regular intervals during the year, and especially about the holidays, Thanksgiving and Christmas, my grandmother made up and baked what she called a "batch" of pies,—mince, apple, and squash predominating. I was very fond of pie, and at these times I was in great demand to peel and core apples, seed raisins, chop meat and suet for the mince; taking a most active part, and a very willing one, in all that was going on in this line.

9

Then came the baking. Our kitchen was large and roomy, and the fireplace immense. This was before cooking stoves came into use. On the left side of the fireplace was a large brick oven, where all the baking was done, and when this occurred it was in large quantities, about thirty or forty pies constituting a "batch." After baking, they were stored in what was called the "back chamber closet," very large and convenient, having tiers of shelves around it, there to remain until wanted. It was a goodly and attractive sight to my eyes whenever a fresh "batch "was stored away. I longed to get at them, but the old lady, probably feeling that I was not to be trusted when pies were around, always kept the closet locked and the keys stowed safely in her ample pocket. My little bedroom adjoined this chamber, and in going and returning I was obliged to pass through it. Always in the morning I invariably tried this closet door, and always found it locked, but this morning my grandmother had forgotten to lock it, although she had taken out the key! I could hardly credit it. Opening the door I looked in, where lay the rows of pies, temptingly displayed in tiers, shelf over shelf. I would not have stolen money, or *anything else*, but the sight was too much, and I yielded to temptation. I did not dare take a whole pie, as that would be missed at once. To cut one would be open to the same objection, *i. e.* discovery. I pondered awhile how I should enjoy the fruits of my "find" and yet escape detection. A brilliant thought struck me. Slipping down-stairs I entered the kitchen. My grandma was busily engaged, and I could see was likely to be, for half or three quarters of an hour, at least. Hastily smuggling a case-knife into my pocket, I passed out of and around the house and entered by the side door. Creeping softly up the back stairs, in a moment I was again in the closet. Standing on a chair, and taking a pie from the top shelf, knowing these would be the last used, I inserted the thin knife between the upper and lower crusts, and working carefully round was able to lift the top crust sufficiently to enable me to get at and eat all the mince from the inside. Carefully replacing the top crust, and patting the edges down, the pie to a casual observer showed no difference, in the looks, from any other pie. Pleased with my first experiment, I proceeded to try another, and did not finish my feast until I had eaten the insides out of six or seven pies.

Each day I visited the closet and regaled myself on mince or apple pie, taking no note of the number; in short, I was just living on pie. No wonder my dear old grandmother thought my appetite was failing and grew anxious about me, but the end was near!

One day, on my return from school, I found we had company to tea, two or three ladies. This was good news, for company days were red letter days to me, as we always had something extra in the way of cake, preserves, and pies; in short, a great addition to every-day fare.

The tea was ready, the table nicely laid, and the guests seated around it, my grandmother at the head to serve the tea, grandpa at her left, and myself at her right. I can see her now, smiling, and beaming upon her guests, as she glanced around the well-appointed board.

Ann, our old servant, had been commissioned to bring down two or three pies, which were on the hearth in front of the fire, warming. At the right moment one of the pies was placed in front of the old lady. As she took the knife and fork in her hands to cut it, she made a few remarks on how she made her pies, how careful she was to select the ingredients, etc., ending with the query whether Mrs. Jones would prefer apple or mince?

"Well, really, Mrs. Appleton," replied the lady, "they look so nice, I believe I'll take a small piece of each."

"Why, certainly," replied my grandmother, laying her knife upon the pie, which crashed through it like an eggshell!

I shall never forget the feeling of terror that seized me, or the look of astonishment on my grandmother's face, as she turned reproachfully to Ann, and said:

"Why, Ann! You've forgotten to put any mince in this pie," adding, rather sternly, "You may pass me up another pie."

Ann's face was a study. She was a splendid cook, and to be called down before company for not putting mince or apple in pies, and baking them without, was past her comprehension. She could not understand it. Another pie was placed upon the table, and again the old lady started to cut it, meanwhile apologizing for keeping her guest waiting. Same result! Laying down her knife and fork, she looked at my grandpa, and then at me.

Although not a word had been said, I could contain myself no longer and blurted out, "I didn't do it."

This of course was a dead give-away.

My grandfather arose, and taking me by the shoulder marched me to the door, telling me to go to bed, and he would attend to me by and by, which he did, and I lost all appetite for pie for the time intervening between this event and my leaving home.

The illustration facing page 13 shows the home of my grandfather Thomas Appleton, once that of the Revolutionary General John Glover.

Now came the bustle of preparation. The carpenter, old Mr. Jerry Smith, was given the commission to make my little blue sea-chest. As no member of the family had ever been to sea, the old folks were somewhat at a loss as to what I would require, but this was got over by pressing into the service old Captain Edmund Bray, a retired shipmaster, who readily entered into the family councils, and, acting on his suggestions, my outfit was soon completed and packed away in my chest.

On Monday morning, I was to leave home, and taking my books from school Friday night for the last time, I bade the master good-by, spending Saturday with the boys in all their games, it being a holiday.

Sunday I attended church all day, and the following morning said the last good-by, and started for the station with my grandfather. Arriving a little before train time, he spent the interval in giving me good advice, which I am afraid was not listened to as earnestly as it should have been, when handing me my tickets for Newburyport, with six new half-dollars, which were very highly appreciated, money having always been a very scarce article during my school days. I stepped on board the train and in a few moments was speeding away toward my future home, at least it would be my home for a year or more.

Arriving at Newburyport, I hired a conveyance and was driven to the wharf with my chest, there obtaining the first view of the ship in which I was to make my start in life, and, as I took in her trim appearance, and looked aloft at her long, tapering spars, realizing that I was really a member of her crew, a feeling of pride came over me, and all regrets, if I had any, were swept away, and I felt I had made no mistake in adopting a sailor's life.

The first and second officers were on board, with the carpenter, who came out to assist me in getting my chest on board and stowed away in the fo'c'sle, where for the time I was the only occupant, the carpenter having his room aft.

Having got my mattress into one of the upper berths, I got out my blankets and sheets, with "comforter "or spread, and proceeded to make my bed after a home pattern. At this time sheets and pillow-cases were unheard of articles in a ship's fo'c'sle, but of this fact I was not aware, so made my bed as near as I remembered it in my little chamber at home. This being done, I went on deck, making the acquaintance of the first and second officers, by whom I was set to work at odd jobs about deck, sweeping up, and anything I was told to do.

As the crew had not come down from Boston, there was no cooking on board, but the officers and myself got our meals at a place called "Brown's Tavern," but a short distance from the wharf.

A week passed, and I had become quite accustomed to being on shipboard. After having received instructions from the second mate before going aloft, I had won considerable credit by sending down the main royal yard, and did the work in a manner that brought a compliment from him, *i. e.* "an old hand could not have done it better."

This pleased me very much, and I began to consider myself quite a sailor.

But, "pride goeth before a fall."

It was the close, of a drear December day. Snow, rain, and sleet had been falling, and about four in the afternoon I had gone below in the fo'c'sle to get ready to go up to the tavern for supper, when I heard a great commotion on the deck overhead. The companion doors were thrown open, and down rained chests, bags, and hammocks, wet and dirty, followed by the crew who had just arrived on the train from Boston.

There were about twenty men, of all nationalities, and as soon as they landed in the fo'c'sle they began pitching the bags and hammocks into the berths, all talking and swearing, for they were not in good humor, being about as wet as their luggage.

I had drawn up, and was standing on my little chest alongside my berth, when, without any ceremony or asking "by your leave," an old grizzled shellback tossed into my clean berth a wet, dirty bag and hammock.

Although I had stood, half in awe, watching the scene, not venturing a word, this act of old Tom's was too much, and laying my hand upon his arm I remonstrated: "Don't do that! You'll soil my sheets!"

Tom gave me a puzzled look for a moment, and exclaimed, "Who in thunder are you?"

I hastened to assure him that I was a sailor, one of the crew, and that was my berth, and my bed was made up. With a queer look he mounted my sea-chest and glanced into my berth. Never shall I forget his look of wonder, and the ineffable scorn conveyed in his tone as he turned around to his chum, and exclaimed with withering sarcasm, "Well I'm blessed, Joe" (only he did not say "blessed"), "if the beggar ain't got sheets!"

I made no reply, but I felt that in his eyes, at least, I was no sailor, and when they had gone to supper, shortly after, off came the sheets and pillow-cases, which were stored at the bottom of my chest, nevermore to do duty as bedding on that ship.

Two days after, the weather having cleared, the crew came on board, also the pilot and captain, and with a fine westerly breeze sail was made at the wharf, the fasts cast off, and the ship headed for the bar. As soon as crossed, the pilot was discharged, and all sail made, topmast stun'sail booms got up and run out, stun'sails got out and sent up, anchors secured, and everything movable about decks made fast.

All was bustle and excitement attendant upon leaving port, and particularly in this case, as the "Ariel "was a new ship, on her maiden voyage, and many a glance was cast over the ship's side to note her speed. Meanwhile the log was hove, and showing better than ten knot, a general feeling of satisfaction was felt fore and aft.

The sea was comparatively smooth, and everything new to me. I was in my element, long looked forward to, and entered into everything with a will. Where I did not fully understand all orders I went with the crowd, and took note of what was going on, managing to get along very well.

At four o'clock the crew were called aft and the watches chosen, after which the port, or mate's, watch went below to supper, while the starboard, or second mate's, cleared up decks. They put everything in order for the night, while the boys swept up.

At four bells,—six o'clock,—the mate's watch again came on deck to relieve the starboard, who went below for supper, remaining until eight o'clock,—eight bells,—when they again came up, relieving the port watch, who went below until midnight.

I will here state that from four to eight o'clock P. M. is divided into two watches of two hours each, and this changes the watches each night; so that the port watch has eight hours below one night, i. e. from eight to twelve P. M. and from four to eight A. M., while the starboard has eight hours on deck, having only four hours below to sleep, i. e. from twelve midnight until four o'clock A. M. The "dog "watches, as they are called, serve to change the long watches, so that the two get their eight hours below every other night, and it is a rule that the second mate's watch always has the eight hours on deck the first night at sea.

I had been chosen in the second mate's watch, Mr. Henry Fabens's, and went to supper at six, with the rest. It consisted of hash, salt meat, hard ship's biscuit, and tea sweetened with molasses. After supper the men filled their pipes, smoked and "yarned" until eight bells, when they again went on deck, myself with them, to stand my first watch at sea.

The wheel was relieved, the lookout man mounted the steps to the to'gallant fo'c'sle, while the remainder of the watch either paced the deck from the break of the fo'c'sle to the stern of the long boat, or picked out a snug berth, sheltered from the wind, to spin a long "yarn" to while away the four hours that must intervene before they could turn into a warm berth.

Old Tom, who since the sheet and pillow-case business had hardly taken any notice of me, started to do a turn of walking, pacing regularly from the fo'c'sle to amidships and return.

BOYS' DUTIES IN THE FORECASTLE.—AT NEW YORK LOADING FOR
LIVERPOOL

ANXIOUS to ingratiate myself in Tom's good graces, and thinking this a favorable opportunity, I hauled alongside, keeping pace, and strove to engage him in conversation, but was not very successful. He was very quiet, occasionally replying to my questions in gruff tones, until I became somewhat discouraged, and lapsed into silence.

Presently four bells (ten o'clock) were struck aft, and repeated on the bell hung at the break of the to'gallant fo'c'sle. The wheel was relieved and lookouts changed at this hour. It was old Tom's lookout, but he thought, probably, that it would be much more comfortable on the main deck if he could shirk it, and send me up to take his place. The officer of the deck, seeing some one up there, would not know the difference unless he came forward on the fo'c'sle, and as it looked fine, this was not likely.

"Boy, have you had a lookout yet? "he asked, suddenly turning to me.

"No," said I.

"Well, you get up on that fo'c'sle deck, and keep a good lookout. Do you hear?"

"All right," I answered, glad to be assigned a position, although I hardly knew what was required of me.

I mounted the steps to the deck, and the former lookout descended, after asking who sent me. "Tom," I replied.

"Oh, he did! "said he, and made no other remark.

I found it much more exposed than the main deck. The night was dark. The topmast stun'sail having been taken in, the yards were braced forward, while the wind began to freshen and the sea to rise. To'gallant sails were handed, and while the ship heeled over to the increasing wind, the salt spray began to fly across the fo'c'sle deck, drenching me, and as I had no oilskins on I was soon wet through. To add to all this, I began to have a squeamish feeling at my stomach, which rapidly increased until I lost all interest in any lookout, and stood clinging to the fo'c'sle capstan, looking aft, towards the cabin, cold, wet and miserable, feeling that, after all, I may have made a mistake in deciding to become a sailor. As I thought of our cozy parlor at home, with its glowing grate of anthracite, in front of which I had spent so many happy evenings reading my favorite books, or sailing imaginary voyages, and contrasted that picture with my present situation, I made up my mind that when the ship arrived at New York, if ever she did, like the prodigal son I would return home, if I had to walk.

Suddenly I was startled by a hoarse cry of "All hands on deck! Reef topsails!" In a few moments the watch below came tumbling up, the topsail yards were lowered on the caps, reef tackles hauled out, spilling-lines and buntlines bowsed taut, the men laid aloft to take in a double reef. These were the days of the big topsails, the double yards not having been invented.

All this was new to me, and as I lay over the capstan-head I listened to the noise made by the flapping of the big topsails, mingled with the hoarse cries of the crew as they hauled out the gear, while from out of the darkness overhead, after they had laid aloft, the stentorian voice of the second mate roared out to "Light over to wind'ard," followed by "Haul out to leeward," terms which at that time were so much Greek to me.

After lying down from aloft, the topsails were again hoisted, and the watch sent below. It had now got to be seven bells (half-past eleven), and while anxiously counting the moments to eight bells, when our watch would go below, I was thoroughly aroused by a yell from the second officer.

"Who in blazes is on that lookout? Don't you see that ship?"

This was followed by some very emphatic language, and rushing forward, he jumped upon the fo'c'sle deck, and sprang towards me, exclaiming, "Who's this on the lookout?"

"Me!" I answered, in faint tones.

"Well! where you looking out to, the binnacle?"

He peered into my face, and with an oath demanded what I was doing up there, and who sent me.

"Tom," I answered.

"Oh! he did!" said he, as the truth dawned upon him, and leaving me, he descended to the main deck, and in a moment more old Tom came flying up on the fo'c'sle, assisted by the second mate in a most vigorous manner, where he was kept on the lookout for two hours in the first officer's watch before being allowed to go below. This was the last straw. Old Tom never forgave me.

At eight bells I went below and turned in as I was, wet clothes and all, covered up well, and was soon warm and steaming.

It did not seem as though I had more than got to sleep, when I was roused by three knocks on the scuttle, and the call of "Starboard watch ahoy." "Turn out!" "Turnout!"

In a moment all was bustle, with the watch turning out to go on deck, but I made no response. Sick and miserable, I lay still, trusting I should be overlooked, but there came a call of "Come, boy, you going to sleep all the way to New York? Turn out!"

I was about to comply, when I heard another voice,—"Oh, let the cub lay, he's no use on deck in this weather. He's sick."

I said nothing, but lay still, and invoking blessings on the head of the last speaker, I slept on, but at seven bells, when the watch were called to breakfast, I was ordered out, without ceremony, and told to go to the galley and hand down the coffee and grub.

In those days it was the custom for the boys to do all the drudgery in the ship's fo'c'sle; to keep the bread barge filled by taking it aft to the steward when empty; to return with it to the fo'c'sle after he had filled it; bring all the coffee and tea as well as food from the galley at meal times for all the watch, sweep up the fo'c'sle after meals, and in hot weather wash it out every morning after breakfast, although in this he was generally assisted by some member of the watch; in short, he was subject to the call of any one while off his watch on deck.

This may seem pretty rough on the boy, but on the other hand, where a boy did his work willingly, without grumbling, the men were always ready to treat him well, teach him the mysteries of knotting and splicing, and everything pertaining to the work on shipboard, doing all in their power to instruct and make a sailor of him.

Pulling myself together, I mounted the fo'c'sle ladder, which was almost perpendicular, and stepped from the hatch, or scuttle, out upon the deck. Since I had gone below at midnight the gale had increased, and the "Ariel "was now hove to, under a close-reefed main topsail and fore topmast staysail, laying over at an angle of many degrees, spray flying over her in sheets, decks wet and slippery, the wind whistling through her rigging with a wail like lost spirits, great waves chasing each other, and looking as if they would overwhelm her, while overhead; patches of lead-colored clouds were scudding across the sky.

The sight was a grand one, and I stood holding on to the fife rail of the foremast, lost in amazement, until admonished by a voice from below that if I did not hurry and get that grub down I would hear of it when I came below. To navigate between the companionway and the galley was a problem, but by making short tacks and holding on, with the help of one of the deck watch, I managed to get the pots of coffee and the "kid" (a small tub) of salt beef passed down safely, and was about to descend, when I was ordered to go and see if the cook had not got something besides "salt boss" for breakfast.

Returning to the cook, he handed me out a long, broad, deep pan, filled to the brim with a compound called scouse, consisting of ship bread broken up and soaked until soft. This, with salt pork fat and

23

molasses baked in the pan, was taken off the stove boiling and seething with hot grease.

Taking hold at each end, I essayed to reach the companionway, which I finally succeeded in doing, and bending over, and holding out the pan, I called out, "Here, somebody, take it, will you?"

Old Tom at that moment was directly underneath, bending over the "kid," engaged in cutting off, with a sheath-knife, a generous slice of beef. Without looking up, he growled, in answer to my call to take it, "Oh, don't be in a hurry, you cub, wait till somebody's ready to take it."

At this instant the ship gave a heavy lurch, my foot slipped, the hot mess ran over and burnt my hand, and I let go! The pan turned over, and with a crash landed on poor Tom's head, the scalding compound flying to every corner of the fo'c'sle. I was horrified. With a yell like a Comanche, old Tom leaped from under, but the mischief was done. From all parts of the fo'c'sle came a volley of oaths and imprecations that scared me. The urgent invitations to come down I respectfully but firmly declined, at least until they should become more calm, and started to argue it out from the companionway. In the meantime the deck watch, having been drawn together by the uproar below, were convulsed with laughter, evidently regarding it as a great joke.

It being now near eight bells, I descended the steps, but had no sooner landed on the deck than I received a tap on the side of the head, which would have knocked me across the fo'c'sle, had I not been held up by a tap from old Tom on the other side. This was getting too exciting to last, however, and eight bells striking, the watch went on deck, grumbling at having been deprived of their breakfast. I went with them, a discouraged boy, and although I was still sick, I was mad, for I felt that I had been "licked" for no fault of mine. My determination to return home the first chance was strengthened, and as the men gathered under the lee of the weather bulwarks, I hung to leeward of the long-boat, keeping out of the way as much as possible.

By four bells (ten o'clock) the gale beginning to moderate, an order was passed to loose the fore topsail and set it close-reefed. Two sailors sprang into the fore rigging to lay aloft and execute the order, while the remainder busied themselves in throwing down the gear and making ready to sheet home when loosed.

Although I had heard the order given by the second mate, I made no response, and as the officer went forward I worked my way aft to leeward until I came to the after, or booby, hatch, the slide or scuttle of which was open, and as I looked down it seemed warm and pleasant below in the between-decks. Glancing hastily around, and noting I was not perceived, all of the watch with Mr. Fabens being busy forward, I slipped over, and down the steps to the between-decks, working my way forward in the semi-darkness, until I came to the bulkhead of the fo'c'sle, on the other side of which were the crew's quarters. Through this bulkhead were bored auger-holes in diamond shape, for purposes of ventilation, thus any conversation carried on either side of the bulkhead could be plainly heard on the other.

Previous to leaving port, all the spare rigging, coils of rope, sails, hawsers, and one or two bales of oakum had been piled up against this bulkhead, and secured. Crawling in over this mass, I stowed myself away in the coil of a big hawser that was laid down over some sails, and taking a bunch of oakum for a pillow, went soundly to sleep.

The between-decks were dark, all the hatches being on except the after one. The slide of that being thrown back, admitted light enough for any one to see after they grew accustomed to it, but coming suddenly from the upper deck, it was difficult to distinguish objects for a time.

When I awoke it was very dark, save that the rays from the fo'c'sle lamp streamed through the holes in the bulkhead, and served to render the darkness a little less dense. As I lay, half awake, the sound of voices in conversation reached my ears. For a few moments I could not remember where I was, but gradually it all came to me, and listening intently, I gathered the conversation concerned myself, not as a creature of flesh and blood, but a boy who had lived and had passed away, been drowned, lost overboard. I heard a voice that I recognized as Joe's, saying:

"When did you last see him?"

"Oh, just as I was going aloft. He was down to leeward, hanging over the swinging boom. He must have gone over with that heavy lurch, when we were all busy with the fore topsail, and no one saw him go."

"Queer he didn't holler," said Bill. "I'm almighty sorry, for he was a likely lad and smart, would have made a good sailor. Did you see him sending down that r'y'l yard, at the dock?"

"Yes," was the reply, "and the next day was cold enough to freeze one, and that bloody second mate had that kid aloft slushing down, and

26

I said he ought to be ashamed to send that boy aloft to slush down in such weather."

"Well," I heard old Tom chime in, "I'm awful sorry I hit him, but the cub scalt every spear of hair out of my head."

"Ah, well," sighed Joe, "he's gone, and perhaps it's all right. He'd been like a young bear, all his troubles to come."

With this the subject seemed to be dismissed, and from the sounds I judged the starboard watch had gone to sleep, so curling myself up in my hawser, I soon followed their example.

When I again awoke I could hear the deck watch washing down. The ship seemed to be very quiet, lying over at a gentle angle. As I became fully awake I suddenly realized that I never felt better in my life, and oh! so hungry! The despised food of the fo'c'sle, how I would have welcomed it! I would have gone on deck had I not been afraid of a most unmerciful trouncing if I showed myself, but something must be done, for I seemed to be literally starving. All at once I remembered there were some four or five hundred barrels of apples in the lower hold, that were being shipped around to New York as freight. Why could I not get some of those apples? To think was to act. Climbing down into the hold, the hatches being off between-decks, and knocking the head out of a barrel, I filled my pockets and shirt all around, climbed out of the hold and into my hawser, and ate apples. Oh, how good they tasted!

After I had eaten my fill, it being yet early, I again went to sleep. The storm had been succeeded by fine weather, and the ship, under all canvas, was sailing steadily towards her destination.

27

The starboard watch were on deck. Mr. Fabens, desiring to strap a block, called old Tom, and gave him a measure, telling him to go below and cut off a piece of rope, as per same, which he would find lying against the fo'c'sle bulkhead. I had awakened, and was thinking what I should do, when I was startled by footsteps slowly advancing towards my retreat. I listened with bated breath. When the footsteps had about reached me they stopped, and I heard a kind of sawing noise. Curiosity impelled me to peep out, and see who it was. Lifting my length out of the hawser, I bent over, just as old Tom finished cutting off his piece of rope, and as he arose our eyes met. I, being on the sails and hawser, came somewhat above him, and as I, being a little cold, had wrapped around me a piece of canvas, I expect my appearance was a bit startling.

With whitened face and bulging eyes he gazed at me a moment, terror in every feature, then dropping rope and knife, and emitting a series of blood-curdling yells that rang through the ship, he dashed for the booby hatch, and disappeared on deck. Every one was aroused, and I could hear the second mate ask, "What's broke loose with you? Where's that block strap?" but for answer all old Tom could ejaculate was, "My God, I've seen him! I've seen him!"

"Seen who?" yelled Mr. Fabens, shaking him.

"Oh! his ghost! his ghost!"

"Whose ghost? What's the matter with you any way?"

"Oh! that boy's ghost, Mr. Fabens," Tom replied.

It was plain old Tom was nearly frightened out of his wits.

"Mr. Fabens," said Captain King, "get a lantern, take that man below, and see what scared him so."

Lighting a lantern, Mr. Fabens descended the ladder, with half the crew at his back, Tom bringing up the rear. As they came forward the second mate called out, "Where's your ghost? I don't see any ghost. Where did you see him?"

"Over that hawser," said Tom, pointing in my direction.

Up to now I had lain still, but feeling that I was discovered, I rose up to step out of the coil. My appearance was greeted with, "There he is! There he is!" from Tom, who with a yell again broke for the hatch ladder, followed by half the men.

Mr. Fabens came up, put his lantern in my face, and with an exclamation, reached over, and taking me by the collar, lifted me out and marched me up on deck, where I was at once surrounded by officers and crew, the latter gazing at me as if doubtful whether I might not be a spook.

Old Tom, suddenly awakened to the fact that he had been fooled, and had made a donkey of himself, started towards me, as if about to administer a cuff, when Mr. Fabens, shoving him back, exclaimed, "You dare lay a hand on that boy and I'll knock your head off!"

Captain King, stepping forward, now addressed me as follows: "Well, boy, where have you been, during the past forty-eight hours?"

"Between decks, sir," I sheepishly answered.

"What have you been doing between decks all this time?"

"Sleeping, sir," I answered.

29

"What! sleeping two days and nights? A mighty fine booby you'd make."

(A booby is a bird that as soon as he alights on a vessel drops sound asleep, instantly.)

"Not all the time, sir," I replied.

"Had anything to eat? What did you live on?"

"Apples," I ventured.

"Apples, where did you get apples?"

"Out of the hold, sir. I got the head out of a barrel."

"Oh, you did! Do you know you've been broaching cargo?"— and then, evidently thinking the farce had gone far enough, as all hands were on the broad grin, the Captain said, sternly:—

"Now go for'ard, boy! and if you cut up any more capers like that you'll get a rope's-ending you'll remember all your life," and turning to Mr. Fabens, he said, "Keep that boy up in his day watch below for a week, and give him plenty of work."

This ended his lecture, and I was glad it was over, and that I had escaped so easily. Going forward with the men, I was set to work, and, what pleased me, I could see they bore me no ill feeling, not even Tom, although in his case he might have been excused even had he done so a little. They all seemed to show a kinder tone towards me; there appearing to be a kind of satisfaction that I was not drowned after all.

Being now all over my seasickness, and feeling strong and hearty, I entered upon my work with a vim, and soon won the good opinion of all by my willingness.

Nothing occurred of note until we neared the port of New York. On the morning of the eighth day after leaving Newburyport, we took a pilot on board, and sailing in past Sandy Hook, through the Narrows past Staten Island, we came to anchor off the Battery. Shortly after, a tug came alongside, taking us to the dock, where the ship was made securely fast, after which the crew went on shore to the sailors' boarding-houses, their time being up, they only having signed articles for the run from Newburyport to New York.

From one home port to another to load, it was customary to ship a crew by the run, to pay them a lump sum, and not monthly wages, while all the work expected of them was to look after the safety of the ship, handle sails, steer, keep lookouts, and keep ship clean under the direction of the officers, and as they received their pay in advance, as soon as the ship reached her port and was made fast to the dock, they left.

This was the last I ever saw of old Tom and many others, although several reshipped with us when we were ready for sea; but of this later.

All now remaining on board were the two officers,—Captain King living at his hotel on shore,—the carpenter, ship-keeper and myself, but in a few days our number was augmented by one, the new boy, from Boston, who had been brought on by his mother to join the ship.

"Abel" was rather older than myself, but not so stout, although a good, sturdy boy. He was received and welcomed by the carpenter and myself, who, having made a voyage, considered ourselves old sailors, and assumed a superior tone towards him, a green hand, who had not

31

passed through the dangers and perils of the sea as we had, and what "yarns" we spun that boy, seated in the fo'c'sle on our chests! His hair would almost rise, and at times he seriously thought of returning to Boston. I now had no thought of going back. There was very little for us to do while in port, the days were so short. We went up near the head of the wharf and got our meals, seldom going any distance from the ship. Meanwhile the cargo, consisting of flour in barrels, was rapidly being taken on board.

CHAPTER III
1845-1846

THE PASSAGE TO LIVERPOOL.—JACK AFLOAT AND ASHORE

IN due course the "Ariel" completed her lading. A new crew was shipped, this time for the long voyage, fifteen months being the limit of time as written in the articles, and the last of December, 1845, the year of the great famine in Ireland, we sailed for Liverpool, England.

The voyage across the Atlantic was wild and stormy. Gale succeeded gale, with furious squalls of snow and hail, but being mostly from the western quarter, gave us a fair wind, before which the good ship scudded under close-reefed topsails and reefed foresail right royally, and although a very heavy sea was experienced, no damage was sustained; the "Ariel" proving herself a splendid sea boat.

During the passage I never missed my watch on deck in all weathers. Abel, however, was not so fortunate, being confined to his berth the entire passage, and not until we were in St. George's Channel did he make his appearance on deck. The officers, being occupied in looking after the safety of the ship, gave very little attention to him, thinking no doubt, sick as he was, he was better below than on deck, in such weather as we were having.

Arriving in the chops of the Channel, we passed a number of vessels, many of them showing the effects of the hard winter passage across.

One, the "Concordia" of the line of New York Packet ships, that sailed before we did, had lost some of her spars, the cargo (grain) had shifted, and she was listed to port very badly.

The following morning the ship was close in under Holyhead, Wales. It opened bright and sunny, though cool. The sea was smooth. The great headland, standing out in bold relief, with its quaint old windmills, and dotted with numerous dwellings, formed a beautiful picture, while the many crafts of all descriptions spread out in every direction, completed a panorama of wondrous beauty, especially so to us boys, who looked upon it for the first time.

Abel made his appearance on deck looking pale, but under the invigorating air and surroundings rapidly pulled himself together, and at once entered upon his duties. That morning ended his seasickness for good.

One amusing thing in connection with Abel's sickness occurred during the passage over. As a general thing seasickness meets with very little sympathy in a ship's fo'c'sle. The members of the crew do not look with pitying eye on the victim of *mal de mer*. Indeed they rather regard him as one inclined to shirk his work, but in Abel's case they were very easy with him, and did not encourage him to get up and go on deck. This seemed strange, as in those days Jack was not inclined to be lenient with a green boy, or show him any favors, but there was a reason for all this apparent kindness. Abel was finely fitted out with plenty of warm clothing, monkey jacket, oilskin suits, several pairs of sea boots, sou'westers, warm neck comforters, etc., etc.

Among the crew were several old packet sailors, a class who, while good enough seamen, are not overburdened with warm, comfortable clothing, the attractions of New York and Liverpool taking all their wages, and warm clothing being a secondary consideration with them until they get to sea and find themselves on a topsail yard, face to face with a wild howling nor'wester, freezing them to the marrow, with squalls of snow or hail beating upon them, and then they would bemoan the fact that they had not taken their hard-earned money, and bought what would have benefited them in times like these, instead of throwing all away in dissipation; but their regrets generally came too late and they rarely gained wisdom by experience.

To these sailors Abel's outfit was a God-send, and they did not scruple to help themselves, or to borrow anything he had that they could use and wear; arguing that as he could not wear them, and they were doing his work, the least he could do was to let them wear his clothes. His mother never would have recognized a large part of his outfit by the time the ship arrived in Liverpool.

Taking a pilot on board and entering the Irish Sea, we reached the lightship that night, and in beating up to it with a strong wind we were kept at quarters, making short tacks.

The boys, ordinary seamen and carpenter were stationed at the braces of the after yards (the yards on the mizzenmast) to brace round at the command of "Mainsail haul!" the carpenter throwing off the braces, while the boys swung round the yards.

The night was dark, and when nearly up to the lightship, Abel took a notion that he could assist the carpenter, and, unperceived, crossed to the other side of the deck.

On the order being given to brace round the after yards, he threw off the belaying-pin, not the braces, but the main topsail halliards, and down thundered the topsail yard upon the cap.

"Who's let go those topsail halliards?" shouted the pilot, and the captain and officers used language that would not appear well in print. Abel was scared out of his wits, and received a most unmerciful cuffing, while all hands tailed on to the topsail halliards, and the yard was again mastheaded.

In the morning we entered the Mersey, passing the Rock Light, and at high water docked the ship in the "Waterloo," one of the numerous docks in the great port of Liverpool.

Stevedores came on board, and preparations were made for the discharge of our cargo.

At the time of which I write, the rules and regulations of the Liverpool docks were very different from what they are at the present day. Then no fires or lights were allowed on board. On shore, near the docks, were a great number of boarding-houses, which catered to the ships' trade. Here the crews obtained their meals, and morning, noon and night might have been seen the crews of all the different ships in port, going and returning to their breakfasts, dinners and suppers.

The days being very short in winter, the men got their breakfast by gaslight, returning to their ship by nine o'clock, and knocking off work by four, or perhaps earlier, in the afternoon, after which the decks were cleaned up, and Jack went to supper, being a free man until the next morning.

As there was no light on board, they generally spent the evenings in the numerous singing-houses or dance-halls that lined the streets adjoining the docks, and here Jack found congenial company, both male and female, who, as long as he had a shilling, were ready to share his pot of beer, "half and half," or something stronger.

There, in these "free and easys," he smoked his pipe, listening to the continuous songs, and the music and performance going on, until about the hour of midnight. When they closed their doors he wended his way on board to turn into his berth in the darkness.

The mates and petty officers also had their separate places of evening resort. The *habitués* of Playhouse Square, the mate's and second mate's quarters, would have no more thought of lowering themselves by visiting "Rossbottom's" on Waterloo Road, than Beacon Street, Boston, would assimilate with the North End.

The captain, of course, lived at his hotel, and came and went at his own sweet will. All these boardinghouses set a good table, and Jack lived well, although the table in the officers' quarters was superior in the quality and variety of the food served. The boys, with the carpenter, took their meals at the officers' boardinghouse, but we did not see them, having a room to ourselves.

We had been but a few days in dock, when Captain King came on board one morning, and informed me that my uncle (Mr. Wm. Courtis), who lived in Manchester with his family and was engaged in business there, had written him asking permission for me to visit them while the ship remained in port. He added that I could go if I wished. Replying that I should be pleased to do so, I was exempted from further work, and getting into presentable shape by putting on my best clothes, I went to the station the following morning and took the express to Manchester, arriving about 10.30 A. M.

Meeting my uncle at the station, he called a cab and we drove to his house, where I received a warm welcome from my aunt and two cousins.

Three weeks in Manchester, visiting, with my uncle and his family, all places of interest, made my stay most thoroughly enjoyable. On my return I was accompanied by him, as he had business in Liverpool. He improved the opportunity to visit the ship and make the acquaintance of Captain King. After his departure I resumed my duties and again fell into the routine of ship's boy.

As it would be a week yet before the "Ariel "would be ready for sea, whenever we could get away from the ship, I improved the time, with Abel, strolling about, and seeing all we could of the city.

Now came the day of sailing or departure from the docks, the ship being bound for Canton, China, in ballast, to load teas for the port of New York.

All being in readiness for sea, stores on board, and two men shipped to take the places of two deserters, about the middle of March the crew warped the ship through the docks into the basin, where she lay waiting for the full tide and the tugboat, to proceed to sea.

The gates being opened, the tugboat made fast, with three ringing cheers responded to by friends of the crew who had assembled to see them off, the "Ariel" passed through the pier heads into the River Mersey, and was again outward bound.

Down the river, past the shipping at anchor, away past the Rock Light at the entrance of the river, into the Irish Sea, past Point Linas until Holyhead was reached, thus insuring a good offing; when sail was made, the tugboat hawsers were cast off, good-bys exchanged, and the tow boat took her departure to look up another vessel to take into port.

With a fair wind and rattling breeze, a fine run was made down channel, and passing Tusker Light, old Kinsale and Cape Clear, we were soon again on the broad Atlantic, bound south for the region of the trade winds and a warm climate.

CHAPTER IV
1846

CROSSING THE LINE.—FERNANDO NOROHNA.—THE MALAYS

FAVORED with strong northerly gales, the "Ariel" swept past Madeira under reefed topsails, and entered the belt of northeast trade winds. The weather was now delightful, continuous fresh breezes, gradually lessening in force as we approached their southern limit. Passing the group of Azores Islands, with the Peak of Pico, on the island of that name, 7,000 feet in height, and the Canaries, with Teneriffe towering above the clouds, we continued on until we lost them in latitude 5 north. The region of northeast trade winds lies between the parallels of 30 north and the equator, although their northern and southern limits vary with the seasons; ships sometimes carrying strong trades within three or four degrees of the equator, and again losing them as high as 10 north. Through these trades is most delightful sailing; steady, fine, fresh breezes, clear skies, bright and sunny; warm, but not too much so, soft patches of light fleecy clouds hanging around the horizon, called trade clouds, water a glorious deep blue, alive with shoals of flying-fish, skipjacks, bonitas and albacore, the former rising in immense shoals close to the ship, and with a whirr like a covey of partridges away they go skimming to wind'ard, their wings glinting and glistening in the bright sunlight for a thousand yards or so, when they drop to wet their wings, only to reappear in a moment. They formed one of the prettiest pictures, that one never wearied in watching.

The flying-fish affords fine eating, having a flavor similar to a fresh sardine, and is one of the finest pan fish that swims.

We had now reached the belt of light, variable winds, calms and squalls, with thunder, lightning, and heavy rains, the last enabling us to fill our empty water casks. Fortunately we were not long in crossing this belt, and striking the southeast trades in latitude 1° north, we crossed the equator and entered the South Atlantic. The visit of Neptune and his wife on board was for some reason deferred, much to the relief of us boys and the carpenter, who was also on his first voyage.

In the old days it was customary on ships, more particularly those flying the British flag, to observe the crossing of the line or equator for the first time by any one on board, by making it a special occasion, and celebrating it as a gala day. Extra grog was served out to the crew, etc. All this was in honor of King Neptune, who was to pay a visit to the ship, in company with his wife Amphitrite, to see if there were any on board, either passengers or crew, who were invading his special domain without having been properly initiated. The green hands had the fact that they were entering the domain of these mythical personage impressed upon them as a reality, and for weeks their minds were filled with the terrors of the ordeal they would have to pass through.

The cabin passengers who were liable could purchase immunity by money or a few bottles of grog, but woe betide the hapless boy, or green hand, who was making his first trip across the equator, old Neptune's home and undisputable possession.

On the morning of the day the ship was to cross the line, these unfortunate victims were blindfolded and shut up until wanted, but were placed where they could hear all that was going on. Preparations were then begun for the reception of His Majesty and His Better Half. Two old grizzled shellbacks were selected from among the crew to act the parts of Neptune and wife. They were painted and decked out in the most fantastic garb, by the crew. They had long, flowing hair and whiskers of rope-yarns and oakum, resembling seaweed, and a crown made from Manila strands and shells, scraps of steel, or iron. Then with the ship's big trumpet, and the five-pronged grains used for catching dolphins or skipjacks, as his trident, his outfit was complete. His spouse was similarly rigged out. Taking their stations over the bows in the head, one of the crew would go out to the end of the flying jib boom with the trumpet and hail the ship, asking her name and where from, ending by stating that His Majesty King Neptune was about to pay the ship a visit, and all hands would prepare to receive both him and his queen Amphitrite.

A half-hogshead of water would have been prepared, with a platform alongside, on which was a chair for seating the candidate for maritime honors. A slush bucket filled with an odorous mixture of slush and tar, using an old paint brush for a shaving brush, with a piece of notched iron hoop for a razor, constituted the shaving outfit.

All being in readiness, the candidate, still blindfolded, was led forward and seated in the chair. Neptune and Amphitrite would then appear, dripping with sea water, which had been previously poured over them to give them the appearance of just having emerged from old ocean. Neptune then propounded to the intruders a series of the most ridiculous questions, ending by ordering him to be shaved and initiated as one of his children in due form; the candidate continuing blindfolded until after his involuntary bath.

Then followed the lathering and shaving, which was of a pretty rough order, but if the poor fellow opened his mouth to utter a protest, it was instantly filled with a brushful of the unsavory lather, amid the delight and jeers of his tormentors. The shaving completed, while answering questions his chair would be jerked away, and he would fall, floundering, into the hogshead of water, after which he was allowed to scramble out, would be given a stiff glass of grog to drink Neptune's health, be permitted to make himself presentable and go his way or take part in the initiation of the next victim. The custom in these days even on foreign ships has become obsolete.

Continuing south, close-hauled, we passed in plain sight of Fernando Norohna, a small, high island off the Brazil coast. That government uses it as a penal settlement, sending hither all its convicts. Here under vigorous discipline they have little chance of escape.

Past Pernambuco and Bahia we continued along the Brazil coast, until we reached the parallel of 23° south, and entered the belt of sou'west passage winds. These winds blow almost continuously from the western quarter, varying from W. N. W. to W. S. W. As the ship draws out of the trade belt the wind gradually hauls round by way of the north, allowing the vessel to come up to her course for the Cape of Good

Hope, crossing the meridian of the Cape on a parallel of 38° to 40° south and sometimes higher.

Being now in the region of the strong west passage winds, the "Ariel" fairly flew before them on her long eastern stretch upwards of 5,000 miles, nearly to the coast of Australia, before again turning north.

During this long run from the Cape of Good Hope to the rocky islets of St. Paul and Amsterdam, there was very little work going on except looking after the ship, hands continually standing by the topsail halliards, clewing down by the run in the furious hail squalls which would come with hurricane force, almost beating one to the deck, with sky nearly as black as night.

This would last perhaps for ten or fifteen minutes, when, presto! the squall would pass, clouds sweep away, while the sun would appear, lighting up the crest of the surges that rolled past. The instant the squall was over topsails were again mastheaded, and with great mountainous billows tumbling after, at times seeming about to engulf her, the "Ariel" sped onward like a frightened deer.

Day after day, and week after week, this continued, until we reached the meridian, when we could once again turn to the north'ard, and entering the region of the trade winds of the Indian Ocean, shape our course for Java Head.

Falling in with the southeast trades, the "Ariel" made fine progress, until, coming on deck one morning in the middle watch, I found the ship hove to for daylight, but with the first peep of dawn she was again put upon her course. At ten A. M. (four bells) the welcome cry of "Land, ho!"

rang through the ship, and all eyes were at once strained to catch the first glimpse of terra firma. Presently from the deck could be seen the outlines of a bold headland, every moment becoming more distinct as the ship sped onward towards it.

All was now bustle and preparation for closing in with the land and entering the Straits of Sunda. Chain cables were hauled on deck after their long rest in the lockers, and bent, lashings cast off, and anchors placed on the bows. Meantime we were drawing in with the land, and from a mere outline it now began to assume shape and color. By three o'clock we had closed in with it and entered Sunda Straits.

Sailing northerly along the coast from Java Head, the land is high, and covered with dense forests having rich tropical foliage. The ship was well in under the shore, and I thought I could never tire of gazing at it.

About dusk the land breeze came off, sweeping over the ship, laden with the fragrance of tropical fruits and flowers so heavy with perfume as to almost intoxicate the senses. This, mingled with the fresh earthy smell, to which we had so long been strangers, was inhaled in deep draughts. Java Head, and my first night in Sunda Straits, remain to-day impressed upon my memory. With daylight, boats from Anger met us and dropped alongside, while the crews, composed of Malays, scrambled over the rails like cats. They were trading boats laden with tropical fruits: green cocoanuts, bananas, oranges, limes, also vegetables,—yams, sweet potatoes, strings of onions and garlic; in short, all vegetables grown in the tropics, with ducks, geese, chickens, fowls, goats, pigs, and many other things, all tempting enough to men who had been deprived of fresh grub as long as we had.

The Malays comprising the boat crews were a source of great interest to me. A small, undersized class of men, tawny, with coal-black hair and small, piercing eyes, well formed and featured, active and springy, as nimble as cats, they sprang from their boats up the ship's side and swarmed on board, the captain, or *serang*, making his way aft, where stood Captain King and officers.

With a bland smile and salaaming to the deck, be presented his "chit" or recommendation given him by the ships that he had supplied while passing Anger, and endorsing him as the one man who could supply all the next ship's needs. There is great rivalry between these boats, but as far as the ships are concerned it is generally "first come, first served."

It is amusing to see the *serang* bowing and smiling while the captain is reading over his recommendations, which he cannot do himself, in many cases denouncing him as a swindling cheat, and the greatest scoundrel that ever went unhung. Of course they are mostly written as a joke, and are so taken by the reader, and no more notice being taken of it, he gets permission to trade, although there may be others. This amounts to considerable, as, besides fruit and vegetables, live stock is taken on board in quantities to supply the ship with fresh provisions, fore and aft, for the voyage up the China Sea, it being more economical, at the prices, to feed the men on fresh meat, saving the salt beef and pork; so Jack lives high, on fresh grub with vegetables daily.

The weather being fine, the "Ariel" ran into the roadstead, coming to anchor off the town or village. Large supplies were taken on board, of fruit, vegetables, and live stock. Never before having tasted bananas, and in fact very little of fruit grown in the tropics, they were a revelation to me, and when the first boat boarded us in the early morning, I traded with a Malay an old pair of trousers for a big bunch, and, taking it into the fo'c'sle, for four or five days I ate little else.

While at anchor Captain King went ashore in his gig, and to my delight I was ordered as one of the boat's crew. This gave me an opportunity of seeing a little of Malay life on shore. We wandered around among the houses or huts, constructed of bamboo with thatched roofs, while swarms of women and children, the latter clad in sunlight only, gazed curiously at us, but we could understand each other by sign language alone.

The following morning getting under way and passing between Sumatra and the N. W. end of the island of Java, we entered the Java Sea, shaping our course for Gaspar Straits.

The Java Sea and Malay Archipelago were at this time infested with pirates, who, in their long, sharp *proas*, were constantly dodging about, looking for some craft that should be so unfortunate as to run ashore on any of the numerous coral reefs or sand banks that abounded in these waters, and woe betide the ship that was caught at anchor in the night time in any of the straits, or passages, with the watch on deck asleep; in which case, although not a thing may have been in sight when she came to anchor, towards morning there would silently steal out of the darkness a fleet of *proas*, each manned by forty or fifty Malays, perhaps more, and once alongside with their deadly creese or knife between their teeth, swarming up the ship's side, in a twinkling they would be on deck, and before the dazed watch could realize it, those not murdered would be driven below, and the ship in their possession, to be plundered and perhaps burnt, while all who escaped would be taken on shore, kept in confinement and held for a good round ransom.

Ships in these waters always carried a good armory on board, consisting of muskets, pistols, cutlasses, and boarding-pikes, and generally two or four large guns on deck, in the use of which the crew were carefully trained.

This did not often occur, however, with American or English ships, as the rascals were generally too cautious to attack a ship in daylight, or under sail, or one that they knew was on the alert. In these days their pirating is about over, the men-of-war of the Dutch and English governments having about exterminated them, showing no mercy.

BOAT TOWNS ON CANTON RIVER.—LOADING TEAS.—HOMEWARD BOUND

Through Gaspar, past Singapore, we continued through the China Sea, and in due course came to anchor in the Canton River off "Bambootown," Whampoa, a boat town on the river some ten or twelve miles below Canton. These boat towns are curious. Here people are born, live, and die, without hardly ever being on shore, living mostly on rice and fish caught from the river. They attend on the shipping, doing the washing for the officers and crews.

Coming to an anchor, our sails were smoothly furled, and the ship moored for a long stay.

The following morning a boat was got ready with a crew of picked men, and Captain King left for the city of Canton, returning in two days and bringing a gentleman with him.

The "Ariel," being in ballast with no cargo to discharge, was soon ready to receive her cargo of teas, to be sent down from Canton in lighters, or cargo boats, and in a week or ten days the first boats came alongside, and were speedily unloaded, others taking their places until our lading was completed. The tea-chests, composed of whole chests, halves and quarters, neat and clean, were encased in matting and marked with the ship's name, "Ariel."

During our stay the crew were allowed liberty on Sunday, one watch at a time, but there was very little to attract on shore, and the crew after one trip preferred to remain on board, or visit the crew of the ship "Chicora," that was anchored within a half-mile.

Abel and myself were not allowed to go on shore at all, it being, in the opinion of the captain, no place for boys, and he was right, no doubt, although we did not see it in that light, thinking it a great hardship.

Our cargo completed, Captain King came down from Canton, bringing with him two gentlemen, who were to make the home voyage with us as passengers.

The ship was unmoored, chain hove short, sail made, anchor tripped and hove to bows, and with her nose pointing down river passed the "Chicora," whose crew gave us three hearty cheers, which were responded to by our men with a will.

This time the "Ariel" was homeward bound!

A pleasant run down the China Sea brought us to the Straits of Banca. Through these we passed, coming to anchor at night to await for daylight.

Being now in dangerous waters, a vigilant watch was kept for pirates; guns were loaded, and all prepared to give them a warm reception should they make us a call, but the night passed without seeing anything, and at the first peep of daylight we were again under way. At Anger, however, I learned that a ship passing Banca some two or three days ahead of us had been attacked while lying at anchor during the night, but the pirates were beaten off, the cook sustaining the loss of an ear while giving them a deluge of scalding water from his coppers, which he had filled and under which he had kept a good fire in anticipation of their attack.

Here, at Anger, we again stocked up with fruits, vegetables, and live stock of all kinds, for the homeward voyage.

Leaving Java, our decks were filled with coops which were stuffed with chickens, fowl, geese and ducks, while pigs and goats filled the pens.

Added to all this, every man forward had his pet monkey, sometimes two or three, while cages, hanging from every point to which they could be attached, were filled with Java sparrows, cockatoos, and birds of every variety of plumage; but very few were destined to reach New York.

In addition to the fo'c'sle stock there were two very large Sumatra monkeys, of a dirty yellow color, standing between three and four feet high. These were kept chained in the stern of the long-boat, and belonged to the two passengers. Some of the monkeys forward were of a good size, but most of them were small. They were a source of great amusement, constantly cutting up all sorts of antics, and being very mischievous, would steal anything they could lay their hands or paws on. As Jack did not tie them up, they swarmed all over the ship's rigging, and if anything on deck took their fancy, they would drop down, seize it, and be aloft again, almost impossible to catch, as they would spring from point to point, chattering and scolding at a great rate. This propensity for thieving cost most of them their lives.

One day the steward had taken the dinner to the cabin table, leaving it to go to the galley. No one was below, and it being warm, the skylight over the table was off. Two of the larger monkeys were about the after rigging. They had apparently been watching the steward, and seeing the coast clear, descended, dropping down through the skylight, and seizing a pair of chickens, on which the captain and passengers were to dine, they sprang on deck, and in a twinkling were aloft, just as the steward returned from announcing dinner. On entering the cabin the chickens were missed, and looking up, the scamps were discovered in the mizzen top, chattering and grinning, while they looked down at their pursuers. Several men had jumped into the rigging to catch them, but their efforts were of no avail; the monkeys were too nimble, and finally running out on a yard arm, dropped the chickens, one going overboard, and the other on deck in a condition hardly fit for the captain's table.

This theft angered Captain King, and sealed their doom, for, after finishing in the cabin, the captain and passengers brought up their pistols on the quarter-deck, and a fusillade began, which picked off monkeys in all directions, many going overboard, until not a Jocko was seen about the rigging. Then the order was given that all monkeys that were not kept tied up should be served in the same manner.

This action of Captain King's almost produced a mutiny. The owners of the monkeys that were shot were furious, looking upon the action as cruel and unjustifiable, and many an oath was registered to get even some day, and two weeks after, when we turned to one morning to wash down decks, the big monkeys in the long-boat were both found dead, having been strangled during the night by some one, whom, no one ever knew, although a reward was offered for the perpetrator. After this, matters quieted down, Jack taking care to keep his pets tied up, but most of them succumbed to the bad weather off the Cape of Good Hope, and only two reached New York safely.

After leaving Java, Charles Johnson, one of the crew, was taken down with fever, and that scourge of the East, dysentery. Day after day he grew worse, and from a strong, well-built man fell away to a mere shadow.

He had been removed from the close fo'c'sle, and a bed was made for him in the bow of the long-boat, where he could have plenty of air. He would lie there all day long reading his Bible, and when off duty the various members of the crew would watch with and read to him, when he became too weak to read himself. Everything was done for him, but in vain. He was fully at peace and longed to go, and one bright, beautiful morning, Johnson's soul took its flight.

After breakfast his wasted body was taken from the long-boat, sewn up in his hammock, and placed on a plank extending from a cask to the rail amidships. The American ensign was placed over him. All being in readiness, the main yard was thrown aback, and all hands called to bury the dead. Sadly, the crew mustered in the ship's waist, grouped around the corpse, with two standing at the head of the plank, and one on either side, the officers at the head awaiting Captain King, who, accompanied by the passengers, presently emerged from the cabin door, prayer-book in hand. Advancing, he took his station at the head, and read the beautiful burial service for the dead at sea. It was a solemn scene, and tears glistened in the eyes of many of the crew, for Johnson was a favorite with all.

With the words, "We commit the body to the deep," the end of the plank was lifted, and the hammock, heavily weighted at the end, slid down, and, with a splash, the blue sea closed over all that remained of our shipmate, while the order to "Fill away the main topsail!" brought us back to a realization that all was over, and our messmate gone forever.

We lost one other under the same circumstances,—fever and dysentery,—committing him to old ocean ere we were up with Madagascar.

With fine, strong, trade winds bowling us along, passing the south end of Madagascar, and later the meridian of the Cape of Good Hope, nothing of note, except the two deaths before mentioned, occurred during our run through the Indian Ocean. Doubling the Cape with a fair wind, and hugging the land which was in plain sight from Cape Agulhas to Table Bay, the "Ariel" again entered the south Atlantic, shaping her course for St. Helena and the S. E. trades.

Up to this point I have made very little mention of the work at sea on shipboard. I have often been asked the question, "What do sailors have to do at sea, with a fair wind and fine weather?"

To this query I answer: In every well regulated ship a sailor has no idle moments, except in his watch below, and on holidays; chafing gear,

54

of which there are large quantities, is being constantly worn out and has to be replaced with new, all of which, in addition to spun yarn, sennit, mats, rugs, fancy work for capstan covers, and many other things, are made on shipboard by the crew, while sail making and repairing, work on standing rigging, setting up and turning in, tarring, painting, with tricks at the wheel, and lookouts, making and taking in sail and attendance to general orders, do not leave much spare time on Jack's hands when on duty, and the officer who cannot find work enough to keep his men constantly employed is lacking in a knowledge of his business. This was not often the case at the time of which I write.

The "Ariel's" rigging being new on her departure from her home port, it took about all the outward voyage to get the stretch out of it, while luff, and watch tackles, were in almost constant use, but now being pretty well out, it was ready to be turned in afresh, and put in a condition that is pleasing to a sailor's eye, also to present a fine, shipshape appearance on arrival in port. To one not versed in these matters, it is almost impossible to understand the labor and care bestowed upon every little detail of this work, and from the time we rounded the Cape and took the S. E. trades it was all hands at work, no more afternoon watch below.

Up to this time I had never been allowed to take my regular turn at steering the ship, although I had often stood at night on the lee side of the wheel, and in good weather I frequently steered the ship by the hour together, under the guidance and eye of the helmsman. I knew the compass, and could box it (repeat it backward) as readily as I could count my fingers, but had never been left alone in charge of the wheel. I was now ordered to take my regular trick, the same as others of the ship's company, being often kept at the wheel four hours, instead of two, when the one who followed me was engaged on some special work.

I loved to steer the ship, and in a short time became an expert helmsman. What glorious weather one experiences within the limits of these trade winds!—a long swell that kept the "Ariel "gently rolling from side to side, the wind being nearly dead aft, steady trades, not varying a half-point day after day and week after week, no squalls, no sails to trim, only an occasional pull at the halliards to bowse everything taut, wind not over strong, but enough to bowl the ship along from seven to eight knots per hour, a cloudless sky o'erhead, with the exception of the light fleecy trade clouds that constantly hung around the horizon, and bright, warm sunshine every day, while the nights were resplendent with the brilliancy of the constellations of the southern hemisphere. This was indeed ideal sailing. The sunrises and sunsets were beautiful almost beyond description, and often, while at the wheel, I would become so absorbed in watching the glory of the departing day, with its gorgeousness of color, as old Sol sank to his ocean bed, that I would almost forget my duties until a glance at the compass would bring me to a realization that the "Ariel" was from a half to a point off her course.

Under a cloud of canvas, with stun'sails spread alow and aloft, the ship swept steadily on, passing close to St. Helena, that small rocky islet, distinguished as being the prison home of the great Napoleon, on, past Ascension Island, until we again crossed the equator, and entered the home waters of the north Atlantic.

During all this long run, the work of the crew upon the rigging went steadily on. I was placed under the various members of the crew, while at their respective tasks, acting as an assistant or helper, soon becoming quite proficient in the knowledge of knotting, splicing, and serving, etc., picking up from the men, by close observation and attention to the manner of doing their work, the knowledge that is so necessary to a thorough seaman. Herein lies the advantage of long voyages to the young man commencing a seafaring life. He may go a lifetime in the western ocean trade or on short voyages, and yet see none of the work that is done on a ship bound home from India or China, while rolling down the trades between the Cape of Good Hope and the equator, or very little of it, much less participate in it. All this work on vessels making short trips is generally done by riggers while lying in port, and their work does not carry the neatness of detail and finish of that done on shipboard. Look over a ship fresh from the rigger's hands, and one just in from Calcutta or Hongkong, and the eye quickly notes the difference between the two in the appearance of their rigging.

All through this fine weather, during my forenoon watch below, I was obliged to go aft and study navigation. In this I became quite interested, getting a good theoretical knowledge of the rules, and in a short time could keep dead reckoning, work the latitude by a noon observation and longitude by chronometer time, but was not allowed as yet to handle the quadrant or sextant, or take an observation myself, which I longed to do, and mentally resolved that on my next voyage I would have a quadrant of my own.

Encountering no calms, we passed from the S. E. to the N. E. trades of the north Atlantic, every day's run bringing us nearer New York, while at night the single stars and constellations greeted us like old familiar faces, the North Star bidding us the first welcome as it twinkled on the horizon's edge. At each watch below, especially the dog-watch, the conversation was principally on future plans when they should arrive in New York, whom they would board with, where they would go, and how dispose of their wages,—which amounted to a good round sum by this time,—interspersed with reminiscences of past experience.

Being now fairly within the trades, came "rattling down," tarring rigging, and painting ship outside and in. This work completed, we were now north of the West India Islands, fast approaching the latitude of Bermuda. Here we looked for a change of weather, and thick clothing was got out and overhauled. Each night, as the watch gathered in the fo'c'sle, would be repeated the old couplet:

> "If Bermuda let you pass,
> Look out for Cape Hatteras."

It seemed to be a fixed fact that we were bound to catch a big gale off one or the other, but there is another old saying, "A watched pot never boils," so, in this case anticipating both, we got neither, but favored by strong southerly and westerly winds, with good clear weather, the

"Ariel" passed the Gulf Stream and struck soundings in seventy fathoms.

Chains up, anchors were again got ready, and the following night we took a pilot on board, and before reaching the Highlands of Navesink we took a tugboat, passed the Hook and Staten Island, where the quarantine officers boarded but did not detain us, and finally dropped anchor off the Battery, our long voyage ended.

Sails having been unbent on our way up in tow of the tug, we were speedily placed alongside of the pier in the East River.

No sooner were we berthed than the runners from the various sailor boarding-houses swarmed on board to induce the men to put up with them, each one extolling the merits of his own particular house,— frequently enforcing his claims with spirited arguments in the shape of a small flask drawn from the hip pocket,—and in less than an hour the ship was deserted by all save the officers, the carpenter, Abel, and myself.

The following morning the captain left word on board that the crew would be paid off the next day. This over, I accepted an invitation from Captain Michael Gregory, of Marblehead, with whom I had fallen in, to make the trip to Boston on his vessel, the brig "Mary Ellen," and the following morning, bidding adieu to the "Ariel," I went on board the brig, sailing that afternoon through Hell Gate and Long Island Sound, past Nantucket, over the shoals, rounded the Highland Light, and after a little brush in the bay arrived safely in Boston. Taking the train to

Marblehead, I met on my arrival with a warm welcome from my sister and the family, but learned with sorrow of my grandmother's death.

My old schoolmates gave me quite an ovation, regarding me as one to be envied, having made a voyage to Europe and China, being absent over a year.

CHAPTER VI
1846-1847

RIO DE JANEIRO.—CAPE HORN.—OTAHEITE

A MONTH on shore, and I shipped as ordinary seaman on the "Tsar," a fine ship of nearly seven hundred tons, just home from Russia, where the ship had been presented with a set of silk colors by the Emperor Nicholas I., as a compliment for the name. Her first voyage completed, she was bound to the north and south Pacific, thence to China. At that time she was considered a large ship, carrying a crew of twenty forward,—including two ordinary seamen, and four boys making their first voyage,—captain (Captain Samuel Kenneday), first and second officers, cook, steward, and carpenter, twenty-six all told.

Sailing from Boston, in the spring of '46, the "Tsar" made a good run to the equator, crossing the same and taking the S. E. trades (fresh), arrived at Rio Janeiro forty-five days from Boston.

The land from Cape Frio to the entrance of the bay runs about east and west, Cape Frio being a very high headland, surmounted by a fine lighthouse. The coast, as one approaches the entrance of the bay, bears a strong resemblance to the figure of an immense man lying upon his back, the peaks of the Gabia and Corcovada with the high hills forming the upper portion of the body, while the Sugar Loaf Mountain on the west side of the bay forms his feet. The contour is perfect when viewed from the right direction. Off the entrance lie two small islands named Pai and Mai. The bay of Rio Janeiro is one of the largest and finest in

61

the world. I shall have occasion to refer to the city and its noble bay later on. The scenery as viewed from the ship was magnificent.

Failing to reach the entrance before the sea breeze ended, we were obliged to remain outside the harbor all night. About 8 P. M. the land breeze struck off in a strong gust, with squalls of wind and rain, accompanied with peals of thunder and vivid lightning, clearing away after midnight, followed by calm.

Taking the sea breeze in the morning, passing the islands and Sugar Loaf on the port hand, the fort of Santa Cruz on our right,—from which we were hailed as to the port we came from, if all were well on board, etc.,—thence past the upper forts, we dropped anchor opposite the city a little below the island of Cobras, where one of the finest dry docks in the world, belonging to the Brazilian government, is now located. Here the doctor came on board, but finding no sickness, and a clean bill of health, admitted her to *pratique*, allowing communication with the shore.

Quite a number of vessels lay at anchor, among them several men-of-war. They were of different nationalities, and I noted the American flag floating from many peaks.

While in port no one visited the shore except the captain. I was one of the boat's crew but was not allowed to leave the boat while waiting for him.

After a stay of four days, the anchor was again weighed, and taking advantage of the land breeze early in the morning, we took our departure from Rio Janeiro, answering the hail from Santa Cruz, and outside of Pai and Mai Islands caught the sea breeze again and were speeding our way south.

Off the Rio de la Plata we experienced a strong *pampero*, which blew with great force. These *pamperos* are violent gales that sweep the plains of Buenos Ayres. They are preceded by heavy thunder and most vivid lightning, and on shore by a dense cloud of fine impalpable dust,—that would penetrate anything that water would go through,—with hailstones of a very large size, or heavy rain.

After passing the parallel of 40° south, the "Tsar" was put in condition to encounter heavy weather off the Cape. Best sails were bent and new running gear rove. In the fo'c'sle, warm, thick clothing was got out and overhauled and the conversation in the watch below savored of past experiences off the stormy Cape.

With the exception of a little brush off the Patagonian coast, all went well, and passing the Falkland Islands, we sighted Staten Land, an island lying east of Tierra del Fuego (Land of Fire), the strait between being called Le Maire.

Staten Land is an island of considerable size and heavily wooded, but uninhabited.

Rounding the east end with a fair wind, with every stitch of canvas drawing, we sped on for Cape Horn, hoping to round it without a setback, but, alas, for our hopes, there was no such luck in store for us.

Away in the southwest loomed up an ominous bank of whitish gray mist, sweeping down upon us. All hands were called, light sails clewed up and handed in a hurry, topsail halliards let go by the run, reef tackles hauled out, while buntlines and spilling-lines were bowsed taut. The ship paid off as it burst upon us butt end foremost, and ere we could jump into the rigging a cold, icy blast with sleet and hail fairly whistled and howled about our ears, as we laid aloft and out upon the yards. This was our first touch of Cape Horn that we were not likely to forget. With the hardest kind of work, it was upwards of an hour ere we could get the close reefs in, and courses furled, but all having been made snug, our watch went below, chilled through to the marrow, and substituted warm and dry for wet clothing, a most agreeable change. Meantime the sea had risen, and the great waves, driven before the gale, gave an idea of what a Cape Horn sea, that I had so often heard talked about in the fo'c'sle, was like.

We were now headed to the south'ard, close-hauled, under close reefs. From this time on, gale followed gale, with short intervals of favoring winds, taking advantage of which, and every slant, at the end of two weeks we had worked up to the meridian 80° west, when with a fine, strong, sou'west gale, the "Tsar "bore away to the north'ard with all the canvas the ship could stagger under. Bidding Cape Horn a long farewell, with no regrets, we fairly flew towards more genial weather and a warmer climate.

During our sojourn off the Cape the ship was constantly surrounded by great numbers of birds,—albatrosses, Cape Horn pigeons, Mother Carey's chickens (stormy petrel), who followed the ship day after day, hanging around for anything in the shape of food thrown overboard. They would drop like a shot from a gun and pounce upon it. Our men caught several with hooks baited with a piece of salt pork, but once on deck they were ungainly and clumsy as they waddled about before they were again given their freedom. No injury is done to them, except viewing them at close range, sailors believing that killing or injuring these birds bodes ill luck. Sailing through the air, poised over the ship, or riding the billows, they present a most graceful appearance. They followed the ship for many days after we bore away north, and we finally dropped them after crossing the parallel of 40° south.

The "Tsar" was now in the south Pacific, with smooth sailing, delightful weather, and fine trade winds, heading for the Society Islands, Otaheite, the largest of the group, being our destination. I was very much interested in these islands, having read in my school days the "Mutiny of the Bounty," a ship sent out by the English government to make a collection of the bread-fruit trees to take to the West Indies. The book contained a fascinating description of Otaheite, or Tahiti, as it is more commonly called.

These islands of the South Pacific always possessed a great attraction for me, particularly Tahiti and Moorea. At this time Tahiti was a French possession, that government having made it a naval rendezvous.

One fine morning the welcome cry of "Land, ho!" greeted our ears, and ere long Tahiti and Moorea were in plain sight.

Beautiful Otaheite! well named the "Garden of the Pacific!" It would take a more able pen than mine to describe your charms!

High, commanding, it rises out from the waves, its hills and vales clothed with rich, tropical foliage, a living green in strong contrast with the sparkling blue waters of the Pacific, encircled with a coral reef upon which breaks the long ocean swell, a snowy white, while beyond lie the still, quiet waters of the harbor of Papatee, the port of Tahiti, its entrance being a narrow channel through the reef.

As we approached nearer a native came on board to pilot the ship into the harbor, where we dropped anchor, off the town, just as the sun was setting.

Sails were furled and decks cleared up, while until gun-fire (eight o'clock) the ship was surrounded by canoes with natives anxious to trade. There were visits to our officers from the officers of the French man-of-war to inquire where from and what news.

Ere darkness settled down I had an opportunity to look at our surroundings, a most beautiful picture. The harbor of Papatee nestles down by the side of a high mountain, the beach forming a crescent, the horn on the seaside being a long point bearing the name of Point Venus. It is covered with magnificent cocoa palms extending all around the beach in front of the town. This beach is a pure white sand, and just in the rear, among the waving palms, orange and banana trees, could be seen the pretty white cottages of the French and English residents, not many at that time, mingled with the picturesque thatched huts of the natives. Some little distance back stood the government house, a more pretentious dwelling, also the residence of the native queen, Pomare.

The whole scene, lighted up with the glory of the departing day, formed a picture of rare beauty.

The anchor watch was set, but it was late that night ere I closed my eyes in slumber.

The next morning was the Sabbath, and we were turned out at daylight to wash down decks and put the ship in shape for a holiday appearance, visitors being expected from shore. Stationed at the head pump on the to'gallant fo'c'sle, I had ample leisure to look around.

In the morning light the scene was beyond compare. The mountains and the hills were bathed in the soft light of the coming day, and the glowing, richly tinted clouds that encircled them. The lighter green of the hillsides contrasted with the deeper shades of the valleys and the graceful foliage of the waving palms that extended around the beach. The groves of orange trees bending with their golden fruit, mingled with the breadfruit trees, and the banana with its great green leaves, while the morning breeze, laden with the breath of flowers, came from the shore, distilling a fragrance rarely inhaled in other lands.

Just as the sun was rising, while drinking in the scene, music from out the groves came to our ears borne on the breeze, not loud and harsh, but exquisitely soft, in complete harmony with the surroundings. The effect was indescribable. For an hour the band played, being stationed in the groves adjoining the government house. I afterwards learned it was the band of the French troops quartered at Tahiti. Every evening and on Sunday mornings they played the most exquisite music.

At eight bells all our colors were thrown to the breeze, with the American ensign at the peak, and the union jack floating from the jackstaff on the bowsprit.

CHAPTER VII
1847

SOCIETY ISLANDS.—HONOLULU.—CALIFORNIA GOLD FEVER

AFTER breakfast, the port watch asked for and received liberty to go on shore for the day, with orders to be at the beach at sunset, when the ship's boat would take them off. Every man was given a few dollars as liberty money, and after washing up and putting on our best shore togs, we were landed on the beach by a boat's crew of the starboard watch, who then returned to the ship.

After landing, the men separated in knots of twos and threes, wandering through the town, scraping acquaintance with the natives, buying fruit and knickknacks, consisting of rare and curious shells, beautiful bunches of coral, sea-fans, embroidered tappa, cloth made from the fibres of the cocoanut husk, and many other curios.

Tattooing was a fine art in these islands. In those days it was almost universal among sailors, to a greater or less extent. It was not long before the crew found an old native who was a past master in the art, and before the ship sailed I do not think there was a member of the crew upon whom he had not exercised his skill. The specimens of his work on my arms to-day, although nearly sixty years have elapsed, are as fresh and bright as when first put in.

In operating the patient lay on his back on the floor of the hut, with his arm bared and outstretched. Old Bob's instruments were a stick, six or eight inches long, with small sharks' teeth inserted or bound to one end, in ones, twos, fours or sixes. Another stick, equally long, was used as a tapper. The ingredients were India ink and vermilion. Squatting down beside the arm, or whatever part he intended to operate on, he would draw his design, generally a ship, a cocoanut tree, a mermaid, or a picture taken from some novel that he had managed to get hold of, such as "Ethwild the Female Pirate," or of that class.

Taking his stick with the keen sharp points in one hand, and the tapper in the other, he would follow the lines drawn upon the skin, tapping, tapping, the blood flowing at each stroke. Every little while he would stop, wipe off the blood, and rub in the India ink or vermilion. This operation was continued until the design was completed. The arm would swell, and be very sore for a few days; perhaps it would be a week before it felt all right, but I never heard of any serious results attending the operation.

In company with the ordinary seaman and the two oldest boys, Barnum W. Field of Boston and Alfred Currier of Salem, after strolling around for awhile we shaped our course for a cruise into the groves back of the town. Following a beaten path, and coming to a spring of sparkling, cold water, we reclined in the shade of a large orange tree, with guavas and bananas in profusion around us, and having eaten our fill of these delicious fruits, we lay back, listening to the murmur of the spring and the soft breeze singing in the tree-tops, and falling asleep, did not wake until the sun was well down its western slope, when we started for the town to be in time for the boat that was to take us aboard at sunset.

At the beach we found about all the watch assembled, one or two arriving at the last moment. Comparing notes, all voted that they had enjoyed their outing hugely. I am sure we did ours, every moment of it. On the arrival of our boats we were rowed on board and reported in good time, thus ending our first liberty day at Tahiti.

The next morning hatches were taken off, and the work of overhauling our cargo commenced, as part was to be discharged here, and the balance at Honolulu, Sandwich Islands.

As one of the boat's crew I spent a great part of the time on shore, or making trips between the ship and shore. When there was leisure, we would let the boat lie, looking over the sides, where the bottom could be plainly seen through the clear, glassy water, many fathoms deep, the waving sea-fans of bright colors, and branches of white coral, through which myriads of fish of almost every hue swam, reminding me of Percival's lines,—

> "Deep in the wave is a coral grove,
> Where the purple mullet and gold fish rove,
> Where the sea flower spreads its leaves of blue
> That never are wet with the falling dew,
> But in bright and changeful beauty shine
> Far down in the deep and glassy brine."

It seemed as if I never would tire of gazing into the depths and admiring the forms of life therein.

The natives were fine specimens of the human family; the male portion of good height and build, and finely featured, complexion a light olive, hair wavy and black. The women were, up to the age of twenty-five, generally very handsome, with a free, upright carriage. As they moved along they appeared, in their light, flowing drapery, as graceful as swans.

The Society Islands were discovered by the Spanish, in 1606, and visited by Captains Wallace and Cook in 1767 and 1769. In 1842, a few years before this, my first visit, they were taken under French protection. The wind'ard group was annexed in 1880, and the leeward in 1885.

As the native population had been in revolt against the French, a military force was deemed necessary to overawe them.

Our stay at Tahiti covered the space of nearly six weeks, when, having put ashore all that portion of our cargo to be landed here, the anchor was weighed, sail made on the ship, and passing out through the reef, we bade a regretful adieu to fair Tahiti, shaping our course for Oahu, Sandwich Islands. How little I thought as I watched it sink beneath the horizon, that ere a few months had passed I should again revisit it, but under different conditions.

A pleasant run of some three weeks brought us in sight of the island of Hawaii, the largest and most southern of the Sandwich group. The lofty peak of Mauna Loa, an active volcano nearly 14,000 feet in height, first appears high up above the horizon. Passing Maui, Molokai, and the smaller islands of the group, we sighted Diamond Head, a high, bold headland, the most southern point of the island of Oahu. East and north some twenty miles lay our destination, the port of Honolulu.

72

The Honolulu of to-day is vastly different from the same place sixty years ago. These islands were united into a kingdom under Kamehameha first in 1791, American missionaries settled there in 1820, and the first treaty with the United States was made in 1826. The first constitution was proclaimed in 1840, and a reciprocity treaty practically establishing free trade with the United States was ratified in 1875. In 1893, the monarchy was abrogated, and four years later a republic was established. In 1902, the republic, under the title of Hawaii, was annexed as a territory to the United States of America.

Closing in with the land, we hauled the main yard aback off the town, outside the reef, with the union jack at the fore, a signal for the pilot.

He soon appeared, in a whale-boat, coming through the channel in the reef, pulled by a crew of Kanakas, as the natives of all these islands are called. Once aboard, I was surprised to learn that he was a Marblehead man, Captain John Meek, who had settled in the islands, married a native woman, and had reared a large family of children, some of the boys being well grown. At this time he held the position of government pilot. Under his guidance we passed through the reef safely, and entered the fine natural harbor, formed by a lagoon, having a depth of from three and a half to five fathoms, and bounded seaward by the reef, with its snowy surf line.

At this time there were no wharves. The "Tsar," having been hauled in and moored stern on to the beach, discharged her cargo into lighters.

There was a large number of vessels in port, nearly all being ships and barques engaged in the whaling business, and, the season over on the nor'west coast, they had called at Honolulu to refit for a cruise for sperm-whales on the equator, or the coasts of Peru and Chile.

Oahu was a great whaling rendezvous, where all the fleet called, both going and returning from the northern whaling grounds, and Honolulu was a lively place, with the harbor full of whale-ships, many lying outside the reef.

After the work was done on board, i. e. putting all rigging and gear in order, tarring and painting, all this work being done in port, on a whale-ship, the crew were given liberty in alternate watches, day after day, as long as the ship remained in port, each man receiving liberty money, from one to two dollars each. This would go a long way if properly managed. Horseback riding was in great vogue. A steed, with saddle, could be hired for from fifty to sixty cents an afternoon, and it was glorious fun for Jack, who generally got all there was in it. While we were hard at work, on the "Tsar," day after day, boat-load after boat-load would pass the ship on their way to the shore to enjoy their outing, until I began to imagine that life on a whaler must be very pleasant. To be sure, we were allowed to go on shore in the evening and on Sundays, generally improving the opportunity, but that was not in the daytime, when we could go horseback riding, and see the country outside of the town.

While lying here a brigantine came into port and anchored close to us. She was named the "Elmira," flying the English flag, and a more beautiful craft I have never seen, but a sad tragedy had occurred. She sailed from Mazatlan, bound for China, and her crew was composed of Spaniards, negroes, and other hard characters picked up on the coast, a captain, first and second officers, a carpenter (a Scotchman) and two apprentice boys. She was in ballast, but had on board a half a million of specie. In the vicinity of the islands the crew mutinied, and took possession of the brig, killing all on board except the carpenter and the two boys. After all was over they got hold of the liquors in the cabin, and entered upon a grand carouse. While part of them lay in a drunken sleep, the carpenter and boys attacked them, "Chips" with his broadaxe taking the lead. They succeeded in killing all the mutineers, throwing their bodies overboard, but, in the melee a big fellow got one of the boys partly over the rail, and was in the act of plunging his knife into him, when the carpenter rushed upon the assailant, severing his arm with the axe and afterwards braining him. Again in possession, one of the boys navigated the brig to Honolulu, and arriving safely, she was taken charge of by the British consul. Many years after, when I was in Port Stanley, Falkland Islands, I saw the same brig, then running as a government mail packet between the Falkland Islands and Montevideo, S.A.

Having discharged the balance of our cargo, instead of proceeding to China in ballast, Captain Kenneday chartered to load oil home to New Bedford, the hold being made ready to receive oil casks, instead of tea chests from a China port as we had anticipated.

We had partly completed our lading, when Honolulu was thrown into a whirl of excitement, by the arrival of the native schooner "Kamehameha" from the coast, with the news of the discovery of gold at Sutter's Mills in California. All who could were getting ready for a trip to San Francisco and the gold diggings. Everything in the shape of sailing craft was chartered and loaded with provisions, or what would pay best, and packed with passengers, who were charged the most exorbitant rates for passage. Every night that we were on shore my ears were filled with the wildest stories of gold discoveries,—fortunes made in a month,—until I caught the gold fever in earnest, and secretly resolved that when the ship was ready for sea I would run away, and manage to work my way to San Francisco. Keeping my own counsel, I made friends with two boat-steerers of the whale-ship "Samuel Robertson" of Fairhaven, who advised me not to leave until the night before the ship was to sail, then get aboard their ship about two in the morning, when they would stow me away until after the "Tsar" left port. This plan I successfully carried out. Separating from my companions about the time they were getting ready to go on board, I lingered about until all was quiet, then borrowing a whale-boat that was lying on the beach, without hunting around for the owner, I paddled off under the bows, climbed on board by the anchor chain, and gained the to'gallant fo'c'sle, from thence descending to the main deck. All was quiet. No anchor watch was kept in port; not a soul to be seen on deck. Descending into the fo'c'sle, I got my clothesbag, and returning on deck, lowered it into the boat, then making the rope fast, I slid down, and casting off, said good-by to the "Tsar," and paddled on board the "Samuel Robertson," that lay but a short distance from the ship. James Barrett, one of my friends, was on the lookout and took me below, where I was stowed away in a locker in the forepeak, remaining there until the "Tsar" sailed the following afternoon.

Coming on deck before she was out of sight, I watched her until hull down. As she sank below the horizon, a feeling of sadness stole over me. I realized that it was the severing of the chain that connected me with home. But this feeling did not last long, for I was naturally of a buoyant and sanguine temperament. Barnum W. Field, a Bostonian, one of our ship's boys, had left previously, with the consent of Captain Kenneday, entering the large mercantile house of Charles W. Brewer & Co. of Honolulu as clerk. At the time I commanded the "Danube," in 1863, I again met him in New York; he was then the head of a large house dealing in western produce.

Finding it impossible, with my limited means, to secure a passage to San Francisco, I shipped on the "Samuel Robertson," for a cruise on the equator to fill up with sperm-oil, thence around Cape Horn home. She was nearly full, and a few whales would enable her to fill up. She had been out from Fairhaven three years, making a most successful voyage.

Having signed articles, for a fortnight I had all the liberty I wished for. Each day one watch would go on shore, receiving a dollar, as liberty money, while on board, the watch would lay around, doing whatever pleased them.

Accustomed, as I was, to the strict discipline of a merchantman, this was indeed a change, but finally, taking our departure, we ran down to Hawaii, where we took on board live stock, yams, sweet potatoes, fruit, etc., after which the ship bore away to the southward for the whaling grounds.

This was an entirely new phase of life, differing greatly from that to which I had been accustomed. After leaving port the boats' crews were chosen, and I was allotted to the first mate's, a large, seven-oared boat, while all the others were but five. The boat's crew consisted of a boat-header, who was either the captain, first, second, third or fourth officer, and the boat's crew of five, or seven, including the boat-steerer, who pulled the harpooner or bow oar.

CHAPTER VIII
1847-1849

WHALING IN '48.—AGAIN TAHITI.—ESCAPE TO THE HILLS.—DINNER IN THE FRENCH RESTAURANT

TEN or twelve days out we sighted our first whales. "There she blows!" came from the lookout stationed at the royal masthead, while to the demand:

"Where away?" came the response:

"Four points off the lee bow, sir!"

Instantly all was excitement. Captain Turner, seizing a powerful marine glass, sprang into the rigging, and quickly ascended to the lookout, from whence in a few moments came the order:

"Keep her off four points!"

This was speedily done, and the yards checked in.

There were many hands to do the work, the ship having a crew of thirty-six, exclusive of officers. Shortly we could see from the deck a large school of sperm-whales, heading eastward, swimming slowly along, little anticipating the reception being made ready for them. Meantime the officers, with their respective crews, were seeing that the whaling gear in each boat was in readiness for lowering. In fact, the gear of a whale-boat when on whaling ground is looked after daily. Harpoons and lances are as bright and sharp as razors. Line-tubs are overhauled, and every kink and turn taken out of the line before being coiled down in the tub, when it is as supple as silk.

Water "breakers" are kept filled, and a lantern keg, with a small supply of biscuit, etc., always ready.

When we were but a short distance from them, the school sounded. The main topsail was now thrown aback, and all made ready for lowering. Though intensely exciting, everything was done very quietly, so as not to alarm the whales. Presently the school broke water about an eighth of a mile astern, and in less than three minutes every boat was in the water, and headed for the whales, while every pound of strength that was in the muscles of the crews was thrown into the oars, until the boats fairly flew through the water.

Just before we reached them, our boat being in the lead, the school again sounded. Lying on our oars, a sharp lookout was kept for their reappearance. In fifteen or twenty minutes they again broke water. No sooner were they sighted than the boats were after them, and shortly the harpooner was ordered to stand up. I could now hear the "choo'o, choo'o, choo'o," as they spouted from their blow-holes.

Fairly quivering with excitement, and turning round to get a good look, I suddenly received a tap alongside the head from the mate at the steering oar, that caused me to see more stars than I ever imagined were made, with a quiet admonition that it was contrary to rules to turn the head to look, when pulling on to a whale.

We were now right between two big whales, at least eighty barrels each. The boat being, in whaling parlance, "wood and black skin "*i. e.* the wood of the boat touching the skin of the whale, by reaching over I could have placed my hand upon one, when the mate shouted to let him have it.

The boat-steerer, who is the harpooner, became gallied (dazed or frightened) from some unaccountable reason. He was too close for darting, and instead of driving, or setting, his iron into him solid, he drove it at him, cutting him down the side, but not fastening securely. Catching up his second iron, he fairly pitch-poled it over him.

It is a singular fact that, as soon as one whale in a school is struck, all the rest know it. In an instant there was not an earthquake, but a waterquake around us, a seething mass of white water, with heads, flukes, and fins in every direction.

Supposing we were fast, the mate roared, "To stern all!" and all the crew thinking the same, the order was obeyed with a will. In less time than it takes to write it, the whole school, having become gallied, were off to wind'ard, going "fin out," like mad.

When the mate discovered that Fred, the Portuguese boat-steerer, had missed his whale, he was furious, and acted for awhile like an insane man. Catching up a paddle, he threw it at Fred's head, and dashing his hat into the bottom of the boat, jumped up and down upon it, in the meanwhile cursing him, and the whole boat's crew. Then, starting on another tack, the boat's head was turned, and we were ordered to row to wind'ard after the whales, the mate offering everything he possessed, if we could only overhaul the school. Standing there bareheaded, with one hand on the steering oar, with the other he would set against my oar with a force that almost threw me over the

81

line-tub at each stroke, while the crew pulled as if for their lives. But it was of no avail, and after an hour's hard work the school was about out of sight, and the ship nearly hull down. The boat's head was then pulled round, and, reluctantly, we returned on board, where poor Fred was "broken," and turned forward among the crew. According to his story, he had only been right-whaling, and was accustomed to a long dart. The manner of approaching a right whale differs from that of going on to a sperm-whale: with the former you approach the fore shoulder, and, after fastening, back off, out of the way of his flukes, that he invariably sweeps from one side to the other, and woe betide the boat that gets within reach of that tail, his fighting weapon. A dart with a harpoon is made from a distance of one to five fathoms. In the latter case, a sperm-whale fights with his head, and rarely sweeps, but when struck with the iron, fans, *i. e.* raises his tail and brings his flukes down with a crack equal to ten thousand coach-whips. In fastening, the boat is run by the corner of his flukes, and alongside, and a dart made from two or three fathoms' distance, but when Fred found himself so close, he lost his head.

It was a bitter disappointment to the captain and officers, as well as the crew, for if he had fastened solid, probably every other boat would have fastened, also, as where one whale is fast the school will hang around generally, giving each boat a chance, and we should have filled up the balance of our casks. The loss of these whales put Captain Turner, officers and crew in bad humor, that cropped out on every occasion. What made it worse, we did not raise another school of sperm-whales, not even a single one, although lookouts were at both fore and main mastheads. Nothing more than a few schools of blackfish were sighted, which we lowered for, and took enough oil to give us some twenty barrels, at the expense of a stove boat. These blackfish are lively fellows, and sometimes give a lot of trouble. They are apt to breach out of water over a boat, and will run one for a short time at a lively gait. They yield, if in good condition, from three to five barrels of oil, according to size, and, unless whales are around, are always taken, as the oil brings a good price.

Thus two weeks passed, and no whales, while gloom hung o'er the ship, and life on the "Samuel Robertson" was anything but "one glad sweet song."

About this time, it was discovered that our fore topmast was badly sprung, and as our water casks needed filling, Captain Turner decided to call in at Papetee, Otaheite, get a spar for the carpenter to make into a fore topmast, and fill water. The ship, being but a short distance from the island, was headed for the port, and the following morning was off the reef with the town in sight, the hills and mountains of Otaheite showing up grandly in the morning light and looking, now, so familiar to me. Passing through the passage in the reef, we came to anchor off the town, with its white beach, cocoa palms waving, huts and houses peeping out from the orange groves, everything looking as I left it a few months before.

Captain Turner was afraid of desertion, and orders were given that no liberty on shore would be allowed. A picked boat's crew to carry

Captain Turner back and forth were chosen, I being so fortunate as to be one of the number. We took him ashore each morning, returning at noon; again after dinner, remaining until nightfall, then returning on board for the night.

Native canoes were allowed alongside during the day, while natives, male and female, swarmed over the ship, trading with the officers and crew, but when night fell they were ordered off.

On the third morning after our arrival, my chum, Jim Foote of Syracuse, N. Y., "turned up missing," having deserted during the night in some way, probably by one of the canoes, eluding the vigilance of the officers. This desertion very much incensed Captain Turner, and a double watch was ordered, the officers succeeding each other in turn.

I had fully made up my mind to run away if opportunity offered, but not until the last night did I see a chance. The port regulations were very strict, no sailors or officers of any ship being allowed on shore after gun-fire at eight o'clock at night, without a special permit. Any one caught between that hour and gun-fire at 3 A. M. was picked up and locked in the calaboose. The native police (kikos) were on the alert for Jack, as it meant a reward. The beach was patrolled by French soldiers until the morning gun. All this made it pretty difficult to escape, but one thing was in my favor. I had picked up the language, during my former visit here, and in Honolulu, and was able to talk Kanaka like a native.

The last day of the ship's stay was spent on shore by the boat's crew, and about dark, Captain Turner, having finished his business, came down to go on board. It was now about 8 P.M.; all the canoes had left the ship, having been ordered off, save one which was lying under the fore channels, the owner, a big Kanaka, with his little *whyenee* (girl), being down in the boat-steerers' quarters, trading with them. Seeing the canoe, a thought that I might get ashore in her flashed across my mind, and slipping into the fo'c'sle, I pulled on an extra shirt, and returning, stood by the rail awaiting his coming. As he passed me I asked in low tones if he would take me ashore, and quickly comprehending the situation, he answered in the affirmative. Slipping through the open port-hole and grasping a rope hanging over the side, I slid down into the canoe, lying flat in the bottom, and was followed in a moment by the *whyenee* and himself. Casting off, and seizing his paddle, a few vigorous strokes set him clear from the ship, and although the officers were watching as well as they could see in the gathering darkness, I was unobserved, and knew that I should not be missed until morning. Passing the guard-boat rowing about in the harbor, which came close to us, the guard speaking to the Kanaka, but failing to see me, we ran alongside some boats moored a stone's throw from the beach. The Kanaka having told me, on my way in, that I must slip into one of these boats and remain until he came for me, I acted on his instructions, and rolled over into a small rowboat and lay down to await his coming, and having dropped asleep, was awakened by a rubbing along the boat's side. Looking up, I saw my Kanaka standing in his canoe signing for silence and for me to get in.

A few strokes sent us to the beach. Leaving the boat drawn up a little, we crawled on our hands and knees, the native leading, up past the sentry, who was sitting on the beach, with his musket beside him, sound asleep. Having got a short distance past him, we arose to our feet, continuing on until we came to several huts, one of which, the roof partly off, was in a dilapidated condition, and nearly filled with leaves fallen from the grove in which it stood. Into this shelter I crept, and covered myself with the leaves, the Kanaka telling me he would come after gun-fire, about 3 o'clock in the morning. Promptly on time he made his appearance, and, taking the lead and telling me to follow, he struck into a path leading to the hills. Two hours' brisk travel brought us to an elevation, where we could look over the town, harbor, and reef. As far as the eye could reach were spread the shining blue waters of the Pacific. The view at this elevation was magnificent. Turning in from the path through a thicket of guava bushes, we emerged into a beautiful grove of orange and other trees. Here he told me to stop, and he would go down and bring me up some food.

As there was an abundance of fruit around, and it was not at all likely that I should remain long, this movement of his appeared singular, and the thought came to my mind that when he returned he would not be alone. No doubt a small reward would be offered for me, and, having hidden, he would know where to find me. In short, I felt that he was going to betray me, and give me up for the reward, and acting on this belief, I went a short distance and climbed a tree having a very dense foliage, making openings through the leaves where I could command a view of the path leading to the grove, as well as one looking over it. I then settled back, and awaited events.

Two hours passed, when, hearing voices, I glanced through the opening, and saw my Kanaka, accompanied by two French soldiers, coming up the path. Leaving them outside, he entered alone, and not seeing me, called softly, but receiving no response, finally called them in. Beating the bushes, they hunted everywhere, but at last came to the conclusion that I had vacated my quarters, for some reason, and giving up the search, returned to town.

After becoming satisfied that they had gone for good, I descended from the tree, and struck into another path that brought me out on the seaward side of Point Venus. Here, hidden in the bushes, I could see the ship lying outside the reef, with her main topsail aback, which meant that Captain Turner was still on shore, waiting for me to be brought to the boat and taken on board, and I inwardly chuckled to think that the "Samuel Robertson" would not have me this time!

At last the boat went on board, and the ship filled away. I watched her until she was hull down, and then, feeling that the chances were very small that she would return, I left my hiding-place and walked boldly into the town, and turning into the American consul's store, I accosted the captain of the barque "George," of Stonington, Conn., U. S. A., a whaler, telling him, frankly, I had deserted from the ship "Samuel Robertson," and asking if he would ship me.

After being badgered awhile, I signed the articles for ten dollars a month, and to help take oil if we saw whales, instead of a regular lay, as the barque was bound home around the Cape, but would lower for whales if we saw any.

The "George" had been out forty-seven months, having had very poor luck, only about twelve hundred barrels of oil, and most of that a poor quality taken in Magdalena Bay, California. She was short-handed, only four of her original ship's company that left home remaining by her.

Having received my advance ($10), I started for the beach, but had not proceeded far when I was arrested as a runaway from the "Samuel Robertson," so, instead of landing on the "George" in a half-hour, I found myself an inmate of the calaboose in company with my chum Jim Foote, who was picked up an hour before.

The following morning Captain George Taber, finding I had not gone on board, came to look me up. This was fortunate for Jim, as the captain not only obtained my release, but his also, shipping him as one of the crew of the "George." We had taken our departure from duress almost famished, I having had nothing but fruit for two days and Jim for about a week. So we made a line for a restaurant just off the beach kept by a Frenchman and largely patronized by the officers of the men-of-war and captains of vessels in port.

With my month's advance in my pocket, we entered boldly, signifying to the *garçon* in Kanaka,—not being well up in French,—that we wished dinner for two. Our appearance was against us, and the *garçon* viewed us with suspicion, but the jingle of the silver dollars set everything right,—and such a dinner! Cleaning off every dish that was brought on, we finished two bottles of wine with our repast, then lay back in our chairs, calling for the best cigars, and finally, as the day was waning, the bill. It was brought. Passing over the items, we glanced at the sum total, forty-five francs,—my whole month's advance, with the exception of five francs, that we magnanimously handed the waiter, who bowed us out, salaaming to the floor, and we went on board without a cent, but full and happy.

The memory of that dinner lingered with us many weeks.

With the exception of one whale, we took no more oil. We were very short-provisioned, and the desire seemed to be more to get home than to see whales. We made a favorable run around Cape Horn and were again in the south Atlantic. Our provisions were getting very short indeed, when we were fortunate in speaking the ship "Martha" of Newport, R. I., also a whaler, and procuring from her two casks of bread, with other stores, but no tobacco. We were all out of tobacco, and on our arrival at Stonington had been without over a month, and every user of the weed knows what that means. We had procured a plug for each man from a schooner, the day before we made port, and from that time all hands were chewing away for dear life.

Taking a pilot, we entered the port of Stonington, when the following day all who had shipped in the Islands were paid off, myself among the number. Paying no heed to flattering inducements held out to me to proceed to New Bedford and join the ship "Betsey Williams," just fitting out for a three years' cruise in the Pacific—having had all I wanted of whaling—I took the train for Boston, where I joined the barque

"Tiberias," Captain Elisha Foster, bound for San Francisco and the gold fields. This was in the rush of '49.

Our crew was shipped for $13 advance, and $2 per month; it being stipulated in the articles that the crew should discharge the cargo in San Francisco, at the going rate of wages at that port.

SAN FRANCISCO.—ASTORIA.—PORTLAND.—GENUINE RED MEN

SAILING from Boston in November, 1849, we experienced a fine run off the coast. The westerly winds prevailing were not long in running our easting down, and we could head south for the trade winds.

Our crew numbered fourteen for'ard, which, with captain and after guard, made a total of twenty, all told. Ten days out insanity developed in John Williston, one of the crew, which caused no end of trouble.

A sailor from Gay Head, Martha's Vineyard, of the name of Charles, had been a shipmate of John's, and knew of these attacks, but had not mentioned it. The discovery was made thus: John had been sick, and confined to his berth two days. Coming from the wheel the second day, I passed the members of the watch getting their supper on deck, and descended the fo'c'sle ladder to get my pot, pan and spoon in order to join them. Securing these, I was about mounting the steps, when there came from, John's bunk one of the most unearthly groans I ever heard. Thinking he must be in great pain, I stepped to the berth, and asked him how he felt. Receiving no reply, I placed my hand upon his shoulder, when like a flash he turned upon me with a demoniacal glare in his eyes. His look was enough to freeze one's blood and in an instant I realized I was alone with a powerful maniac, endowed with the full use of all his limbs, and possessing at least five times his natural strength. I turned to escape by the companionway, but with a roar like a wild beast he sprang to the fo'c'sle deck, making for me ere I could reach the foot of the ladder. The big oak bitts came through the centre of the fo'c'sle, and around these I sprang, followed by John, who was as nimble as a cat. Finally, on the fourth or fifth round, he caught his foot in the becket of the bread-barge and fell. I reached the companion ladder with a bound, and was part ways up, when he grasped my foot, but a vigorous kick in the head with the other foot caused him to loosen his hold and fall back into the fo'c'sle, where, seizing the barge in one hand, he started in, smashing everything in general. At that moment Charles, his former shipmate, came from the wheel, and looking down, exclaimed:

"My God! John's got his fits again!" adding, "He must be secured. He'll kill all hands if he gets out of the fo'c'sle."

As only one man could go down at a time, it was apparent that the first one would have anything but a picnic before the others could assist him, but something must be done, for John was creating havoc among the chests and berths, and the carpenter, a big man, volunteered. Springing into the fo'c'sle, he grappled the madman, and for a couple of minutes poor "Chips" was knocked around like a shuttlecock, and until we could get down and overpower him by force of numbers. Then, having bound him so he could do no damage, we let him lie while Charles enlightened us. It seems that these attacks would come on daily for several weeks, then every other day, finally every third day for ten days or a fortnight, and then pass away entirely. He would have no more unless some fit of passion, or other reason, caused a return. The worst feature was that when he felt them coming on he would conceal the fact, and before we were aware of it, he would be a raving maniac, with a desire to kill some one, so it became necessary to keep a very careful watch upon him, so as to have him confined in time in a strait-jacket and f rapped down on a four-inch plank, some seven feet long, with a row of holes bored on each side, through which ratline stuff was passed, making a complete lacework over him. Even bound thus, he would grip with his toes anything coming in contact with his feet, while a rope swung by his face he would snap with his teeth in the most vicious manner. It was much feared he would have an attack at night, and get hold of a hand-spike or knife, in which case he would probably have had to be shot. When he came out of these attacks, he would be as weak and almost as helpless as a kitten for about two hours, after which he would recover his strength, and be as well as any one until the attacks came on again. They would last from one to two hours. Before we reached Cape Horn the fits passed away entirely, but they cost us many a scare, and kept all hands on the qui vive for nearly two months.

Just before sailing from Boston a week of very severe cold weather was experienced, and on breaking out stores when we got part ways to the equator, it was found that twenty-five barrels of potatoes had to be thrown overboard, having been frozen while being taken on board. It was a keen loss, as we had counted on potatoes for a long time.

On the equator we spoke an English ship bound from Sydney, N. S. W., to London, and it being nearly calm, the captains visited each other, and some of the passengers of the Englishman wishing to go to California, Captain Foster got two men from her. They were good, able seamen, and on John's account we were glad to have them. We made a good run to Cape Horn, with fifteen days of stormy gales off the Cape, and we were again in the south Pacific.

Passing the belt of S. E. and N. E. trades, nothing of note occurred until we arrived off the heads of San Francisco.

Sighting the Farralones, a cluster of small, rocky islands, in the morning, we took a pilot on board, and entering the Golden Gate, we passed up the bay, coming to an anchor among a fleet of shipping of all nationalities, one hundred and forty-five days from Boston.

Glorious California! El Dorado of the Pacific slope! What successes, struggles and hardships have you witnessed in the mad rush for gold during the early days, after the discovery of the vast amount of mineral wealth within thy borders had been made known to the world, and the Golden Gate of thy magnificent bay was opened wide to young and old, rich and poor alike, sturdy adventurers from every land, bidding them welcome to a participation in the treasures to be harvested from thy rivers, streams, and mountains!

Such a gathering could only be found in San Francisco during these early days of '49 and '50. One met very few old men in the city streets, but young to middle-aged, full of life, brawn and muscle, eager, and all dominated by one thought, in the wild headlong scramble for wealth: Gold! Gold! Gold!

Although our crew had shipped to discharge the cargo, all hands except the captain and mate went ashore the following morning, landing at Clark's Point.

94

Wending my way up the hill, I was so fortunate as to meet a "Marbleheader" I knew well, who, after a hearty handshake, informed me that I would find a restaurant just over the hill kept by a townsman, Mr. Benjamin Dixey, adding, "You will find all the 'Marbleheaders' there, and get all the news."

For a few moments after I had entered the restaurant it seemed as if I had struck the old town again. Here I obtained all the news about the mines, who had gone, cost of outfit, what townsmen were in port, and general information upon other matters, then I started for the ship to get my sea chest, which had been left on board. Half way down the hill by the roadside stood a shanty built of rough boards and canvas, with a sign over the door bearing the name of one of the swell hotels of New York City, "Delmonico's."

Stopping a moment to glance inside, I noticed a young man in a red shirt, standing in the doorway, looking intently at me.

"Why, Jack! "he suddenly burst out with, "where in thunder did you spring from?"

It dawned upon me in a moment, it was my old schoolmate and chum, Ambrose Allen, whom I had not seen since my first voyage.

Mutual congratulations and comparing of notes occupied the next hour, at the end of which it was agreed that I should stop there, at the shanty,—hotel, I mean. The terms were $50 per week, plenty to eat if one was not too fastidious, and a good bunk to sleep in; what more would one wish? Of course the bar made it a little noisy, and a free fight, now and then, made everything exciting and lively. Although

95

about every man carried a revolver, or some weapon, they were seldom resorted to. Each man knew his opponent was armed, and the drawing of a knife or gun was the signal for a battle to the death, or at least severe wounding. Men would hesitate before being killed or perhaps permanently disabled for any small quarrel, and generally settled the matter with fists.

My chum said if I did not find anything to do in a few days, he would speak to Capt. William Stacey, his prospective father-in-law, and get me work on board his ship as cook at $200 per month, until we should make up our minds what we would do, whether to go to the mines or not.

I worked on shore at odd jobs for a week, but not having money to purchase an outfit, I abandoned the idea of gold digging. My chum got his discharge, his pay amounting to quite a sum, and we fell in with a Marblehead captain (Captain Hector Dixey), who was in command of a small schooner named "Eagle," between 80 and 90 tons burthen, that had come out in '49 during the excitement and was then owned by Dunbar & Co., merchants in San Francisco. She was bound to Portland, Oregon, with freight and passengers, who were going to take up land offered by the United States government. To encourage settlers the government was for a short time giving out grants of 320 acres of land to one person, or if two, 640 acres, as a homestead to all who would settle on it and improve the land. A great many from San Francisco availed themselves of this offer. Picking up another "Marbleheader" (William Swasey), who acted in the capacity of mate, and four others whose acquaintance we had made, one acting as cook, we shipped for a trip to Portland, wages $100 per month. Sailors were hard to get, at this time, even for short trips, and wages ran from $100 to $150 per month, high wages for Jack, but this was more than balanced by the high cost of everything on shore. A sailor, or any one who could turn his hand to anything that came along, although not an expert, could always command high pay; while on shipboard, food costing nothing, $100 a month was very good. Jack in San Francisco, in these days, was a very independent character, who dictated his own terms.

Sailing from the bay, we encountered head winds and fogs, and two weeks passed before we arrived off the mouth of the Columbia River. We crossed the bar a little after noon, and arrived at Astoria, fifteen miles inside, before sunset.

Astoria, named for John Jacob Astor, of New York, had been until recently the trading post of the old Hudson Bay Fur Company, which had removed to Vancouver's Island. It contained one little frame house, a few log huts, and the fort of the old trading company.

The forest extended to the beach. Save a few whites, the inhabitants were Indians, genuine red men of the forest, but fast disappearing before the onward march of civilization.

> "Where swam the squaw's light birch canoe,
> The steamer smokes and raves,
> While city lots are staked and sold,
> Above old Indian graves."

Sickness, diseases of the white man that they knew not how to treat, was decimating their numbers, and our pilot pointed out a neck of land on which he said there were over a thousand Indians only a year before, but now, not one, almost all having been swept off by smallpox and other forms of disease, while those who had not died had moved away from the stricken spot.

Sailing up the Columbia, we passed Coffin Rock on the right. This was a large, flat rock or small island, which was used as a burial place for the Indians. It was covered with canoes, each containing the corpse of an Indian, with his implements of war, bow, arrows, pottery, etc. It had been burnt off by the whites, and the pilot said would be again, when the Indians would no doubt abandon it as a place for burial.

A singular rock stood near the middle of the river, rising like a shaft from the bed of the stream to a height of forty or fifty feet above the surface, perpendicular on all sides, with shrubs growing on the top. The scenery was magnificent. The river banks, rising from the water's edge hundreds of feet in height, were crowned with giant pines, extending heavenward a hundred and fifty feet or more, while each turn and bend of the river opened up new beauties, which at night, under a full moon, formed a picture long to be remembered.

Entering the mouth of the Willamette, we arrived at Portland City, making fast under the bank.

Portland, at this time, was a city only in name. The site was laid out, but the virgin forests extended nearly to the river's banks, which were from thirty to fifty feet above the stream. The trees had been felled, and the ground cleared for five or six hundred yards back from the river's bank, but the stumps were standing in every direction. There were a dozen or more log houses, no streets, and one small frame building only, which served as a general store for whites and Indians.

After landing passengers and freight, the fo'c'sle hands became restless, and having had a difference with Mr. Swasey, the mate, we left in a body, rented a log house, and settled down to enjoy life on shore. I employed, to cook for us, the cook of a barque who had been left on shore sick but had now recovered. We lacked nothing in the food line, for we had laid in a liberal stock of provisions at the store; also guns and ammunition, for the river was alive with game,—ducks and geese,—and its waters were teeming with fish, the finest salmon being daily speared by the Indians at the falls just above the city.

Here we remained, leading a sort of nomad life, for a month, until, tiring of its monotony, we shipped on the barque "Susan Drew," Captain Drew, for "Frisco."

No men being obtainable in the port for the voyage, we asked and received two hundred dollars per month, with the contract to discharge the cargo at the same wages.

A short, pleasant run brought us again to port in San Francisco, where two weeks were used up in discharging the cargo of round timber, after which we took our discharge from the vessel.

Some two months were spent in port, most of the time working on board ships in the harbor at big pay.

September 9, 1850, California was admitted into the Union, the 31st State. It was a gala day, and was celebrated with all the eclat that could be contributed by brass bands, parades, burning of powder, and firing of cannon, with illuminations and fireworks at night. Every one entered into the spirit of the occasion and the whole affair was voted a grand success.

We were now pretty well in funds, and as everything was so high in San Francisco, it was agreed upon by the six of us to take a run to Valparaiso, S. A., have a general good time, as we looked upon it in those days, then return to San Francisco and make a lot more money.

Looking back through the vista of years, I can now see how foolish and improvident was the course we were pursuing, but I can only say that we were like thousands of other sailors, living only for the day and hour, with no thought of the morrow, or of laying up our earnings against the time of need.

Shipping on the barque "Zingari," of Salem, Mass., Captain Eaton, we dropped down the bay, and crossed the bar, bidding adieu to the Golden Gate, for a few months, as we then supposed, I little dreaming it would be ten or twelve years before I again passed its portals, and then as captain of a fine ship.

Discharging our pilot, we shaped our course south.

CHAPTER X
1850-1851

CHILE AND PERU.—ITALY.—COTTON SCREWING AND "CHANTIES" ON NEW ORLEANS LEVEES

AFTER a pleasant run of six weeks with nothing of note occurring, we entered the spacious harbor of Valparaiso, a fine bay, but open to the "northers," which at times blow with great violence, and cause a heavy sea, or ground-swell, making communication between the ship and shore difficult, and at times dangerous. The holding ground is good, however, and unless a ship breaks from her anchorage, disasters seldom occur.

The view of the city and surrounding hills, from the bay, is very fine.

As we had only shipped for the run to Valparaiso, we were discharged the following day, taking up our quarters at a boarding-house bearing the cognomen of "The Old House at Home," at the foot of the "Main Top Hill," so called. Here we remained for several weeks, until, our funds getting low, we sought an opportunity of returning to California, but found this no easy matter.

We worked on board ships in the bay for a month, and finding no chance of returning to San Francisco, we shipped on a large centreboard schooner, called the "Sarah," flying the Chilian flag, for a trip down the coast and return to Valparaiso. The cargo consisted of provisions and mining supplies for the ports of Coquimbo, Huasco, Copiapo, Cobija, Chile, and Iquiqui and Arica in Peru.

We landed our cargo on the beach with boats, most of the ports being nothing but an open roadstead. The surf was high, at times, rendering landing with an open boat a ticklish and frequently a dangerous undertaking, but with great care our cargo was all gotten on shore safely.

On the eastern side rain is abundant, but along this part of the coast rain never falls; the high peaks of the Andes forming a watershed that draws every drop of moisture from the clouds passing over. There are heavy dews at night. There is no vegetation, no drinking-water, except that distilled from the salt water at the works that supply the inhabitants. The town wore a dry and arid look. Earthquakes are of frequent occurrence. We experienced many shocks while at Valparaiso, some very severe, shaking down a number of dwellings, but we became so accustomed to them that they occasioned no alarm unless of very unusual severity.

We returned to Valparaiso, after five weeks absence, and finding no opportunity of going back to California, we shipped on the barque "Antelope," Captain Zenas Crosby, bound for Coquimbo, Chile, to load skins and pig copper for New York. The cargo was taken on board and stowed by the crew. It was hard, backbreaking work, carrying the big rough pigs of copper with their jagged edges,—some weighing a hundred pounds or more,—from one part of the hold to another.

It was not stowed in a solid mass, but first dunnage, consisting of planks, then a layer of pigs,—not close together, but a foot apart,—then a layer of bales of skins over all, and on top of these another layer of pigs, and so on, in alternate layers, until the lading was completed. Although it was a heavy cargo, the manner of stowing made it springy.

Sundays we had liberty, one watch at a time, and embraced the opportunity of visiting the city of Coquimbo, situated about nine miles from the port or roadstead, and hiring horses with saddles, for a dollar each, we set out on the gallop over a good road. The day was bright with sunshine, a fine brisk breeze blowing, an ideal day for horseback riding. Being a fair horseman, I thoroughly enjoyed it, but several of my companions cut but a sorry figure on horseback, and several tumbles were the consequence, but no serious mishap. Arriving at the city, we rode around awhile, but found not a great deal to interest us, streets not over clean, low flat-roofed houses, one and two story, and a strong odor of garlic pervading the atmosphere everywhere. We visited a few of the churches, after which we purchased some delicious white grapes and other fruits, for luncheon, while our horses rested, and again mounting, arrived at the port just at sunset, having greatly enjoyed the trip.

Our lading completed, all was made ready for sea. It was now near midwinter in the southern hemisphere, and anticipating severe weather rounding Cape Horn, our best sails were bent, and running gear carefully looked after. We sailed from Coquimbo with a strong northerly wind, and passed the latitude of Cape Horn in ten or twelve days from port, when, taking a strong, westerly gale, we scudded past under a close-reefed main topsail, and reefed foresail, with a fearful sea sweeping after, every wave having a most ominous look as it rose high above the taffrail, but our good barque seemed to realize the danger, and rose to each mountain of water as light and graceful as a bird. Squalls of snow and hail, beating fiercely upon us, followed each other in rapid succession, while two men at the wheel had all the work they could do to keep the barque before it, yet she was not a hard-steering craft.

It was at this time I met with an accident, which but for a merciful providence would probably have ended my career.

About four bells, in the mid-watch, during the height of the gale, the head of the main spencer blew adrift, and an order came instantly from the mate, for one of the watch to take a spare gasket, lay aloft, and secure it. This was no easy matter, as the shrouds were cased with sleet and snow, while the running gear was stiff with ice. The ship was rolling heavily as she drove before the blast, while the night was dark as Erebus, save momentary gleams of phosphorescent brightness from the surges as they swept past. Standing near the main rigging, I procured a gasket, and started aloft. I was very heavily dressed, in thick clothing and monkey jacket with oilskins over all, thick sea-boots and mittens. Opposite the spencer gaff, just under the maintop, I was obliged to swing out from the rigging, grasp the running gear, and with legs wound about the sail to smother it. I worked with both hands at getting the gasket passed. As I could do nothing with mittens on, I dropped them, and during the sharp heavy rolls I would cling on with my fingers like fish-hooks. Just as the last turns were passed and the sails secured, the barque gave an unusually heavy roll. My benumbed fingers, stiff with the cold, refused to hold on, and down I went by the run, and now my thick clothing and heavy sea-boots saved me. Striking the edge of the pin-rail around the mainmast with my heels, and breaking a piece out, I shot into the scupper, striking my shoulder, but not my head.

Although not seriously injured, I lay there, stunned, the breath being about knocked out of my body, and picking me up, the watch carried me into the cabin, where I soon recovered my wind. Captain Crosby, after an examination, finding no bones broken, and nothing worse than a severe shaking up, administered to me a stiff glass of brandy, and I resumed my watch on deck, though feeling the effects in a general soreness for days after.

Having passed the Horn and rounded Staten Land, we sped on with favorable gales under all the canvas the "Antelope" could carry, towards the belt of S. E. trades, and crossing the equator, and entering the N. E. trades, passing the Windward Islands, Bermuda, Cape Hatteras, and the Gulf Stream, struck soundings on Yankee land once more, and taking a pilot off Barnegat Light, the "Antelope" arrived safely at New York, without the loss of a sail, spar, or man, eighty-two days from Coquimbo.

We were paid off the following day, and my chum Ambrose Allen and I parted from our shipmates and took the steamer that night for Newport and Fall River, thence by rail to Boston and Marblehead, where we received a warm welcome from our friends.

This voyage ended the seagoing experience of my schoolmate. His father wished him to go into business with him on shore, so Ambrose abandoned the sea. He was a loyal, staunch friend through life. He married the sweetheart of his boyhood days, a lovely girl, and when at home from my voyages in after years, we spent many happy hours at his house or at his store, recalling our early experiences in California, or along the Pacific coast.

After a short stay on shore, I shipped on the barque "Kepler," for a voyage to the Mediterranean, with a cargo of naval stores for the port of Spezzia, Italy, at that time a naval rendezvous for our fleet in Mediterranean waters. A pleasant run brought us to the Strait of Gibraltar, through which we passed in daylight, having a fine view of the Spanish coast with the island and light-house of Tarifa, and the mountains of Spain, while on the south towered the giant peaks of the African shore, ending with the high bluff promontory of Cape Spartel, marking the western entrance of the straits, and Gibraltar standing like a giant sentinel guarding the eastern entrance. We sailed past Malaga, and the sunny shores of Spain with its mountains in the background, past Cape de Gata and the Balearic Islands, and crossing the Gulf of Genoa, entered the port of Spezzia, passing between an island on our right and the mainland, a narrow channel through which a strong tide ran.

Having discharged our cargo at the government dock, the "Kepler" sailed in ballast for Palermo, Sicily, to load fruit for Boston. A run of a few days brought us to that port, and drawing in under the high land, the strong gusts from off the hills obliged us to take in our kites in a hurry, but once around the long mole, we were in a fine harbor sheltered from all winds.

Off this port will be seen in the illustration the barque "Cornelia L. Bevan," owned by Isaac Jeanes of Philadelphia. It is copied, by courtesy of Mr. Joseph Y. Jeanes, son of the owner, from a painting made at Palermo, and is a good specimen of a Baltimore clipper of sixty years ago. She was built in that city in 1847, for the Mediterranean trade, although she did make a voyage to San Francisco and back. Her dimensions were: registered tonnage, 330; length 108 feet; beam 25 feet, 7 inches; depth of hold 13 feet, 3 inches; square stern and female figurehead.

Sicily is a large island, with an area of nine thousand nine hundred and thirty-six square miles, lying off the southern and western end of Italy, and belonging to that government. A fine view of Mt. Ætna can be obtained from the harbor, towering high above the rest of the island, with an elevation of a little upwards of ten thousand eight hundred feet. The day after our arrival, its summit was white with fresh snow that had fallen during the night, presenting a beautiful appearance in the sunlight, contrasted with the vivid green farther down the slope of the mountain. Palermo and Messina are the principal ports, from which large shipments of fruit, principally oranges and lemons, are made to London and Liverpool, as well as the United States. Trapani, on the northwestern end of the island, is also a great shipping port for salt brought from Marsala, where there are extensive salt-pans, the salt being heaped in great mounds resembling snow-drifts when viewed from the water with the sun shining on them.

Having completed our lading,—oranges and lemons,—the "Kepler" took her departure from Palermo, and after a quick run from Gibraltar with a fair passage of thirty-six days across,—not bad in the month of February,—we took a pilot, and were shortly fast alongside Central Wharf, Boston, where the crew were paid off.

I made a run to New Orleans on the barque "Ionia," and then joined the ship "Governor Davis" of "Train's White Diamond Line." We loaded cotton for Liverpool, and returned to Boston with emigrants, some three hundred in the steerage. Very rough weather was experienced on this passage over, and the passengers suffered accordingly. Gale succeeded gale, with a frightful sea, and it was necessary to keep the passengers below, with hatches on, for days at a time. When they were removed the men were sent below with buckets of tar and red hot irons plunged in them to fumigate the hold and between-decks. Two deaths occurred and one passenger had his leg broken by a cask breaking away in a gale. With the record of sixty-eight days from Liverpool, we anchored in Lighthouse Channel, Boston, badly iced up, with crew frost-bitten and thoroughly fagged out.

From the "Governor Davis" I went to the "Tirrell," a large ship, commanded by Captain Thomas Hyler, as third mate, and made another voyage to Liverpool, returning to Boston with four hundred and twenty emigrants. This was another long, hard passage. We had heavy gales, with plenty of snow and hail squalls, with high seas. Sixty days was our record this time, between Liverpool and Boston.

I left the "Tirrell" in Boston, and having had enough of western ocean winter voyages, I signed the articles of the ship "Emperor," Captain Knott Pedrick, as third mate, bound to New Orleans. The "Emperor" was a ship of seven hundred tons burthen, having fine accommodations for cabin passengers. Sailing from Boston in ballast, we arrived safely, and loaded cotton for Havre, France.

New Orleans, at this time, was the great shipping port of the South for exporting cotton to Europe, although Mobile, Savannah and Charleston also shipped great quantities.

In the winter months, all along the levees at New Orleans lay tiers of shipping of all nationalities, loading cotton for the northern ports of the United States, as well as the various ports of Europe. The river front is shaped like a crescent, and from this fact New Orleans takes its name of the "Crescent City." For miles along the banks, or levees, extends the shipping, lying in tiers, loading cotton, staves, or tobacco, but principally cotton. The bales were rolled from the levee by the stevedores' gangs, generally roustabout darkies, up the staging, and tumbled on deck and down the hold, where they were received by gangs of cotton-screwers, there being as many gangs in the ship's hold as could work to advantage.

The bales were placed in tiers, and when they would apparently hold no more, with the aid of planks and powerful cotton-screws, several bales would be driven in where it would appear to a novice impossible to put one.

Four men to a screw constituted a gang, and it was a point of honor to screw as many bales in a ship's hold as could possibly be crammed in, and in some cases even springing the decks upwards, such a power was given by the screw. All this work was accompanied by a song, often improvised and sung by the *"chantie"* man, the chorus being taken up by the rest of the gang. Each gang possessed a good *"chantie"* singer, with a fine voice. The chorus would come in with a vim, and every pound in the muscles of the gang would be thrown into the handle-bars of the cotton-screws, and a bale of cotton would be driven in where there appeared to be but a few inches of space.

The songs or *"chanties"* from hundreds of these gangs of cotton-screwers could be heard all along the river front, day after day, making the levees of New Orleans a lively spot. As the business of cotton-screwing was dull during the summer months, the majority of the gangs, all being good sailors, shipped on some vessel that was bound to some port in Europe to pass the heated term and escape the "yellow Jack," which was prevalent at that season. When they returned in the fall they could command high wages at cotton-screwing on shipboard. Some would go to northern ports, but generally the autumn found them all back, ready for their winter's work.

"Chantie" singing was not confined to the gangs of cotton screwers. In the days of the old sailing ships almost all the work on shipboard was accompanied by a song or *"chantie."* My old friend Captain George

110

Meacom, of Beverly, nephew of my old commander, Captain Edward Meacom of the ship "Brutus," in an able article in the Boston *Transcript*, says in regard to the old time *chantie* songs:

"Fifty years ago, in my early sea life, when the American merchant marine was at its zenith, and the deep-water clipper sailing ship carried the broom at its masthead, no first-class well-appointed sailing ship would think of shipping its crew without having at least one good 'chantie man' among them. For with the old-style hand-brake windlass for getting the anchors, the heavy, single topsails and courses to handle, it was necessary, in order to secure the combined power of the men, that unison of effort should be made, especially while heaving up the anchor, mastheading the topsails, getting the tacks of the courses aboard and the sheets aft, or pumping ship, and this could better be well done by the assistance of a good 'chantie' song. With twenty-five or thirty men's efforts worked as a unit, this great, combined power would be sure to bring desired results in all heavy work. Noticing an article recently published, the writer said, 'I have passed many miserable hours pumping out leaks from wooden ships, but I was never so fortunate as to hear a pumping *chantie*.'

"In my early days of sea life ships were driven hard, and sail carried on the vessel to the utmost limit, that quick passages might be made, with the result that the vessel often being strained,—it not being uncommon for the whole body structure of the ship to quiver,—would leak considerably, and in order to keep her cargo from being damaged, it would be necessary to pump the water out of the vessel at stated

111

periods, and at these times the pumping 'chantie 'song came in place and served its purpose admirably. Among these songs were the following:

" 'MOBILE BAY

Were you ever down in Mobile Bay,
  Johnnie, come tell us and pump away.
A-screwing cotton by the day,
  Johnnie, come tell us and pump away,
Aye, aye, pump away,
  Johnnie, come tell us and pump away,' etc.

" 'FIRE DOWN BELOW

" 'Fire in the galley, fire in the house,
Fire in the beef kid, scorching scouse;
Fire, fire, fire down below: fetch a bucket of water.
Fire down below,' etc.

" 'ONE MORE DAY FOR JOHNNIE

" 'Only one more day for Johnnie,
  Only one more day:
Oh, rock and roll me over,
  Only one more day,' etc.

"All of the named 'chanties' the writer of this once took pride in singing as a *chantie* man when before the mast as a sailor, and, in later years, after becoming an officer and captain, he found that the early acquisition was valuable as a critic of good 'chantie' singing, and although more than one half of a century has passed, yet the old 'chantie' song will start the blood tingling with the vim of the days of yore."

112

The phrase "carried the broom at its masthead," in Captain Meacom's letter, is a reference to a custom of the old Dutch ships, signifying their ability to sweep the seas.

Ships were constantly coming and going, the great tows nightly leaving for their long journey down the Mississippi to the sea, or rather to the bar, for it was a problem whether a ship, after arriving at the mouth of the river, would be able, if she drew much water, to cross the bar, and I have known ships to be weeks aground before the powerful tugboats could drag them through the mud, three or more tugs often being hitched on to one ship. All this has been changed since Eads completed his jetties, deepening the channel so that ships of heavy draft enter and leave without trouble.

The "Emperor," being loaded, left the city at eight P. M. in tow of the tugboat, and arrived at the bar the following morning. Here, finding a high stage of water, we crossed without difficulty, and proceeded down the Gulf of Mexico, en route for Havre, France. The "Emperor" carried three passengers, a lady, child and servant.

After a pleasant passage of forty-six days, we entered the basin of the docks of Havre, and discharging the cotton, some four hundred steerage passengers were taken on board, over three-quarters of whom were women and girls, with ages ranging from seventeen to thirty-seven, a fine lot, mostly French and German, with a sprinkling of Swiss, who were bound to New York, and thence to a western State to work in a factory or mill, on some special line of goods. The run across was most delightful. Quartering winds and a smooth sea produced no seasickness,

113

and having a good band on board amongst the men passengers, Captain Pedrick invited the girls, in the evening, to dance; allowing the crew, mostly Germans and Swedes, to join them from seven to nine P. M. as partners. The ship, having a full poop deck extending to mainmast, afforded splendid facilities for dancing, which was improved by the girls on every opportunity, and the kindness of Captain Pedrick was appreciated by all on board.

A quick run of nineteen days brought the "Emperor;; to the port of New York, and taking a pilot, we passed Sandy Hook, receiving the doctor on board, who detained us but a short time. Captain Pedrick received the compliment of having the finest lot of steerage passengers ever brought to the port of New York.

CHAPTER XI
1851-1852

ASHORE ON TERRA DEL FUEGO.—CAPE PEMBROKE.—PORT STANLEY.—AN INTERNATIONAL INCIDENT

HAVING a desire for long voyages in preference to the Atlantic trade, I left New York for Boston, where I joined the ship "Revere," Captain Howes, as second mate, for a voyage to Callao, Peru. The cargo consisted of ice in the hold, and lumber between decks. The "Revere" was a fine ship of about seven hundred tons.

A quick run was made from Boston to the equator, when, taking the S. E. trades, we continued on until in the latitude of the Falkland Islands; from thence the course was shaped for the Straits of Le Maire, between the island of Staten Land and Patagonia.

Although the weather was thick and no observation had been taken, or any land sighted, Captain Howes, feeling confident of his position, shaped his course to pass through at night.

I had the first watch on deck, from 8 P. M. until midnight. It was very hazy, but the sea was smooth, with an eight to ten knot breeze blowing, no indication of bad weather, and with a favoring wind we set the foretopmast stunsail.

At eight bells, Mr. Bird, the first officer, came on deck to relieve me, taking the course, and we passed some ten minutes in conversation, congratulating each other on the fine prospect for a quick run around the Cape.

Going below, I turned in, but before dropping off to sleep I heard the order to brace forward, and take in the stunsail; then turning over, I fell into a sound slumber, from which I was suddenly awakened, hearing four bells strike, and was wondering what woke me, when the ship struck with a shock that brought my head in contact with a beam, causing me to see more stars than I ever imagined were made, but gathering my senses and thinking we were in collision with another ship, I sprang from my berth and rushed for the deck, meeting Captain Howes in the companionway, who, emerging from the cabin door, ran to wind'ard. Hearing the order to haul aback the main yard, I sprang to leeward, throwing off the lee braces. The night was black, and coming from the light of the cabin, I could for a few moments distinguish nothing. The ship was lying heeled well over on her port side, and with her yards thrown aback worked and pounded with such force that we expected every moment the spars would come about our ears.

In the meantime, becoming accustomed to the darkness, I jumped on a spar, and looking over the side, could see the white sand and huge boulders by which we were surrounded, and I then knew we were ashore on the bleak coast of Terra del Fuego, an island off the southern end of Patagonia, inhabited by the lowest type of cannibalistic savages.

The shore was bold, and we could now make out the high land looming black through the fog almost directly over us. Our only salvation lay in getting the ship afloat; unless we did, the probability was we should have to take to our boats and effect a landing on Staten Land, on the eastern side of the straits, taking the chance of being rescued by some passing vessel, or else make for the Chilian settlement of Sandy Point, Straits of Magellan.

Fortunately we were not brought to this pass, as the strong gusts of wind swept down from the high land, and every sail being thrown aback, the ship began to careen and work, jumping until we trembled for the spars. Everything held firm, however, and in the course of from twenty minutes to half an hour, she gave one final jump, and slid stern first into deep water. As she swung around, the yards were trimmed and she was steered offshore by the sails. Our steering apparatus was disabled, for a time the rudder was useless, both arms that worked the rudder-head with a system of cogs having been smashed.

By the time we had made an offing of a half-mile or so, the courses were hauled up, and pumps sounded by the carpenter. Anxiously we awaited the report that came in the ominous reply of "Chips "to Captain Howes' interrogatory:

"Two feet nine inches, sir!"

All knew our condition was now serious. The carpenter was set at work fitting spare arms to the rudder-head so the ship could be steered, while the pumps were rigged with brakes to which to hitch the lines, making the task of continuous pumping easier for the men. This done, the pumps were manned, and a rousing song started, which never stopped for ten hours, or until two o'clock in the afternoon.

At this time, the rudder-head being in order, the pumps, which had shown no indication of sucking, were again sounded, and a gain of the leak was reported. It was then four feet!

A consultation of all hands was called and the consensus of opinion was that it would be folly to attempt a passage around Cape Horn in our condition, the unanimous verdict being to bear up for the Falkland Islands, and make Port Stanley, if possible, so the pumps having been manned with a fresh gang, the "Revere's" course was shaped for Cape Pembroke, F. I.

All boats were put in order with provisions and water, with tackles on the yards ready to hoist and swing should it become necessary to leave the ship at any time, and, all being in readiness, the crew relieving each other at the pumps in gangs, it was nothing but clang, clang, clang of the pumps, day and night, the water gushing from the scuppers as clear as alongside.

No other work was being done but to trim sails.

During the three days before we sighted Cape Pembroke, the weather was delightful. A fine eight or ten knot breeze blowing, with the wind dead aft, and a smooth sea. All hands had cabin fare: canned meats and cabin stores were served out freely to the crew, as it was not known at what moment we might have to abandon the ship. It might be a change of wind that would—owing to the quantity of water in her— throw her on her beam ends and render her unmanageable, or a storm might arise at any time in this latitude, that would bring matters to a climax.

The wind holding steady, and the sea continuing smooth, we sighted Cape Pembroke the third day, rounding which, the ship entered a long reach of smooth water,—like a mill pond,—between Green Island and

118

the cape. Bringing the wind abeam caused her to list heavily to starboard, and the sounding-rod showed some nine feet of water in the hold just before rounding the cape. We had now an opportunity to look at our surroundings, being in comparative safety. The reach was narrow, and the shore was lined with penguins, standing on one leg, as regular as a troop of soldiers drawn up in line, which they very much resembled. The whole of Cape Pembroke was covered with nests of sea-fowl, or rather the eggs, which lay in every direction about the rocks.

Working up into Port Stanley, the inner harbor of Port William, we entered the snuggest haven that a ship was ever in.

Stanley Harbor is oblong in shape, about four miles long, by a mile and a half wide, with a depth of from five to eight fathoms, completely landlocked save the narrow entrance from Port William, with good, sandy beaches, an ideal spot for a disabled ship to undergo repairs. Dropping anchor, we were at once visited by old Captain William H. Smiley, our American consul at the Falkland Islands, who carried on, in addition to consular duties, a sealing business on the coasts of Patagonia, Terra del Fuego, and adjacent islands, as well as the South Shetlands. He had a brig and two or three small schooners, with a number of whale-boats.

After a conference, it was decided to haul alongside an old hulk lying in the port, put our stores on board, raft the lumber and throw the ice that was in the hold overboard, heave down and examine the amount of damage, hold a survey, and decide what was best to be done.

The town, situated on the opposite side of the entrance to the harbor, was small, consisting of a hundred dwellings,—a story and a half and two story buildings,—with a court-house and jail, and at the lower end of the bay the more pretentious residence of the governor. The population numbered from six hundred to eight hundred, largely composed of pensioners of the English army, old soldiers, receiving a pension of sixpence or a shilling, and perhaps more, per day, placed there with their families and given a house and land to cultivate. Here in this far-off corner of the earth, they could eke out an existence.

There was no lack of food. Sea-fowl were abundant, and the islands were overrun with hares and rabbits. Rabbit served in every style was the regular bill of fare while we lay there.

Having disposed of our lumber at a good price to "Dean & Co.," the only mercantile house in the port, we hoisted out the cakes of ice, dumping them in the harbor until the waters around the ship looked like a small section of the Arctic Ocean!

All the stores, with the belongings of officers and crew, were removed to the hulk, where we now lived.

From a whaler coming in homeward bound, we procured her cutting in falls and blocks, and reeving purchases at our ship's fore and main mastheads, hove down to Captain Smiley's brig, bringing the "Revere" out of water on the port side to her keel, which was found to be nearly gone. The garboard-streak was cut half through, lower part of rudder gone, the stem knocked off, and pieces gouged out of her bilge a fathom or two in length, not leaving but an eighth of an inch thickness of plank.

The copper was wholly torn off of her port side, with great copper bolts driven up through the kelson six inches and more. She was a sorry sight, and had she been loaded with any other cargo than ice and lumber, it would have been impossible to have saved her. Procuring a piece of English oak for a stem, and heavy oak plank for the keel, replacing plank where gouged out, we caulked all seams, pitching over all, fitted lower end to the rudder, and nailed down the ragged ends of copper, and the good ship "Revere" was again tight and sound as temporary repairs could make her.

The work on the ship was done by the officers and crew, under the supervision of the ship's carpenter.

Our stay at Port Stanley covered four months, the weather during that time being very changeable; bright sunshine followed quickly by sharp squalls of snow or hail. Eight or ten times during repairs it would come on to blow so heavily as to oblige us to let her up, and all were heartily rejoiced when the work was completed.

During our stay a man was hung for murder, the first execution that had occurred on the island.

One incident took place while we were there, that illustrated what a little thing may sometimes stir up ill feeling between two nations.

Captain Smiley, in former years, had let loose a few hogs upon the West Falkland, an uninhabited island of the group, which multiplied until at this time there were large numbers of them running wild.

A whale-ship named the "Columbus," having a tender called the "George Washington," was cruising on the whaling grounds about the

Falklands and Patagonia, and a boat's crew, landing on the West Falkland, shot a number of the hogs. A week after this occurrence, six men from the "Columbus" deserted in a whale-boat, and came up to the East Falkland (Port Stanley), where they reported to the governor that the captain of the "Columbus" and "George Washington" had been guilty of shooting and stealing hogs from off the West Falklands, possessions of her Majesty Queen Victoria.

The governor of the colony, who had been recently sent out, and felt the importance of his position, was horrified, and at once wrote to Montevideo, Uruguay, for an English man-of-war to be sent down.

In the meantime, Captain Smiley, getting wind of what was going on, employed the boat's crew who deserted from the whaler on board his brig, and when he got them there he kept them there, allowing no communication with the shore, and the next sailing of the mail packet carried a note to the American consul at Montevideo, requesting an American war vessel and stating the facts.

About ten days passed, and there sailed into the harbor of Port Stanley a ten-gun English brig. Salutes were fired and visits exchanged between the governor and the brig's commander. The following morning the brig sailed.

The English brig had been gone but a few days when the tall spars of a Yankee war vessel loomed up over the point, and the American sloop of war "Germantown" sailed into the harbor, and anchored above the point, housing her upper spars, so they could not be seen from Port William, the outer harbor.

Captain Smiley immediately went on board in full consular uniform, and a mysterious interchange of visits began, between his brig and the sloop of war.

Another week had passed, when about three o'clock in the afternoon, the tender "George Washington" sailed into the harbor, in charge of a lieutenant of the English brig and a prize crew! The "Columbus" was following, with an officer from the brig in charge, but came to anchor outside of the entrance, neither of them dreaming of an American sloop of war waiting to receive them.

They were hardly inside, when a lieutenant and boat's crew from the "Germantown" boarded the tender, and asked who was in charge.

"I was," said the captain of the tender, "until this officer was put on board with men, and I was ordered in here."

"Very well," said the American lieutenant, "you can take command again of your vessel, and come to anchor under the guns of the 'Germantown.' Lieutenant," turning to the English officer, "you will give over your charge, and the boat is at your disposal to go on shore, or we should be most happy to entertain you on board our ship until yours arrives."

The same scene was enacted on board the "Columbus," with the exception that a number of the crew of the "Germantown "boarded the ship, and brought her into the inner harbor, anchoring her near the schooner.

All this was great fun for us, who were now fully alive to the situation.

The next morning the English brig came in.

The two war vessels saluted each other, and visits were exchanged between the officers.

The governor went on board, U. S. Consul Smiley, also, and there was a constant pulling back and forth, the officers and crew of the U. S. sloop of war "Germantown" and the English man-of-war fraternizing in the most cordial manner, the governor seeming to be ignored, somewhat.

In a few days both war vessels sailed.

The whaler "Columbus" recovered her men, Captain Smiley delivering them on board with the boat they had stolen. A full report of the affair was sent by our ship to Washington, and it was also brought to the notice of the British government, by whom, I afterwards understood, the governor was recalled. A few days after, the "Revere" sailed for Boston, taking, as passengers, Captain Smiley's wife and child, and in fifty-eight days we again entered Boston Harbor, where all hands were paid off, and the "Revere" went into the dry dock for full repairs.

The day after our arrival, on taking up the paper, my eye caught a head-line in large type, "Insult to the American Flag," and then followed a long account of the almost "international affair" in the Falkland Islands.

As I shall not have occasion to refer to the Hon. William H. Smiley again, I will say that he was in many respects a most remarkable man, and worthy of a more than passing notice. Four months at the

Falklands, passed in his company, gave me an opportunity of obtaining an insight into the character and studying the peculiar traits of the man.

Tall, possessing a massive frame, a face that would not have taken the prize for beauty, being seamed and scarred, but having a firmness about the jaw and mouth that indicated an iron will; fearless in the face of peril and always cool in the hour of danger, he was a man most admirably fitted for the position he held in his little world in a far-off corner of the earth, from which as a friend of humanity, and a benefactor to mankind, his deeds were heralded in both Europe and America, being recognized by both nations.

He was the owner of a number of small schooners and whale-boats, and in his occupation of sealing about the Patagonian coast and South Shetlands, as well as trading with the Indians of Patagonia, Captain Smiley, with his crew, was exposed to many perils. At one time, having his men all out sealing, he sailed alone around Cape Horn; it being said that he was the only man that ever doubled Cape Horn alone in a fifty-ton schooner.

His adventures among the South Shetlands were most thrilling, and many nights, in Port Stanley Harbor, I have lain awake until long after the midnight hour listening to Captain Smiley's yarns that were being spun to Captain Howes, who would sit up all night to hear them.

Captain Smiley died of cholera at Montevideo, in the year 1871, at the store of the United States consul, Mr. Parsons, where he was stricken. Mr. William D. Evans, a ship chandler of Montevideo, and his manager, Captain Joseph W. Clapp of Nantucket, a great friend of Captain Smiley, were with him to the end. As characteristic of the man, it was said that at the last, a clergyman was brought in, who started to read a passage from the Scriptures, but the captain, being in great agony, waved him back, saying, "Don't read me anything, I am in too much pain to listen. I am not afraid to die. I've kept a straight log."

The following obituary notice by the editor, Mr. Mulhall, appeared in the Standard of Buenos Ayres:

"It is with profound regret we have to announce to our readers the death of Captain W. H. Smiley, a worthy American citizen whose connection with the River Plata dates so far back as 1808. During the Chilian War of Independence, Smiley served with great distinction under our lamented countryman Admiral Browne, and in subsequent years played a very conspicuous role in the waters of the south Pacific and Atlantic. He was born in Rhode Island in 1792, in the city of Providence, and well may that little State be proud of her sailor boy, who in his extraordinary career won the friendship and esteem of the savages in Patagonia, and the first statesmen of Europe and America. A man so universally esteemed must have had high claims to great philanthropy, and have proved himself in every sense a benefactor to humanity.

"Captain Smiley was one of the most whole-souled fellows that ever breathed, and possibly no more noble epitaph could be inscribed over his grave than the long list of vessels, with their passengers and crews, which he has been instrumental in saving.

"For upwards of forty years he acted as commercial agent for the United States at the Falkland Islands, where he established his headquarters. Although not belonging to the United States Navy, so highly did his country prize his services, that his little barque, the 'Kate Sargent,' carried her own guns, and her worthy commander wore the uniform of the service which his name adorned, yet not in commission. Mr. Seward (U. S. Secretary of State under President Lincoln), when a boy, was cared for by the subject of this memoir, and Lord Palmerston (English Prime Minister), in his long connection with foreign affairs, was so frequently brought in contact with the noble acts of the lamented Smiley, that he often expressed a hope that he might some day or other have the pleasure of meeting this extraordinary man.

"The loss of Captain Smiley will be long felt, not only by the immediate circle of his friends, at home and abroad, but by the mercantile marine navigating the Straits of Magellan, where he was a sort of Neptune, intimately acquainted with every spot on the Patagonian coast, and the best pilot extant for the difficult navigation of the Straits. Captain Smiley ever found constant appeals for his services, either from suffering humanity, to further science in her discoveries, or forward commerce in her onward march. Success ever crowned his exertions, and he won the thanks of a trading world whilst he amassed a fortune for his family. We knew him, and proud are we to think that one of the privileges of an editorial career is to be thrown into contact with such men. Last year he visited this city in company with two little orphans, the children of a dead friend,—whom he brought up at his own expense,—to see the cities of Buenos Ayres and Montevideo.

"The first gun that saluted the Fourth of July, 1867, in our harbor, was from the 'Kate Sargent,' and two years previously he joined the Fourth of July banquet at the Hotel Provence, and astonished the company by the *naïveté* of his eloquence.

"Men like Smiley pass from among us, but they leave their footprints. At his funeral in Montevideo, on Friday, the flags in the harbor hung at half-mast, and the American admiral attended with a full staff of officers, to pay the last tributes to one of the worthiest sons of New England. The Rev. Mr. Adams read the funeral service, a long line of carriages followed in the procession, and he who saved so many, at last found eternal salvation."

FISHING ON THE GRAND BANKS.—MAYAGUEZ, PORTO RICO.—SAVANNAH, GA.—ASHORE ON THE DRY TORTUGAS

STOPPING at Marblehead, my old home, for a few weeks, I passed the time in watching the fishermen fitting out their schooners for a "fall fare" to the Grand Banks and Quereau and taking aboard stores and water, and while in conversation with them I chanced to remark that I had never taken a trip to the Banks, as a boy, but would like to go very much.

The next afternoon, which was the Sabbath, just after tea, there came a knock at the front door. There were no electric bells in those days, but we used the big old-fashioned brass knockers. Opening the door, I confronted Skipper Joshua Nickerson, of the good old schooner "Ceres." I asked him in, and he stated that he understood that I would like a trip to the Banks, and he would be pleased to have me go with him as navigator. Although in the science of cod-fishing he was a past master, he had not mastered the science of navigation. Considering a few moments, I quickly made up my mind, and asked the skipper what there would be in it.

"A full share, and half the skippership," said he.

This last was an extra remuneration of $75.

I replied, "Well, skipper, I'll go," and the bargain was made.

After a short conversation as to what I would require, this being a new business for me, he took his leave, and the following morning I went to work on board the "Ceres," as one of her crew, getting her ready.

Fishing on the Banks at that time was very different from the present day. Then all fishing was done from the vessel, not with trawls and dories, as now carried on; the big moses boat at the stern davits, and perhaps a single dory on deck, were all the boats carried. I am now referring only to the Marblehead men; the French vessels on the Banks were all trawlers.

The "catch" was divided into shares, the vessel taking three-eighths, while the remaining five-eighths were divided among the skipper and crew. In fitting out, the vessel found what was called the "big general," consisting of beef and pork, bread, flour, bait, salt and water barrels, while each man furnished his small stores, known as the "small general," his tea, coffee, sugar, molasses, vinegar, and whatever his fancy dictated, in addition to his fishing gear, not forgetting a small brown jug of fine old Medford rum, as medical stores.

The day for sailing having arrived, sweethearts and wives were bidden good-by, and with colors flying, we rounded Point Neck Light, the men glancing lingeringly back for a final look at the old town, and, perchance, a last look at the dear homes of some of the crew, where wives or mothers would anxiously wait the passing of the sad, weary days, ere they would again see their loved ones, if ever, for the Bank fishing, especially "fall fares" with the September gales, was a dangerous calling, as the town records of old Marblehead will show; but "men must work and women must weep," and however dangerous, there never lacked brave, hardy men to man her fishing fleet and take the chances, nor women to watch like "poor lone Hannah" in Lucy Larcom's poem, while

> "Round the rocks of Marblehead
> Outward bound a schooner sped."

We passed Marblehead Rock and Half-way Rock, the latter near enough to enable each man to throw on it a few copper cents, for good luck, a custom religiously observed, in those days, by every Bank fisherman sailing from Marblehead, and was supposed to guarantee a good fare, if not "wetting their salt," *i. e.* using it all up.

Arrived on Quereau, we sighted the fleet, coming to anchor just at sundown, and throwing over the lines, found the fish were biting well.

The deck fittings when on the Banks were kids, or receptacles to hold the fish when caught. There were three on a side, even with the rail, extending to the deck, and they would hold two or three hundred fish.

Fishing was done mostly at night; unless they were very sharp in the daytime, we improved the daylight to change our berth and throw over the gurry (refuse). The night watches consisted of two men at the lines for three hours and twenty minutes, when they were relieved by two more.

The cook was called at four A. M. At six o'clock, all hands breakfasted while the cook tended the lines, after which came "dressing down."

In the waist were high plank in squares, to hold the fish caught during the night, that were taken from the kids. These squares prevented the fish from slipping about the deck, and in them were

131

stationed one or two men with sharp knives who cut the throats, and split the fish, passing the same to the heading and splitting table, which extended about four feet from the rail to which it was attached. On one side stood the "header," whose business it was to sever the head and remove the refuse, dropping the livers in the baskets placed underneath to receive them, from which when full they were emptied into the cod liver butt lashed alongside the rail just forward of the main rigging, to try out in the sun for the cod liver oil, a fine odorous compound after standing a month or so, but not unpleasant after one became accustomed to it, and very healthful.

The fish having been passed across the table to the splitter, he, with two cuts, removed the backbone, sending it to the main hatch to the man who shot him down the hold to the salter. This position was only held by an experienced hand, as too free use of salt would waste it, while not enough would cause the fish to burn or turn red, something that would hurt its marketable value. The tongues and sounds were generally cut out and cleaned by any of the men who wanted them for home use, as a delicious food supply for the family during the winter months. They packed them down in kegs or kits in their off hours.

Great halibut were often caught, and besides furnishing a food supply, the "napes" were always saved by the crew, for smoking, after being cured. They hung them in the network under the deck of the forepeak. On the "Ceres" we had taken a new departure in having a stove in the cabin, all hands living aft, where all the cooking was done.

This innovation was the death-blow to the old-fashioned Marblehead smoked halibut, although adding to the comfort of the crew.

The old-fashioned forepeak, which was the fo'c'sle, was fitted with a fireplace built of brick directly under the fore scuttle, from whence the smoke escaped, or was supposed to, but as a matter of fact, the forepeak was generally so filled with smoke that one could not see across it. Above the fireplace hung a heavy iron crane, from which was suspended a huge iron pot in which all the cooking was done. The tea and coffee were made in it, the chowder and meat were boiled in it, and it was put to every other use required in the culinary art. To get up and down one had to clamber over the steps made directly over the fire, as best he could. An unlucky slip might land him in the pot, but it was an ideal place to smoke halibut, as any old Marbleheader can testify. My old friend and schoolmate, Captain Eben Graves, used to tell many stories of the times when, as a boy, he went to the Grand Banks fishing in the old quarter-decker "Decatur."

Saturday nights at six o'clock the lines were taken in, and not put out until six o'clock Sunday night, the cook being ordered to prepare a pot of rice chocolate. The big kettle was filled two-thirds full of water in which rice was boiled, with chocolate added. It was sweetened with molasses, and imbibed during the evening, hot, as a great treat, the occasion being a gala one, interspersed with song and story. Sunday was a day for general visiting among the fleet if the weather was good, as no fishing was carried on.

For awhile the fishing continued good, and we were doing fine work, then it fell off, and we almost daily changed our berth. Gales and rough weather succeeded.

At the end of three months we had salted down nearly sixteen thousand fish. We had lost all our fishing-anchors, and as the snow was beginning to make its appearance in the squalls, it was decided by Skipper Nickerson to bend "Big Ben" (the large mainsail) and head for home. With strong northeast winds the "Ceres" scudded before the gale for two days, then light pleasant weather, with variable winds, succeeded. We spoke the American ship "Esther Barnby," bound for New York, with passengers for Liverpool, supplying her with fish and firewood, in return for which the captain sent on board two cases of assorted liquors, which were divided up among the crew and taken home for household use.

Sighting Boston Light, we bore away for Marblehead Harbor, which we entered early in the morning, home again!

Not stopping to wash out the fish, but employing a man in my place, I left my account to be settled with the owner in a friend's hands, and afterwards received some $300 as my share.

Shipping as mate of the brig "L. & W. Armstrong," I made a voyage to Mayaguez, Porto Rico, loading salt at Turk's Island for return cargo to New Haven, where we arrived after an absence of fifty-eight days.

Returning to Boston, I engaged as first officer on ship "James Guthrie," Captain Chase, bound in ballast for Savannah. The crew were colored, with a colored boatswain, a very good set of men, and good sailors. A week from port the "Guthrie" encountered a very heavy gale. The steamer "San Francisco" was lost in this gale, and her passengers were rescued by the British ship "Three Bells," Captain Creighton. For ten hours we scud before it, under a close-reefed fore topsail, with the sheets eased off a fathom or so, and two men at the wheel with an officer conning them to see that they did not allow her to broach to, in which case, being so high out of water, she would undoubtedly have been on her beam-ends in a moment.

There was not a high sea, the wind being so strong as to prevent its rising. It was covered with foam, snow white. We passed through the gale without the loss of a rope-yarn and made the land, coming to anchor in the Savannah River off Tybee Island. Captain Chase went up to the city on the tug, and returning the following day, we got under way and proceeded to Mobile Bay, rounding Abaco (Hole in the Wall), one of the Bahama group.

We crossed the Great Bahama banks, as the ship, being in ballast, was of light draught. The moon was nearly at its full, and the white sand, only about twelve or fourteen feet below the surface, reflected in the bright moonlight, made the ship appear to be sailing through a sea of milk. The effect was beautiful.

Passing Havana, we continued along the Cuban shore until, having rounded the Dry Tortugas, a few days more took us to the bar of Mobile Bay, which we crossed and came to anchor off Grant's Pass, when the tug coming alongside, Captain Chase took his departure for town. He returned the second day and informed me that the ship was chartered to load square timber for Ferrol, Spain.

Five weeks passed ere our timber lading was completed. It was rafted alongside, and taken in at the bow ports, the work being done by a stevedore and his gang. The weather was extremely cold for a southern climate, ice forming nights as thick as window-glass, and sometimes a half-inch in thickness. Once a week, taking a boat's crew, and pulling into Grant's Pass, we would load the boat with the largest and most delicious oysters ever tasted; these we took on board, filling barrels with them, and all hands were allowed to help themselves until they were gone, when another trip would be made to load up. Captain Chase and family remained in Mobile, during the ship's stay in port, the captain coming down on the tug weekly, and returning at once to town.

Our second mate having been discharged while in the bay, I had been deputed to go to New Orleans and select a man to fill his position. I fortunately succeeded in finding a most capital officer and brought him over with me.

We were now in readiness for sea. Stores were taken on board, the captain and his family came down on the tug, we weighed anchor, and in tow we again crossed the bar, outward bound. With a fine northerly wind we ran down the gulf, and on the third day after leaving port, while engaged in changing the fore to'gallant mast, the bos'n and two men being aloft, the cry of "Land, ho!" was called, and looking ahead, we could see the high part of the Dry Tortugas above the horizon.

Glancing aft, I saw Captain Chase with a spy-glass looking at it, and gave it no more thought, being busy with the work, until suddenly the ship struck, bringing up on a sand-bar with a force that drove her well on, where she lay, heeled over, hard and fast.

Sail was kept on for an hour, but with the appearance of a wrecking schooner beating up to us, Captain Chase gave the order to clew up and furl everything. On the arrival of the wrecker, the captain refused assistance, but next day made an arrangement to take Captain Chase to Key West, while I commenced discharging the timber, rafting it alongside, after which anchors were carried out, but all efforts to move her failed.

After sticking on the bank a week, a towboat came up from Key West, and with the assistance of the wreckers, taking advantage of a very full tide, she finally succeeded in pulling the "Guthrie" off the bank, and took her in tow for Key West, where we safely arrived and proceeded to discharge cargo and hold a survey.

I knew the delay was going to be a long one, and I did not relish a stay of months at Key West, so I applied for my discharge, the crew having received theirs, and it was granted by Captain Chase, the second mate taking my place, and I took passage on the barque "Wheeler" for Boston, as passenger.

CHAPTER XIII
1854-1855

CALCUTTA.—JUGGERNAUT.—CEYLON.—MAURITIUS.—ST. HELENA. NEW ORLEANS

ARRIVING safely in Boston, after spending a week on shore I joined the "Elizabeth Kimball," a fine large ship of between eleven and twelve hundred tons, half clipper, as first officer, Captain Freeman commander, for a voyage to Calcutta and return. Loading ice at Tudor's Wharf, Charlestown, the stores were taken on board, and the crew brought over from Boston, the ship leaving the wharf in tow of a tugboat. We had one passenger, Mrs. Ladd, who was going out to join her husband, who was a merchant and in charge of the ice-houses at Calcutta.

At this time the ice business with the far East was a great trade. Ice was carried out at a low rate of freight, preferably to the ship's going in ballast, and bringing high prices when retailed from the ice-houses, it became a complete monopoly and paid big profits. We had a pleasant voyage out to the equator in the Indian Ocean, crossing which, and passing Ceylon, we entered the Bay of Bengal.

The southwest monsoon prevailing, we encountered high winds, with heavy squalls, thunder and lightning with rain in torrents, thick gloomy weather. We sailed along the west shore, passed Madras, and made the land on the coast of Ganjam, where are located the three Juggernaut pagodas, the central one containing the great car of Juggernaut upon which is seated the god himself. This temple is two hundred feet in height. The three are a fine landmark for ships making for the pilot brig lying at anchor on the tail of the sand-heads at the mouth of the Hoogly River, upon the banks of which stands the city of Calcutta, the capital of India. The pagodas of Ganjam are the Mecca for pilgrims from all parts of India, who make annual pilgrimages to see and worship their god Juggernaut.

In former times, in the presence of tens of thousands, the great car, to which were attached huge coir cables, was drawn forth. The platform on which the image rests is thirty-four feet square, and the sixteen wheels are six and a half feet in diameter. The upper part is decorated with broadcloth in red and yellow stripes. The strong box near the idol is the depositary for his gold hands and feet, which, together with his shawls and jewels, are locked up in it at night.

The ropes were seized by the assembled throng, and—the land about the pagodas being perfectly level—the immense image was drawn over the plains, with the great multitude shouting and singing, and beseeching their god to grant them his favor. Every little while some devotee would cast himself before the wheels, which would pass over and crush him, when hundreds of the worshippers would rush forward to dip a handkerchief, or some other article, in the blood of the victim, while a mighty shout would go up from the throng, at this act of devotion. The British government has long since stopped these self-sacrifices, and India, to-day, through a wise government, and the efforts of the missionary societies, has greatly altered.

Leaving Ganjam, we made out the pilot brig the following night, and taking a pilot on board, passed Saugor Island, and entered the Hoogly River, coming to anchor off Kedgeree, the pilot station. A fine lighthouse stands on Saugor Island, surrounded by an iron fence as a protection against the tigers with which the island is infested. The Hoogly is a dangerous river, having a very swift current, with obstructions in parts of it, which might prove fatal to a ship if she took the ground. The pilots are a most skilful class of men in the management of a ship, having to serve a long apprenticeship as leadsman, second mate pilot, mate pilot, and finally master pilot, their term of service to master pilot covering some twenty years, during which time it is necessary to make two voyages to England, to become perfectly conversant with the workings of a ship. What they did not know about the working of a ship in a tideway, or swift current, was not worth knowing. From the moment they stepped on board, followed by their leadsmen and servants, their orders were law.

Leaving Kedgeree, the ship proceeded up the river, at times doing tide work, and passing Diamond Harbor, and the James and Mary Shoals, safely, we arrived off Garden Reach, lined with elegant residences, among them the palace of the King of Oudh, passing which we came to anchor off Calcutta.

Along the water front of the city are great mooring buoys, where the ships lie in tiers of twos or threes. The landings opposite these tiers, running up the bank from the river's edge, are called "ghauts." Going into moorings in the inner tier to discharge our ice, a bridge of boats was made, with a plank walk about four feet wide, from the bank to the ship, the ice blocks being hoisted from the hold and lowered over the ship's side upon the heads of three coolies stationed to receive them. It was very hot, and the moment the cold ice water began to trickle down their black backs, they would shiver, and strike a bee line for the ice-house, never stopping until their load was off their heads. During the discharging our ship was a popular resort for all the officers of the surrounding ships, and iced drinks were concocted in every shape. Barrels of apples that were buried in the sawdust in the hold were found when opened at the ice-house to be in good condition, the apples readily bringing from fifty to seventy-five cents each.

While the ice lasted, we had no end of visitors.

Captain Freeman lived on shore while the ship lay in port, and drove down daily in his buggy, coming on board for an hour or so.

Calcutta, the capital of British India, is the chief commercial centre of Asia, and contains many institutions of learning. The spirit of caste is strong, and the contrast between the wealthy class and the masses, who suffer the most abject poverty, is very sharply drawn and painfully evident.

Here is situated the residence of the English viceroy, a building of great magnificence, built on four sides of a beautiful garden. The Maidan, an esplanade extending a few miles along the river, forms a fashionable promenade, and parade ground for the military. One of its finest streets, otherwise unexceptionable, but without shade trees, is called "Clive" after a British nobleman who was prominent in the

141

acquisition of the territory of India, and the subjugation of her people to the British Crown. In the heated term most of the English residents leave the city, in which the mercury sometimes rises to 120 in the shade, and breathe the cooler atmosphere of the Himalayas, the nearest range being about 1,200 miles from Calcutta. Those who are compelled to remain in the city, seek after sunset the cool breezes of the esplanade.

The natives moved about freely in the extreme heat, being clothed entirely in white as a protection from the sun's fierce rays, their heads protected by immense white turbans. Although the presence of European characteristics might be noted in almost every prominent street, Hindooism forced itself upon the attention against the strong background of English prejudice and customs, and bodies were cremated at the burning ghauts, while the ashes and partly burned remains were thrown into the river as of old. It was a common thing in the morning to clear away four or five corpses from the ship's gangway.

With the exception of a ride along the strand on Sunday afternoons, there was very little shore visiting, it was so hot and sultry. The atmosphere, charged with moisture, made it anything but pleasant to go around sightseeing, and the officers found it much more to their taste remaining on board, or visiting from ship to ship among themselves. These gatherings in the evenings on board some of their respective ships were jolly affairs, and highly enjoyed by all.

Having taken on a cargo of jute, saltpetre, and other products of India, in due course our lading was completed, and the ship unmoored, and hauled into the stream in charge of the harbor pilot. Dropping down to Garden Reach below the city, we came to anchor, awaiting the coming on board of the captain and river pilot, who made their appearance on the following morning, when the anchor was weighed and the ship proceeded down the river.

Five days later, we passed Saugor, discharging our pilot at the pilot brig, and the ship commenced her beat down the Bay of Bengal, against a strong southwest monsoon. Very bad weather prevailed, with high winds and fierce squalls, copious rains accompanied by vivid lightning and heavy thunder, compelling the carrying of short canvas, double and close reefs a part of the time, while the heavy seas made progress slow, and three weeks elapsed ere we were up with Ceylon. Gradually the weather grew better after getting south of the Andaman Islands.

One night, when off the southern end of Ceylon, we were sailing with a smooth sea and an eight-knot breeze, the moon being near its full, and about four bells in the mid-watch, while sitting on the weather side watching the ship's progress, and admiring the beauty of the night, the ship suddenly seemed to stop, the sails that had been rounded out asleep flapped violently, back and forth, and there was a rumbling sound that seemed to proceed from the hold, with a trembling throughout, as though the keel was dragging across a reef. For a moment I was startled, thinking we had struck a shoal, but an instant's reflection convinced me there were no shoals in that vicinity, and it flashed upon my mind that we had experienced a submarine earthquake, and a severe shock at that.

143

Captain Freeman rushed on deck, as well as the watch, but finding no cause for alarm, again went below.

Taking the S. E. trades fresh, the course was shaped for the south end of Madagascar, when the ship sprung a leak that made lively work at the pumps. The heavy seas in the Bay of Bengal, against which the ship had been driven, had started the wood ends about the waterline, causing the oakum to work out, developing a leak which grew worse daily until it took two thousand strokes per hour to keep her free. As the leak was known to be just below the water-line, alongside the stem, Captain Freeman decided to touch at Mauritius, an island in the Indian Ocean about five hundred miles east of Madagascar, and without entering Port Louis, come to anchor in smooth water just outside the port, when, by shifting everything aft, bringing the leak out of water, it could be got at and stopped. This was successfully accomplished. Raising the island in the forenoon, we ran in for the port, and dropped anchor in smooth water.

Rolling all water casks aft, bringing the stem out so the carpenter could get to work, before night the leak was stopped, and gave us no more trouble during the homeward voyage. It was a good piece of work.

Mauritius was discovered by the Portuguese in 1505, and came into possession of the British in 1814. Port Louis, the capital, has a population of about 65,000. It has a considerable trade, its chief export being raw sugar.

Getting under way in the early morning, we passed Reunion, or Bourbon Isle, lying one hundred and ten miles southwest from

Mauritius, that evening. This island has an active volcano, upwards of 10,000 feet in height, which was in a state of eruption as we passed. The molten lava was distinctly visible running down its sides in rivers of flame, presenting a most beautiful appearance, as seen from the ship.

Passing Madagascar, we soon sighted the land east of Cape Agulhas, and taking a stiff gale, we stood to the southward, and rounding the Cape of Good Hope, two days later, the "Elizabeth Kimball" passed St. Helena in ten days from the Cape.

This island, famous for being the prison of Napoleon I. from 1815 to the time of his death, in 1821, lies about 1,200 miles west from the coast of Africa. It has an area of 47 square miles, with a population of about two thousand, and is an important coaling station.

Fine S. E. trades prevailing, we made good progress towards the equator, all hands being busily employed in the usual ship's work described in the foregoing chapters. Crossing the line, we experienced a few days of light winds with rain squalls, then the trades, when tarring down, painting and putting the ship in fine shape for our home port was the order of the day.

Having passed the Bermudas and the Gulf Stream, we struck soundings, heading for the South Channel between Georges Banks and Cape Cod.

Favoring winds, but foggy weather, prevailing, we were bowling along about eight bells in the last dog-watch, when the ship struck on the south shoal of the island of Nantucket, with a force that startled all hands.

145

"Hard up!" came the order, and the "Elizabeth Kimball "responded. She never fully stopped, but dragging through the sand, paid off, and in a few moments was clear from the shoal, having just scraped its outer edge, and sustained no serious damage. The fog prevented our seeing anything. It was a narrow squeak, but in this case, "a miss was as good as a mile."

Rounding Cape Cod Light the following morning, and taking a pilot on board, passing Boston Light and the islands of the harbor, we let go our anchor one hundred and twenty-two days from Calcutta.

The cargo having been discharged and crew paid off, I spent a few weeks at Marblehead, and then joined the barque "Glen "as mate for a voyage to New Orleans. We loaded at Rockland, Maine, with lime. Nearly four months were occupied on this voyage, the greater part being spent at New Orleans, where an epidemic of yellow fever was raging. Captain Samuel Prentiss having left the barque in Rockland, he was succeeded by Captain Green of Portland, who was laid up in hospital at New Orleans for over a month, with the yellow fever. The second officer and myself were the only ones on board, the crew having left on arrival.

Neither of us took the fever, which may have been on account of our cargo. The lime having shrunk the barrels so that they literally fell to pieces, the best part of the cargo had to be shovelled out. The lime was all over everything, and in every corner and crevice of the ship. Owing to the scarcity of men, it was a long time before it could be discharged. The death rate, while we were lying in the port, was from five hundred to seven hundred daily, but by the latter part of September it began to abate.

Loading molasses for Boston, on October 12th, we took our departure from the city in tow, and reaching the bar the next morning, I never sniffed anything so delicious as the cool, salt breezes that came from the gulf, laden with a saline fragrance that we inhaled in long draughts, grateful enough to our senses, after having been penned up in New Orleans nearly all summer with an epidemic of yellow fever raging. We came to anchor for twenty-four hours to see if any new cases developed, and finding none, we got under way, and proceeded on our voyage.

Entering the bay, and making Boston Light, when within two or three miles we hove to for a pilot.

The weather was cold and raw, with indications of snow, and shortly after midnight it began to fall and the wind to rise, when, seeing no chance of a pilot and the light beginning to shut in with the snow, Captain Green, after a consultation with me, concluded to run in without a pilot. Keeping her off, we passed the light and kept a sharp lookout for the buoy on the tail of the Centurion Shoal, when picking it up, the barque was rounded to under the lee of George's Island, coming to anchor in the roads. By daylight it was raining and blowing hard, but procuring a towboat, we picked up our anchor, and inside of two hours made fast alongside of Battery Wharf.

CAPTAIN MEACOM'S IDEAS.—OBSERVANCE OF THE SABBATH.—SOCIAL LIFE IN CALCUTTA.—ANIMAL LIFE ON SHIPBOARD

ABOUT ten days after my return, I met Captain Edward Meacom of Beverly, then commanding the ship "Brutus," and I engaged with him as first officer, for a voyage to Calcutta and return, reporting for duty on the ship, which lay at Charlestown, loading ice at Tudor's Wharf. The "Brutus "was a fine ship of about a thousand tons burthen; a regular Calcutta trader. This would be Captain Meacom's seventeenth consecutive voyage to that port. It proved to be one of the most pleasant and agreeable voyages I ever made as chief officer.

Captain Meacom was the most genial and gentlemanly of shipmasters.

A sailor, every inch of him, a good disciplinarian, never profane or overbearing, treating officers and men in a manner that endeared them to him, yet exacting perfect obedience to orders, and permitting no undue familiarity.

Our ice lading completed, and stores taken in, the crew came on board. It comprised fourteen able seamen, two ordinary, and four boys, the latter from Beverly and all known to Captain Meacom, who took a great interest in them. The officers, besides myself, were Mr. Edmund Kimball, second, with Mr. Frank Rogers, a nephew of Captain Meacom, as third mate. A carpenter, cook and steward completed our ship's complement. Sailing with brisk westerly winds, rounding Cape Cod, and passing out of the South Channel, we entered the Gulf Stream, where the nose of the "Brutus" was pointed to the eastward, and, favored by fresh, westerly gales, the old ship made good time towards the region of the N. E. trades.

Getting into good steady weather, one evening in the dog-watch Captain Meacom and I had a long talk, and he gave me his ideas relative not only to the work on shipboard, but the course to be pursued with the boys and crew, to make everything pleasant on a long voyage, saying that much depended on the officers. He would give the men all privileges consistent with good discipline, but a firm, steady course of the same to be adhered to, and no abuse of men, no cursing or profanity allowed or practised by officers. An order given must be obeyed at once, and while kind to the crew, the officers should permit no familiarity. They should have good food and plenty of it, with plenty of work and no idle moments for the men when on duty.

Saturday afternoon was to be given Jack to get the fo'c'sle washed out, and do his own washing and mending, so there could be no excuse for doing this work on the Sabbath. Sunday was to be a day of rest, no work permitted except making, taking in, and trimming of sails, while Sunday morning, weather permitting, divine service was to be held on the quarter-deck, which all hands, dressed neatly, would be required to attend.

The booby hatch, covered with the American ensign, on which was to be placed the Bible and prayer-book, would be the reading-desk.

All this was something new in my seagoing experience, I never having served on a ship where services were held on the Sabbath. I, however, acquiesced, telling Captain Meacom that I believed the idea a good one. He wished, also, to have a school for the boys to attend and study navigation, open to any one who wished to do so. Mr. Frank Rogers, third officer, who was a good scholar and a fine mathematician, was to have charge and coach the boys, while I superintended the arrangement generally.

The steerage under the booby hatch having been cleared, a room with bunks around it was fitted up by "Chips "(the carpenter) as quarters for the boys, ordinaries and carpenter; Captain Meacom deeming it better for them, as well as for the purposes of study, that they should live separate from the crew, but in no sense as an afterguard.

Taking the trades, the weather was superb, flying-fish in shoals, while dolphin, bonita and albecore were caught almost daily, affording a table supply of fresh fish, fore and aft. The first Sabbath for Sunday service arrived, causing a ripple of excitement throughout the ship. I had notified the crew Saturday afternoon that services would be held on the quarter-deck the following morning from ten to eleven o'clock, and every man was requested, unless sick, to be present, neatly dressed. Every officer would attend, and they would expect to see every man present.

Sunday was a beautiful day, trades steady, not over strong, light, fleecy clouds around the horizon, and a quiet Sabbath hush pervading the ship.

At 9.30, chairs for Captain Meacom and officers were brought from the cabin by the steward and placed about the booby hatch, and on the stroke of four bells (10 A. M.), the order was passed by Mr. Kimball, "All hands aft to attend service!"

The men responded by filing aft, seating themselves on the spare spars lashed along the waterways. All were clean, and neatly dressed, presenting a good appearance, an expectant look on most of their faces, showing this was an entirely new departure in their logs, but with all a most respectful demeanor.

Captain Meacom, when all were seated, made a good, fatherly address, pointing out to the men how much time was wasted in a sailor's life, that could be put to a good use; the desecration of the Sabbath, both ashore and afloat; that the day was appointed by God as a day of rest, and for the worship of the Heavenly Father; that when they spent the day seeking their own pleasure and gratification rather than in a manner suitable to His holy will, they were robbing no less a personage than the Almighty Himself. If they would only take this to heart and impress it upon themselves, there would be no danger of their trifling away the hours that God had set apart for His own glory, and His creatures' good.

He dwelt upon the brevity in general of a sailor's life, and the importance of being at all times prepared for the great change, and said he would read some selected passages of Scripture and prayers from the ritual for "services at sea," ending with a hymn, after which good books from the ship's library would be distributed among them, to be exchanged each Sunday, or as soon as read.

The men listened respectfully throughout the services, and at six bells (11 A. M.) all hands were dismissed, seeming to have enjoyed the meeting very much.

These Sunday gatherings were observed weekly, until the weather rendered it inconvenient to hold them, and the library was always open for books.

In the meantime the school of navigation prospered. The boys could "fudge" (get through) a day's work, while all were required to keep a log, or journal, which was open to inspection by Mr. Rogers, and looked over by myself as often as once a week, all errors corrected and suggestions made.

Entering the doldrums (the space between the northeast and southeast trades at the equator), light airs from all quarters were experienced, with calms and rain squalls, accompanied by thunder and lightning.

Waterspouts were frequent, no less than eight being sighted one afternoon; one of them quite near the ship. Waterspouts, being miniature tornadoes on the water, are ugly things to come in contact with, a wreckage of spars, at least, is a pretty sure result of one crossing a ship.

After a week's delay, taking the S. E. trades fresh, the "Brutus "made good time south.

Each night new stars and constellations appeared in the heavens, while the "Southern Cross "and "Magellan clouds "shone resplendent in the dark blue sky.

From early boyhood astronomy possessed a fascination for me. I would pass hours at night studying the heavenly bodies with the greatest delight, and in later years, at sea, to me it was the greatest mystery how any one who had had the privilege of looking upon the nightly glories of the firmament, in the northern and southern hemispheres, could ever doubt the existence of a divine being, an all-wise ruler of the universe.

It was a pleasure to talk over with the boys the names of constellations, with the magnitudes of different stars and planets, and impart what little knowledge I possessed of astronomy, but the approach to the Cape of Good Hope, and the advent of strong gales with rough weather, put an end to our star-gazing for the time being.

Crossing the meridian of the Cape, the "Brutus" drove on before fine westerly gales, accompanied by snow and hail squalls, covering between two hundred and three hundred miles daily.

Passing the rocky islets of St. Paul and Amsterdam, which are of volcanic origin, we bore away north for the S. E. trades and the equator. The youngsters by this time had made good use of their hours below, and could take a meridian observation and find their latitude at noon, take a morning or afternoon sight, finding their longitude by chronometer time, and keep the run of the ship almost as well as the officers. Their journals were well kept, much to Captain Meacom's satisfaction, who often remarked, "The time given to these boys, Mr. Whidden, will be repaid in the knowledge that they will be fitted for their profession. These boys in time will become officers and rise to the command of our ships, and in case of trouble with foreign nations, our ships will become the nurseries of seamen for our navy, and if every shipmaster would take three or four boys each voyage, good boys of good families, give them time to study, and devote attention to their training, in a few years a change for the better would appear, a great improvement in our merchant marine would result, and in time of war our country would be the gainer."

These words of Captain Meacom, in 1856, seemed prophetic in view of the breaking out of the war, in 1861, when the United States Navy was largely recruited from the merchant marine.

We passed up the Bay of Bengal on the last end of the southwest monsoon, and experienced light winds and generally pleasant weather. We made the pilot brig, and taking a pilot on board, an old acquaintance of Captain Meacom, entered the Hoogly, proceeding up the river. A Hindoo religious festival was being held at Saugor Island, and the river was covered with boats decorated with flowers containing gaily dressed natives, male and female, all bound for the island to take part in the rites. These consisted, in part, of offering their female children to the immense crocodiles that swarmed in the waters of the

Hoogly and especially around Saugor at this time. The cries and shrieks of the victims were drowned in the music and shouting of the multitude.

This custom of sacrificing female children has since been done away with by the government.

Arrived at Calcutta, the "Brutus" went into moorings, and made ready to discharge her cargo of ice, and the northeast monsoon setting in, the cool season was inaugurated, making life more endurable than on my former visit.

Calcutta in the northeast monsoon is a very different place from what it is when the southwest monsoon prevails. It was now cool, delightful weather, and we indulged in more shore excursions than on my former trip. On a visit to the botanical gardens lying on the opposite bank and down the river a few miles, we saw, among other objects of interest, the great banyan tree, described by Milton, as,

> "Branching so broad and long, that in the ground
> The bending twigs take root: and daughters grow
> About the mother tree; a pillared shade,
> High overarched, with echoing walls between."

An army of ten thousand could repose beneath its branches.

Although called a single tree, in reality it is a great many. As the branches shoot out from the parent stem or trunk, offshoots from them descend into the earth and take root; these in turn grow and send out more shoots, which descend and take root, until from a single trunk an immense space is covered, and the banyan tree becomes the home of millions of birds of every description, with colonies of monkeys, while

155

beneath its grateful shade the native finds protection from the scorching rays of the midday sun.

During the discharging of our ice cargo, as in the "Elizabeth Kimball," we had lots of visitors, and iced lemonade and other concoctions were much in evidence while the ice lasted. The reunions aboard each other's ships in the evenings were scenes of hilarity and good-fellowship. The ship on which a gathering was to be held on any particular occasion was always in readiness to receive, the officer taking a pride in having everything in good shape, generally a nice spread, with all incidentals conductive to a jolly time, but everything within the bounds of decorum and good order. Well I remember our visits to the good old ship "Walpole," Captain Woodbury of Beverly, whose specialty was baked beans, and his first officer always had several pots ready baked to set before us. They were cooked in old New England style, that could not be obtained outside its limits except by a cook who had served his apprenticeship in Beverly or Marblehead, and the cook of the "Walpole" was a native of the former town. With what gusto we cleared the table; after which Mr. Lovering might have made use of the exclamation attributed to old Mrs. Humphrey of Marblehead. Mrs. Humphrey kept a boarding-house in the old town, and when one of her boarders asked for more beans, while several others waited expectantly, she ladled out the last spoonful in the dish, and beaming around the table, exclaimed, "There! I calculated on just enough to a bean!"

The buggy rides along the strand (river front), on a Sunday afternoon, were charming. The road leading along the river's bank gave

156

a fine opportunity of viewing all the shipping in port, each ship decked out with its national colors and numeral flags, making a fine show. One was constantly passing the most elegant equipages of the wealthy English residents. Fine carriages containing army and navy officers in their rich uniforms rolled smoothly along over the finest of roads, while wealthy natives and baboos (merchants), in gorgeous costumes, mingled with the throng, each carriage having its native coachman and footman clad in immaculate white with great snowy turbans, while the native syce, or groom, that accompanied each equipage, carriage or humble buggy, ran ahead of the vehicle, waving his arms and shouting in Hindostanee:

"Clear the way, clear the way! make room for the Sahib!"

After the afternoon drive the English residents take their bath and prepare for dinner, the meal of the day. In fashionable society these are generally "swell" affairs.

Both officers and boys on the "Brutus" had ample opportunity of shore visiting while in port, and the crew had their shore leave each Sunday in alternate watches, being well supplied with liberty money. During our stay in port I never saw any drinking, or a crew less inclined to dissipation on shore.

We loaded with the usual Calcutta cargo, jute butts, etc., and were again ready for sea. Captain Meacom, who always liked fresh milk night and morning in his tea and coffee, brought from home a milch goat, and another was procured for the return voyage, in addition to which was a large stock of pigs, goats, geese, ducks, chickens, and a big

157

flock of pigeons, fantails and other kinds. Captain Meacom believed in having plenty of live stock on board, and when it could be obtained as cheaply as in Calcutta, always laid in a big supply. The decks were literally packed with coops and pig-pens.

In addition to stock, the boys and crew had great numbers of pets,—comprising cockatoos, parrots, minas and Java sparrows, besides a few monkeys of various sizes.

Sailing down the river with a fair wind, we passed the James and Mary Shoals, Diamond Harbor, Kedgeree, and Saugor Island, discharged the pilot at the pilot station, and with fine weather and a fair wind proceeded down the bay.

What a change from our passage down in the "Elizabeth Kimball," when gales, torrential rains, thunder and lightning prevailed, with tremendous seas into which the ship drove, straining in every timber day after day. Now, fine, beautiful weather with clear skies, sea as smooth, almost, as a pond, and great water snakes swimming about in all directions, with occasionally a big turtle asleep on the water.

We passed Ceylon with its spicy breezes, and crossed the equator in ten days from the pilot brig; taking the trades not over strong, our course was shaped for the Cape of Good Hope. Nothing of note occurred until nearly up with Cape Agulhas.

On our passage down the Bay of Bengal, Captain Meacom conceived the idea of building a model house for the stock that would do away with the great number of coops scattered about the deck, and confine all in one space, yet have them separate from each other.

158

Utilizing the capstan on the main deck, the carpenter inserted joists into the handspike-holes. These joists extended nearly to each side, leaving a good passageway between, and coming, also, within two feet or so of the fife-rail around the mainmast, and within four feet of the cabin entrance; in short, the house took up pretty much all the main deck abaft the mainmast. On each side were very large coops that drew out and pushed in, like a chest of drawers. On one side were kept the geese, the other ducks, and the other two chickens and fowls. In the centre were the goats, while the whole upper part was devoted to pigeons, who roosted on the joists, and flew around the ship, passing back and forth through the holes made for them, always returning at night to their coop. By the time we were up with the Cape, the cook had made large inroads upon them, but there still remained a goodly number, besides the pigs that were kept in the large sties forward by themselves.

Just east of Cape Agulhas, the "Brutus "took a sharp, short gale, with very high sea. Under a close-reefed main topsail and foretopmast staysail, she had been standing to the south'ard, when the order was given to "wear ship." With the wheel aweather, she came gracefully round on the port tack, heading to the north'ard. This brought the sea well on our port bow.

Half an hour passed, when glancing up from something I was about at the time, I saw towering high above the bulwarks a great curling wave just ready to break. With a yell to the men to look out for themselves, I seized a piece of running gear, passing several turns around my body, and a spare spar. The next instant the crash came. Driving with the force and fury of an avalanche, the wave swept over us, starting the forward house, filling the decks with water, and knocking the model stock house into smithereens, while the live stock were in a moment swimming and floating around the deck.

Finding no one was injured or swept overboard, all hands were ordered to save the stock and throw them into the cabin doorway, so wading into the water and grabbing what they could lay lay their hands on, the crew threw geese, chickens, ducks and pigeons into the cabin companionway, while large numbers were lost.

Between the forward part of the after house and main cabin was a wide passageway, with my stateroom on one side and the second mate's on the other, mine unfortunately being to leeward.

Knocking out two side ports, the ship quickly freed herself from water.

I had taken with me on that voyage a dog, named "Dash." In bad weather he usually took up his quarters in my stateroom, the door to which was a sliding one. Before the catastrophe this door had accidentally been left open, and afterwards had been closed by some one, and on opening it when I went below, after all was in order again, to change my wet clothes, a comical sight met my eyes.

My pillow was occupied by a big goat, who glared defiance at the dog, who stood at the foot of the berth, and a pig reclined in the centre, while all around were chickens, geese, and pigeons wringing wet, and everything in the room, bedding and bedclothes, were soaking. There was about six inches of water washing about the deck. Calling several of the men, I had the stock cleared out and everything righted. This was the only unlucky sea we shipped for the voyage.

Shortly after the gale moderated sail was made, and, the wind favoring, we slid by Agulhas, with the land well aboard, to catch the strong westerly current that prevails close alongshore.

Having passed the Cape of Good Hope and Cape Town, the south Atlantic seemed like again entering home waters. Fresh breezes soon brought us up to St. Helena, and from now on the youngsters got a good insight into ship's work, besides being put through a course of instruction in lunars, Captain Meacom daily taking a series of distances, and having the boys work them out for the longitude under the guidance of Mr. Rogers. Before they reached the equator, they had attained great proficiency in taking and working out lunar observations.

The ship, in common with all Calcutta traders, was infested with cockroaches of enormous size, some of them being two and even three inches, in length.

Although only cockroaches, they were most destructive. Just before rain they would swarm out of the after hatch in clouds, the helmsman being obliged to keep his hat or cap waving to keep them clear from his face, while the decks at night would be almost covered with them, and in stepping on them an explosion would follow with a report similar to the crack of a small pistol. When painting ship they would eat the paint from the planksheer and waterways at night, about as fast as it could be put on, seeming to thrive and grow fat on a diet of white lead and

"Paris green." Holes were eaten through the plank-sheer, and, on discharging our cargo in New York, we found they had eaten holes in the solid oak bitts between decks into which one could almost insert one's fist. Beyond biting at sleeping Jack's hair and fingernails, which latter they would often gnaw to the quick, they did not trouble us with their carnivorous propensities, but the odor from them was most offensive. Nothing but drowning them out by sinking the ship seems to have any effect in killing them, and that is not always convenient. In the "Elizabeth Kimball" we had a few, but nothing as compared with the "Brutus," that had been for many years in the East India trade.

Carrying the trades across the equator and experiencing neither calms nor light airs, the wind gradually drawing around to E. N. E. and freshening, sliding into the N. E. trades without an effort, we now came to the last quarter on the home stretch. All hands, fore and aft, were feeling in good spirits, and all, especially the youngsters, eagerly looking forward to a safe and speedy arrival at New York and old Beverly, where the joyous "welcome home" awaited them. I would frequently hear the boys in the dog-watches rehearsing their plans of what they would do after they should arrive; wondering whether this or that girl had been staunch and true, and if so-and-so were married? A day of particularly fresh trades always elicited the remark, "Ah! the Beverly girls have got hold of the tow-line sure."

The fields of floating gulfweed had a home look, while every vessel sighted was a subject of speculation as to where she was from, how long out, and where bound. We would often signal, if convenient, by

162

Maryatt's code, and all these questions would be answered, with many others.

Passing the Bermudas and Cape Hatteras, we crossed the Gulf Stream with a rattling breeze, heaving to at midnight for soundings which showed ninety fathoms. We took a pilot on board off Barnegat Light, and he received a most royal welcome. He brought the papers with him, giving us all the news, and they were passed around to all hands.

Sandy Hook passed, we hove to at quarantine for the doctor, but his visit was short. He made an examination of all hands, and finding every one in good condition, and being shown a clean bill of health from Calcutta, which was an open sesame, he passed us to the city of New York, off which we dropped anchor opposite the Battery until it was known where we were to dock.

My second voyage to Calcutta was ended.

Runners from the sailors' boarding-houses now came on board to make arrangements with the crew to stop at one or the other of their houses, but not a man was allowed to be taken out of the ship until she was fast at the dock. I also gave the men a little advice against drinking with them, almost every runner having a bottle of spirits, and I was pleased to see my advice generally followed. When the ship was taken by tugboat to dock the following day and tied up to the pier, every man, when he left the ship with the runners, was sober, the only ones at all intoxicated being the runners themselves.

The youngsters, with ordinaries, got their meals at a restaurant but a short distance from the ship, until all hands were paid off, two days later, when they took their departure for their homes.

Remaining on board until the cargo was discharged, I took my meals on shore, and slept on the ship.

It was a queer sight at the dock when the bales of jute were hoisted out of the ship's hold. Each one was black with the most enormous roaches, and the instant the bale touched the dock they would scamper in all directions.

The ship was lying at the foot of Wall Street, and people who had met swarms of them travelling up the street, evidently bound up "on change," came on board to inquire what species of bird they were, never having seen their like before.

The cargo being all right, I was paid off, and taking passage for Boston on the Fall River line of steamers, arrived safely and took up my residence there for the time being.

This practically ended my services as first officer. I was now on the lookout for a command, which was hard to obtain without influence or money to buy into a ship.

Becoming an owner of a small portion, an eighth, sixteenth, or even a thirty-second ownership in a craft, may insure a captaincy, but this I did not have, and so had to depend upon my record as first officer.

CHAPTER XV
1857-1858

CAPTAIN OF THE "LITTLE LIZZIE."—HURRICANE OFF RIO DE LA PLATA.—
BUENOS AYRES IN WINTER.—DINNERS, LUNCHES, HORSEBACK RIDING.—
BARQUE ON FIRE

A MONTH passed, and though I kept watch of all ships arriving, making inquiries if there would be a vacancy, and applying if there was one, I was either too late, or found that almost every ship-owner had some one he knew who wanted a position, and for every vacancy there seemed to be ten applications; but, never relaxing my efforts, I called one day at the office of an old-time ship-owner whom I knew, Mr. Daniel Deshon, who was located on Doane Street. Finding him alone, and at leisure, I asked him frankly if he had or would be likely to have a vessel for which he would want a captain, and if he should have, would he give the command to me, knowing me as he did; and I referred to Captain Meacom and others, as to competency, etc.

He replied that it was not necessary to give references, he had known me a long time, and did not question my ability, ending by telling me that he had the barque "Little Lizzie," about four hundred tons burthen, that he had been trying to sell, and if not successful the coming week, he should load her with lumber and send her out to Buenos Ayres, and would be pleased to give me the command, adding that in addition to her freight out, I might get a chance to sell her at the river (Rio de la Plata) at a better price than could be obtained in Boston. Going out from his office, I went home happy, the only concern I had being the fear that some one might buy her before she was taken off the market, but no such calamity occurred. I was informed, in due course, that she would load for Buenos Ayres, and I could at once take command. This I lost no time in doing, and having shipped my officers, I made out a list of stores needed for the voyage, and ordered the shipping master to engage a crew, also purchasing such instruments and charts as were necessary.

The lading completed, the crew were ordered on board and the pilot notified, and taking my final instructions from Mr. Deshon, the owner, I repaired to the barque, where I found all in readiness for sea.

Although she was a little craft, I stepped over the gangway with as much pride as though she had been an eighteen-hundred-ton ship, and giving orders to cast off, sail having been made at the wharf, the "Little Lizzie" was pointed down the harbor, passed the islands, and through the narrows, and arriving at Boston Light, the pilot, after wishing me a pleasant voyage, took his departure.

In addition to the lumber below, a deck-load had been added which came just even with the rails, leaving a space around the mainmast and pumps. Stanchions were placed around the barque's sides through which life-lines were now rove as a precaution against any one going overboard in a blow or seaway. Passing Minot's Light, we were soon up with the highlands of Cape Cod, and our course shaped out of the South Channel, clear of which, the barque was pointed to the eastward.

On trying the pumps the first night it was soon apparent that either they had been standing a long while, or the "Little Lizzie "was sadly in need of caulking below the water-line. It gave me no uneasiness, however, as I felt it might take up, and loaded with lumber, there was no danger of her sinking. If it was pump to Buenos Ayres, why, pump it should be! It would never do to put in with a leak on my first command.

Getting a stiff gale with a high sea, ere we had been a week out, it was found that the barque made no more water in rough weather than in smooth water; that the leak was a steady one; that with hourly spells at the pumps she could easily be kept free. But pumping so frequently gave little time for much else besides making and taking in sail, and attending to ship generally. There was no grumbling, and all was pleasant on board.

Favored with good winds, we struck the N. E. trades fresh, and bowled along, with all the canvas that could be piled on, for the equator.

Before leaving, I had undertaken to keep a log for Lieutenant M. F. Maury, U. S. N., superintendent of wind and current charts for the government at Washington, with notes and observations on tides, sea currents, clouds, storms and winds, with all the phenomena of the sea. This, with my own journal, and looking after the ship, occupied my time pretty well, and the days passed rapidly with no idle moments on my hands. A week in the doldrums, with squalls of wind and rain, with light airs, kept the watch on deck busy with the sails, when, taking the S. E. trades, we again crossed the equator.

Sighting Fernando Norohna and Cape Frio, ten days later saw the "Little Lizzie" off the Rio de la Plata, where she encountered her first setback. The weather became very bad, gale succeeded gale for seven or eight days, blowing us offshore a long distance, at the end of which time the wind moderated, the weather cleared, and the barque coming up nearly to her course for Lobos Island, the sea gradually growing smooth, with a fine breeze blowing, two reefs were shaken out and to'gall'nt sails set, and the barque was soon bowling along from eight to nine knots, making good time towards Lobos, now distant about sixty miles.

Although the weather was warm for the season, with bright sunshine, I did not like the looks or feeling of it. The barometer was very low, with a falling tendency, but aside from this there was no indication of bad weather, or any change after nine o'clock (two bells), except a steady fall of the glass; otherwise the night was so fine, and being anxious to take advantage of the favorable slant of wind, I was 10th to shorten sail.

It was perfectly clear, not a cloud to be seen in the heavens, the stars shining with a brilliancy seldom equalled, water smooth, but each time I looked at the barometer I would find it a little lower, and I felt that something out of the ordinary was coming, yet it seemed impossible not to have time to get sail off.

At four bells, feeling tired, having been up a long time, I told Mr. Lovett, the mate, I would lie down on the lounge in the cabin, and if there was any indication of a change, or any increase of wind, to call me at once. Going below, I lay down, but not to sleep, being too anxious, as the barometer was now 28.

About six bells (11 P. M.) I heard Mr. Lovett descending the steps.

"Well! any change?" I inquired.

"No sir," he replied, "with the exception that the wind is a little stronger, I think."

"All right, sir, I'll be up in a moment," I answered.

Mounting the steps, as my head came out of the companionway I detected a faint flash of lightning in the southwestern quarter. I gave the order to braid up the spanker, clew up the to'gallant sails, furling them, and to haul up the mainsail before they laid aloft at the main. Before the sail could be handed the wind increased rapidly. Telling the helmsman to put his wheel up and keep her dead before it, I also hailed the second officer to get on deck instantly, Mr. Lovett having gone aloft to assist the men. Running forward over the deck-load, letting go the topsail halliards on the way, I called to the watch to hurry on deck, not stopping to put on many clothes. By the time they made their appearance, the men with the mate were down from aloft. With all sail clewed up, and although running dead before the wind, over two hours of the hardest kind of work elapsed before everything was furled, and the barque hove to on the port tack under a mizzen staysail made of No. 1 cotton canvas, entirely new. By this time the wind was blowing with hurricane force; above a cloudless sky, but everything now snug, with the exception of the fore to'gallant sail that blew away ere it could be furled. The sea had risen, but the wind was too heavy to permit its rising very high. The barque lay almost on her beam-ends, the spars lying at such an angle the wind passed over, her masts not offering much resistance to its full force. Lying with her lee rail in the water, the men doing nothing, but holding on for their lives, eight hours passed, after which the wind began to abate in violence. From the time the wind struck us at eleven the night before, the barometer had risen rapidly, the lowest being 27.70, which had gone up by daylight to nearly 29, and was still rising.

From this time the gale moderated very fast, and by 10 A. M. sail was again made. By night the main to'gallant sail was set, and a new fore one bent, and the wind favoring us, we were soon up with Lobos Island, passing which, we shortly sighted the Mount, coming to anchor outside the harbor of Montevideo. A boat from shore in the early morning came on board bringing fresh beef and vegetables, also a river pilot who had been signalled for, and we were soon under way for Buenos Ayres.

The Rio de la Plata, from the junction of the Parana and Uruguay Rivers, is very wide, about thirty miles between Buenos Ayres and Colonia, and increasing in width as it approaches the ocean. It is a muddy, turbid stream, having at times of freshets a strong current. Anchorage for shipping at Buenos Ayres, unless the vessel is of light draught, is in the outer roads, about eight or nine miles from shore. Between the outer and inner roads lies a wide bank of shoal water, but vessels of from eleven to twelve feet draught can cross it to the inner roads about a mile from the landing mole. The water there is much smoother than in the outer roads, the bank breaking the sea, although in a winter southeaster, the Plata can get up a very respectable sea even in the inner roads. In the strong southeast gales of the winter season the waves run high, and a ship needs good ground-tackling, but the holding ground is good. It is sometimes a week at a time when no work of discharging cargo can be attempted, it being impossible for a lighter to lie alongside a ship; even communication with the shore would be cut off, although it must be pretty rough weather when the shore boats that supply the ships with fresh beef and vegetables, take the mails, and carry the captains back and forth once a week or so, cannot go off. All the captains live on shore, boarding at some of the many boarding-houses. These are kept mostly by Americans or English. Mine was presided over by Mrs. Bradley, formerly of Portsmouth, N. H., who with her three daughters conducted one of the best establishments in Buenos Ayres. It was patronized almost entirely by American shipmasters with their wives, if married and accompanied by them.

Taking advantage of high water, the "Little Lizzie" crossed the bank, anchoring in the inner roads among a number of light-draught vessels like herself. This was much more convenient, as it was but a short distance from the landing mole, and communication with the shore could be had daily, or at any time that it was necessary. .

The water front of the city of Buenos Ayres was very different from the present day; then all discharging was done by lighters, but of late years docks have been built at Ensenada, below the city, to accommodate the shipping, or a portion of it.

The population at that time was upwards of three hundred thousand, while to-day it numbers nearly a million. It is the capital of the Argentine Republic, and is the first city in size in South America. Its export trade is very large, besides having important manufacturing interests.

Rosario, lying northwest of Buenos Ayres, on the Parana River, is second only in commercial importance, its population being today upwards of 125,000. Stock raising is its chief industry,—cattle, sheep, horses, etc., in vast herds. The pasturage afforded by the central plains is practically unlimited. The production of wool, also, is one of its greatest industries, and of this Buenos Ayres Province is the chief seat.

Sailing up the Parana River, from Buenos Ayres to Rosario, from the deck of the vessel can be seen immense grassy plains, one great level as far as the eye can reach, covered with seemingly countless numbers of horses and cattle, grazing. It formed a sight worth many miles of travel to see.

The illustration shows La Boca del Rio Chaco circa de Barracas (the mouth of the River Chaco near the warehouse) at Buenos Ayres, 1856. The old established house of Samuel B. Hale being my consignees, as it was of almost all of the American ships in port, I made daily visits to the offices at the Barracas lying at the lower part of the city. Here the captains not only met each other, but joined the consignees and the employees of the firm in social intercourse. Here they received their letters and newspapers, and if any one was not so fortunate as to receive any mail, he learned the home news from others. There was always a nice lunch set out, of which all who chose were invited to partake. Frequent invitations to dine were given to a few at a time, and these dinners were very sociable gatherings, enlivened by music and witty conversation, all serving to make the time pass most agreeably.

Meanwhile the work of discharging our lumber proceeded. On account of the shallowness of the water along the city front, the laden boats or lighters could not approach within a long distance of the Custom House mole, where all goods were landed, and everything had to be carried on shore from the lighters in high carts, drawn by horses. It was a queer sight to see the teams going out nearly a half-mile from shore, coming in loaded, and returning empty. In addition to the Custom House mole, there was the landing mole, where all boats from the shipping landed. It was, I should judge, about an eighth of a mile in length, making a fine promenade, always well filled with people in fine weather, but when there was a heavy sea on, landing from boats was a difficult and hazardous operation. All along the mole were davits with boats hoisted, hanging ready for an emergency. Along the water front on each side of the mole was built a fine sea-wall, in front of which, extending a long way out into the river, were large lumps called "*toseas*," highly dangerous to a boat getting among them in a seaway.

Our cargo having been discharged, the barque was now put into fine condition as to appearance, painted outside and inside, spars scraped, and everything polished up until she shone like a fiddle, and as she lay with her royal yards across, she much resembled a yacht. It was my intention to sell her if possible, and the consignees were looking out sharp for a customer. In the meantime there was very little to do but enjoy myself.

Horseback riding was the favorite amusement of the captains, among whom was my old friend Captain William Gregory of Marblehead, commanding the barque "Albers," and almost every afternoon we took long gallops into the country from ten to fifteen miles, sometimes much farther when we started earlier. This was not only most enjoyable and exhilarating sport, but very inexpensive, horse-flesh being at a low figure. A good horse could be bought for five or ten dollars, and a superb animal for fifteen. Our stay in port on that voyage covering four months, I bought a fine animal the second month for fifteen dollars. I had him fed, and taken care of, and used him almost daily, and on leaving gave him away in payment for his "keep."

One of our most enjoyable excursions was in company with six or eight genial fellows to the *estancia* of an old German, who kept a sort of tavern for travellers, or parties making him a call from the city for a good dinner, or a bottle of fine old Hock or Moselle, of which he had a large supply in his cool cellars. Leaving Buenos Ayres at about two P. M., a brisk ride, or leisurely gallop of an hour or so, brought us to his place, when dismounting and having had the dust removed, we seated ourselves at tables in a most pleasant arbor with rich clusters of grapes hanging in luscious pendants from the vines overhead, our leafy covering protecting us from the sun's hot rays.

Ordering a bottle or two of cool, sparkling Moselle, we would sit chatting for an hour, enjoying our wine and fragrant cigars, while our horses rested. The sun meanwhile would be getting lower, and as it neared the horizon's edge abating much of its fervor that had made it oppressively warm at noontide.

Again mounting our steeds, a brisk gallop would soon take us back to the city, to pass an entertaining evening at our boarding-house with music and the companionship of the ladies of our party.

During my stay many pleasant acquaintances were formed, friendships that lasted for years.

On my going to the office one day Mr. Hale informed me that he had a prospective customer for the barque at a price nearly double what the owner would have taken for her in Boston, and said he would be on board the following day to inspect her. Since her cargo had been discharged her bends and upper works had been caulked, previous to painting. Early the next morning I went on board, followed shortly by Mr. Hale with Captain Manuel, a Portuguese, who wished to buy, to command. I showed him over the "Little Lizzie," after which he partook, with Mr. Hale, of a nice little lunch in the cabin, with a few glasses of wine. Pleased with the barque and all on board, the next day the sale was consummated, Captain Manuel taking possession and command as soon as papers were made out and signed. He altered her name to "La Chiquita Paulina" (Little Pauline), after his daughter.

The officers and crew were paid off and berths for the former found on vessels homeward bound, while the crew shipped on various craft bound for the United States and elsewhere. A fortnight later I engaged passage on the barque "Swallow" of Salem, Captain Stephen Upton, bound for that port. I bade my consignees good-by, took leave of my genial landlady and her family, and with a hearty handshake from my fellow shipmasters, embarked with Captain Upton from the mole. A run of an hour and a half placed us alongside the "Swallow," lying in the outer roads. Anchor was at once weighed, and with a leading wind we took our departure from Buenos Ayres, landing our pilot at Montevideo the following morning. Passing Lobos Island, Maldonado, and Cape St. Mary, we were soon again on the south Atlantic, homeward bound.

The "Swallow" was a very pretty barque of five hundred tons, quite sharp, with good sailing qualities, flush fore and aft, with the exception of a break in the deck abaft the mainmast, having a foot rise from that aft, all her cabin and forecastle accommodations being below deck.

With fine weather and steady trades we were in the latitude of Pernambuco, when about four bells in the morning watch, we experienced a sharp earthquake shock.

The following afternoon, while sitting by the companionway aft, reading, for which there was now plenty of leisure, Mr. Connor (Thomas Connor of Salem), the first officer, being busy with something about the wheel, we were both suddenly startled by the cry of "Fire," forward.

Glancing towards the fo'c'sle scuttle, I saw the watch below rushing on deck, followed by a cloud of smoke. In an instant I followed Mr. Connor, who bounded by me and, diving into the fo'c'sle, called loudly to pass water down. Two men were ordered to draw water, and the others quickly passed down bucket after bucket, which Mr. Connor received and slashed around perfectly regardless of Jack's bedding or belongings. In a few moments the fire was extinguished and the scare was over. Mr. Connor then used some very emphatic language in addressing a few remarks to the watch that had been below.

It turned out that the seams around the barque's bows on the insides of the bunks of the fo'c'sle were the home and abiding-place of innumerable bugs, which, especially in warm weather, were a source of great annoyance to Jack. He had tried various expedients to get rid of them, all of which were of no avail, they were so deep in the seams. That day a brilliant idea had struck one of the watch, and going to the paint locker without asking leave, he smuggled down about a quart of spirits of turpentine, then getting a piece of oakum, he proceeded to saturate the seams with the spirits. He was anxious to see what effect it had, and it was too dark to see plainly, so he lit a match and held it close to the seam. The effect, if startling to the inhabitants, was much more so to Jack. In an instant the flames ran around the two tiers of bunks, scaring the watch so that, without attempting to extinguish it, which they might easily have done, they piled on deck, yelling "Fire!"

It is, I think, safe to say they never tried that experiment again.

After a fine run through the northeast trades, one pleasant morning found us in Boston Bay, between Thatcher's Island and Half-way Rock, with light airs fanning along, until we were but a short distance from the entrance of Marblehead Harbor, when it fell away calm. Putting out a dory we had on deck, I pulled to a fishing-schooner just back of the Neck, bound to Boston for salt, got the news, and a morning paper, returned on board, and shortly after we were boarded by a Salem pilot. At noon we were fast alongside Derby Wharf, the voyage ended.

Upon seeing Mr. Deshon, the following day, he expressed himself well pleased, adding he was sorry I had not arrived sooner, for he had

had a new barque for me. She had sailed the week before, but as soon as he had a command I should have it. All of which, though very gratifying, would not warrant my remaining idle.

NEW ORLEANS IN WINTER.—BALLS, OPERAS, ETC.—THE FRENCH MARKET AT
SUNRISE.—TO MARSEILLES.—THE SHIP "J. P. WHITNEY"

I COULD see no opening for a command, and after a short stay on
shore, I engaged with Captain John Devereaux of Marblehead, as first
officer on the ship "Carnatic" for a voyage to New Orleans. He stated to
me, at the time, that if he could get a stave freight for Bordeaux, he
would place me in command at New Orleans, and take a run up around
Tennessee with his wife and see his son, whom he had not seen for a
long while. This I considered a good opportunity, and shipping Mr.
Horace Broughton, also of Marblehead, as second officer, with Mr. John
Bartol, a nephew of Captain Devereaux, as third, we left Boston in
ballast for New Orleans. Making a quick run to the south end of Abaco,
one of the Bahama group, the "Carnatic" rounded the "Hole in the Wall"
and entered upon and crossed the Great Bahama Bank as described in
a previous chapter. There is a uniform depth in the fairway of from
fourteen to sixteen feet of water, with a bottom of white sand as level as
a floor, while the ship being in ballast and of light draught, could easily
cross, thus making a great saving in distance. The Bahama group
comprises twenty inhabited, and many uninhabited islands, the Great
Bank being fringed with small islands and keys. Running off the edge of
the Bank, and sighting "Dead Man's Keys" and the Cuban shore, we
speedily entered the Gulf of Mexico, the course being shaped for the

Southwest Pass of the Mississippi River, and on arrival off the Pass, Captain Devereaux engaged a tugboat to tow the ship to New Orleans.

Towing from the gulf to the city is very interesting. In the first part, after leaving the bar, the banks are low and swampy, fringed with reeds and bushes, large portions of which at a high stage of water are often partially submerged. These are the homes of the mosquito, gallinipper and "green-head," a large fly that will bite a piece out of an animal very quickly.

About sunset, in the summer months, when the tow is gliding along the banks, the mosquitoes come off in swarms, almost darkening the air, but farther along, the land is higher and more uniform, houses and cabins come into view, and still farther on plantations with their blooming cotton fields, stretch far away, white as snow, ripe for the picking by the darkies in the fields, and near, the shining black "mammies" with their "pickaninnies" are mustered up to see the tow pass by, shouting and waving their colored bandannas. This was in the old slavery days, before the emancipation of the blacks, and a tow on the Mississippi from the bar to the "Queen City of the South" was quite an event. On our arrival at New Orleans the towboat placed the "Carnatic" alongside the levee, lying outside the ship "Ocean Pearl."

During our stay the captain and Mrs. Devereaux lived on shore, the captain coming on board daily. Not being able to procure the freight he wished, he gave up the idea of going to see his son, and chartering the ship to load tobacco and staves for Marseilles, France, told me he would like to have me continue the voyage, which offer I accepted.

Captain Devereaux was the most genial of men, a good shipmaster of the old school, and a most agreeable man to sail with. Our relations at all times were very pleasant.

Mr. Hooper, our passenger, remained in New Orleans for a fortnight and then took his departure for Boston by rail, having during his stay visited the ship almost daily with Captain Devereaux.

At this season New Orleans was very gay; theatres, operas, balls, and drives on the shell road to Lake Pontchartrain were in full swing.

A visit to the French market in the early morning was a rare treat to any one not familiar with the habits, manners, and customs of the Creoles and elite society of New Orleans in that day.

Here one could sit at any of the numerous coffee stands, and while sipping his cup of the most delicious coffee or cocoa, with delicate coffee cakes and cream,—or, if his tastes inclined that way, a tiny shell glass of the finest old cognac to take in his coffee,—watch the passing throng, of every shade of color, clad in garments varying from all the variegated hues of the rainbow to a spotless white, all smiling and joyous, engaged in animated conversation fraught with jest and repartee thrown from one to another, in a breezy, light-hearted manner, only to listen to which was most exhilarating. This was a favorite stroll of ours at this hour during our stay in port.

As soon as the ship was loaded, she dropped out of the tier and down to the lower levee, making up a tow of four vessels for the bar the following night.

The last of the stores having been taken on board, with water, about 7 P. M. the crew made their appearance, all sober, for a wonder, and at 8 o'clock the fasts were cast off, and the "Carnatic" swung into the stream, being headed down river for the bar, where we arrived the next morning, and crossing at once, sail was made, and with a light northerly wind, we proceeded down the gulf.

Rounding the Tortugas, we passed Key West and the Florida Keys, with a leading breeze, and aided by the strong current of the Gulf Stream, which here runs with its greatest force, rapidly passed Florida, with Abaco on our starboard beam. Once to the north'ard of Abaco, the wind, hauling to the sou'west fresh, gave us a fine run for a week, and meeting with little easterly weather, the ship's passage was a good one to Cape St. Vincent, where a strong easterly gale was encountered, bringing the "Carnatic" down to close reefs. Running down under Cape Spartel, we lay off and on, for two days, when, the gale moderating, we stood over towards the Spanish shore, and the wind falling light, morning found us at the entrance of the Straits of Gibraltar, Spartel bearing about south half east.

A Spanish fishing-boat coming alongside, a lot of fresh sardines were purchased, which made a great addition to our table fare. They are a most delicate pan-fish, sweet and delicious.

Fanning along with light westerly winds, about 1 A. M. (two bells), we made Tarifa Light on the port bow, and as I knew Tarifa to be a revolving light, and this was a fixed one, I was puzzled. The night was dark but clear, and after satisfying myself that it was a light on shore, and no other than Tarifa, I went below, and calling Captain Devereaux, told him Tarifa Light was a little forward of the port beam.

Coming on deck, he took a good look at it, and for the first time our opinions clashed.

"That's not Tarifa, Mr. Whidden," said he.

"I think so, captain," I answered.

"But I tell you it is not. Tarifa is a revolving light, and that is steady."

"That may be so," said I; "it's a fixed light, sure, but it's Tarifa."

Looking through my glass, which was a good one, at the light, which by this time had got well abeam, I could make out the dim form of the lighthouse below it.

With a long look through his spy-glass Captain Devereaux exclaimed:

"A steamer's light; I can see her smoke-stack," to which I made no reply, and Captain Devereaux went below.

I remained on deck until daylight, when Tarifa showed plain in sight abaft our beam, with the mountains of the African shore looming up grandly in the morning light, and looking aft from forward, I saw Captain Devereaux come on deck, take a look at the lighthouse, and go below at once, where he remained until nearly seven bells.

Passing Gibraltar, we again encountered a strong easterly wind, making it a hard dead beat to Cape de Gata, but rounding the cape the wind became more favorable and we made Planier Light but a short distance south of our port, and taking a pilot, the "Carnatic" entered the basin of the docks at Marseilles, a very old city, located in the southeastern part of France, but a short distance from the Italian border. It has a population of nearly half a million, and is the principal seaport of France, and of the Mediterranean. The harbor is composed of two big basins or docks, the old and the new. Entering the old basin, we hauled alongside the pier and commenced the following day the discharge of our tobacco and staves.

The second day after docking, Captain Devereaux came on board in the afternoon, and after talking with me in a general way, "By the way," said he, "I see that Tarifa Light is undergoing repairs, and, for the time, the revolving light has been changed to a fixed light. That was something I did not know, when we passed it. Mr. Whidden, go to your tailor's and get a suit of clothes, and tell him to send me the bill. Don't you get a Prince Albert suit."

I laughed and thanked him, and gave my order for a nice suit, and Captain Devereaux paid the bill. This was characteristic of Captain John,—blunt, stubborn, he always hated to acknowledge he was wrong, but once convinced, he was ready to rectify an error, and generous to a fault.

Fruits of all kinds were abundant, and as it was the season for them, we literally feasted, while in port, on the largest and most delicious grapes.

The barque "Azof," off the port of Marseilles as shown in the accompanying illustration, was an Eastern built vessel of 295 tons register, and a fair type of the smaller class of freighters of our

184

merchant marine of sixty years ago. She hailed from New York previous to being purchased by Messrs Isaac Jeanes & Co. and Messrs Chamberlain, Phelps & Co., large ship-owners of Philadelphia.

She was commanded by Captain William Chipman, a native of Barnstable, Mass., who in 1859 commanded the fine ship "Isaac Jeanes." She was principally engaged in the Mediterranean trade, plying between the various ports in the Sea and Philadelphia, New York, and New Orleans. Her eighth voyage was made from Philadelphia to New Orleans with coal; thence to Cronstadt, Russia, with cotton; from there to Plymouth, Eng., with general cargo, where she was wrecked in October, 1859.

The cargo having been discharged, and the ship ballasted, we cleared for New Orleans, taking as passengers the former American consul who had been stationed at Nice, with his wife, son and daughter.

A few days later the "Carnatic" sailed from Marseilles, passing Gibraltar and the straits with a strong levanter (a strong east wind prevalent in the Mediterranean Sea), and in due course entered the trade belt, and from now on fine, steady winds, with bright, beautiful weather, accompanied the ship all the way to the Windward Islands. Past Guadeloupe, and through the Caribbean Sea, we held our way, passing south of Jamaica, getting a fine view of the Blue Mountains, thence along the Cuban shore and past the Isle of Pines with its rich, tropical growth of trees and foliage, rounded Cape San Antonio, the west end of the island of Cuba, and with course shaped for the Southwest Pass, a few days later we dropped our anchor outside the bar

185

of the Mississippi River. Taking a pilot and towboat, we were just in time to complete a tow, and at once were off for New Orleans.

On arrival at New Orleans the "Carnatic" loaded cotton for Boston, also taking on board ten barrels of "Old Rye" whiskey, which were stowed directly under the after hatch. We had good weather and favorable winds until past the latitude of Bermuda, when the ship encountered a hard gale from the northwest, obliging her to lie to, for eight or nine hours, but no damage was sustained, for the "Carnatic" as a sea-boat was a gem. With a favorable slant, good time was made to the South Channel, when the wind, falling light, finally died away to a flat calm, then breezing up from north northeast, it rapidly increased in force until at midnight the ship was under close reefs clawing off Nauset, the wind blowing a hard gale with snow and sleet. It was a wild night and all hands suffered much with the cold. About six bells (midwatch) the wind suddenly veered into nor' west, and although blowing heavily, the weather cleared, while the air became intensely cold, ice making fast, and the rigging becoming stiff very rapidly.

Captain Devereaux had left orders to call him if any change occurred, and this was now done. Daylight had just broken, when from for'ard, where I was busy with the men, I saw the captain emerge from the cabin door, and running up to wind'ard, take a look for some two or three minutes. Returning, he called out, "Mr. Whidden! Mr. Whidden!"

"Yes, sir," was my response, going aft.

"Where did you stow that whiskey you took on at New Orleans?"

"In the after hatch, sir," said I.

186

"Do you think you could get out a barrel?"

"Certainly, sir." And calling the watch aft, in less than fifteen minutes a cask was up and secured in the cabin gangway. Tapping, and drawing off a small demijohn, Captain Devereaux ordered that the men have a drink each watch while the extreme cold lasted, then disappeared below.

Two drinks, however, were sufficient, as after the first the weather moderated wonderfully.

Having passed Highland Light, we took a pilot on board, and arrived in Boston the following morning, and the cargo of cotton having been discharged, I bade good-by to Captain and Mrs. Devereaux, leaving the old "Carnatic" with regret, and having received instructions from New Orleans to proceed overland to that port and take command of the ship "J. P. Whitney," 1,200 tons burthen, I left at once for New York, and there purchasing tickets for New Orleans via Savannah, Montgomery and Mobile, I embarked on the steamer "Alabama," Captain Schenk, for Savannah.

A fine run down the coast brought the "Alabama" to her pier at midnight, and engaging a carriage, I drove across the city to the railroad station. The moon, being at its full, made objects almost as light as day, and the drive enabled me to get a fair idea of the city, from which I took my departure by the train which left at 3.30 A. M. The trip across country was very interesting, the stops for meals at the various stations serving to make an agreeable break. On my arrival at Montgomery, I learned at the hotel, that the "St. Nicholas," one of the big river steamers, would leave for Mobile the following day at noon, and having engaged my stateroom, I took the opportunity of looking over the city, which is the capital of the State of Alabama, situated on the banks of the Alabama River, having a population, to-day, of over 30,000. It was then, as now, an important shipping point for cotton. The banks are high along the river front, but at this time there was a very high stage of water. The streets of the city, which covered a large area, were very wide, bordered with spreading shade trees having the most beautiful foliage. Shrubs and flowers were in full bloom and in the greatest profusion, distilling their grateful fragrance upon the soft and balmy air. Leaving at noon, the boat took her course down the river, midstream, for Mobile.

The "St. Nicholas" was one of the old-time Southern river boats, of light draught, with a spacious saloon and a bar. The management furnished good accommodations and set a fine table. The captain and other officers were courteous and obliging, sparing no pains in looking after the comfort of their passengers.

Approaching Mobile, we found the river banks overflowed, making the surrounding country look like an inland sea. All this sort of sailing was something quite new to me, and the trip from Montgomery to Mobile was most enjoyable. At its close, I took the boat for New Orleans, via Lake Pontchartrain, where we arrived the next morning, and boarding the steam-train I was landed at the railroad station in New Orleans about 11 A. M.

I found the ship had been chartered to load tobacco for Marseilles. The first and second mates, Mr. Henry P. Connor and Mr. Saunders, were on board, and on recommendation of Captain Gray, the former captain, their services were retained, and the selection was fortunate, as they proved most competent and efficient officers. (Mr. Connor at this time of writing has been retired from the service of the Pacific Mail Steamship Company for ten years. He had commanded the finest ships for a long term of years, his last command being the steamship "New York," which he took from New York to San Francisco when the Pacific Mail Steamship Company retired from the Atlantic trade to the Pacific.)

Our lading completed, the gangs of cotton-screwers, who had been employed on board, wishing to get out of the city for the summer months, made application for the crew's positions. They were a fine set of men, and all being good sailors, they were given a note to the shipping-master, and by him were duly enrolled on the ship's articles.

For a better crew I could never wish. Only one fracas occurred during the voyage, and that was occasioned by the action of the steward, a little fellow, but a capital man for his position. His only failing was a tendency to be arrogant and overbearing towards the forward hands, when he came in contact with them.

While serving dinner one day in the cabin, a sailor brought the bread-barge aft for him to fill. It should have been brought at night or in the morning, when he was not busy, so he kept the man waiting until he got ready, then filled the barge, and as he gave it to him, told him not to come again at that hour, using some abusive language. This Jack

189

resented, and told him if he would come out from the cabin he would polish him off. In a moment there was a mix-up on the quarter-deck in front of the cabin door. Mr. Connor, the mate, was in his room, heard the row, and stepped out. When he saw the steward on the deck with the man on top, pounding him, he promptly knocked Jack over, and then ordered the steward to the cabin, and the man forward. This would have ended it, but the steward, after Mr. Connor had gone back to his room, foolishly went forward and the altercation was renewed.

The steward, being in the enemy's camp, was now having a bad time of it. The second mate was at dinner, and Mr. Connor, again hearing the noise, went forward on the lee side, where, taking in the situation, he started to interfere, but this was resented by the crew and all hands pitched into *him!* He knocked down two men, but finding the odds against him rather heavy, he seized a handspike, and having backed against the house, was doing good work, while with heavers, belaying-pins, and fists the crew sought to reach him. Knowing nothing of all this, I came from the cabin to take a smoke, when I was accosted by the steward, who had deserted Mr. Connor and came aft. "Mr. Connor is having trouble forward, sir," he said. I walked past the house on the lee side, and the scene for a moment was startling. Five or six men were stretched out, bleeding freely, and Mr. Connor, bloody and thoroughly aroused, was standing off a half-dozen who were trying to get in a blow, the rest having retreated to the fo'c'sle. Perceiving that it was no time to ask questions, I grasped a heaver, and the men, seeing the captain and second officer, who at that moment came round the house from the wind'ard side, retreated to the fo'c'sle, followed by the officers. Bringing the heaver across the arm of one in the act of drawing a knife, I caused him to drop it; a stampede was made from the fo'c'sle to the deck, and the excitement was over.

The mate's head, which was badly cut, was bandaged, and all hands were ordered aft, while the two ringleaders were placed in irons, below, in the half-deck, and kept on bread and water for forty-eight hours.

The riot act was read to the others, who were then sent forward, after which the steward was called into the after cabin and received the "talking to" of his life, with the assurance that he richly deserved the thrashing which he would get, if the like happened again. On the promise of better behavior, the two men were taken out of irons the second day and everything settled down to its usual routine.

Off Cadiz the ship encountered a strong levanter, and ran down under the lee of Cape Spartel. Here, fully protected from the violence of the wind, she backed and filled around, in company with a dozen sail of other craft, who had also sought shelter under the cape. On the second day, standing out towards Spartel, and seeing an English man-of-war wear ship and head to the north'ard, the "Whitney" was put under close-reefed topsails, whole foresail, and lower staysails, and heading from the cape to the Spanish shore, running well in, tacked ship in smooth water. Again standing over for Spartel, we found we had gained a little. It was a hard beat, but midnight found us off Tarifa, from then until daylight barely holding our own. Day broke with dense masses of vapor, or fog, shutting off the view of land on either side of the straits, the wind still blowing heavily. By 10 A. M. the fog lifted, when, the mainsail being given her, she began to gain, and by four in the afternoon passed Gibraltar, from Spartel to Europa Point, the southern point of the Rock, taking thirty hours, but we had the satisfaction of arriving at our port seven days in advance of those left under the lee of the cape. Half-way between Gibraltar and Cape de Gata a favorable slant of wind was taken, carrying us to Marseilles, making the passage fifty-four days from New Orleans.

Docking in the new basin, and obtaining pratique (passing the board of health), we were at once besieged by every class of tradespeople and artisans who had anything to do with shipping to solicit the ship's patronage. The first day we had consignees, stevedores, and tradespeople selected, and commenced discharging the second.

A large number of American ships being in port, many captains having their wives with them, there was no lack of company, while drives and sightseeing made the time pass very pleasantly, and one could hardly realize it, when the time for our departure had arrived.

While lying in the basin, a most amusing incident occurred, more amusing to the onlookers than to myself. It was Sunday morning and I had made an engagement to drive out with several ladies and gentlemen and to dine with them afterwards. Having dressed with unusual care, a short time before starting I remembered something I had on board that I wished for, and taking a carriage and driving to the dock, I obtained a shore boat and started for the ship, that lay moored to the buoy with chains from her stern to the pier. The cargo being out brought her high out of water, while a French ship had hauled alongside, shutting our gangway off, and the only way of reaching it was by crossing over her decks. She was deep in the water, while the "Whitney" towered above her. She had just been painted, and a ladder was hanging over the bows to accommodate any one wishing to get on board, an awkward place to climb up, but the only way to reach my gangway. Mounting the ladder carefully, to avoid the paint, and starting aft, I had reached the main hatch, when, with a tremendous howl, a dog that looked very large and fierce came bounding towards me. He looked wicked, and not a soul in sight. Putting my dignity in my pocket, and making a spring to the main rigging, I never stopped until I was half-way to the top; then looking down, I saw a small boy who had come out of the cabin administer a cuffing to the dog, that I now perceived was securely muzzled. To make it worse, the rigging had been freshly tarred, besmearing me from head to foot. As I descended the rigging I could see my men lying around the to'gallant fo'c'sle chuckling, and all on the broad grin at the "old man's" dilemma. This, of course, I pretended not to see, and went to my cabin, where a complete change was necessary.

No suitable freight offering, the "J. P. Whitney" took her departure for Trapani, Sicily, to purchase a cargo of salt on the ship's account for New Orleans.

Trapani, a very pretty city, nestles down at the foot of Mt. Julian. On this mountain the ancient city of that name, founded by the Saracens about 300 A. D., was built. I visited the ruins, which are very interesting, several times during my stay. Only one other American ship, the "Isaac Jeanes," Captain William Chipman, was in port. She was lying close in at the landing.

The ship "Isaac Jeanes," a photograph of the model of which accompanies this sketch, was built of white oak in the city of Philadelphia, by William Cramp: dimensions, 160 feet long, 33 feet beam, 21 feet 6 inches hold, 843 tons register, 1,150 tons dead weight. The Philadelphia *Public Ledger* of April 1, 1854, thus records the event of the launch of this fine ship as having taken place on the day previous, which happened to be on Friday:

"Thursday was originally fixed for the launch, but the tide not being sufficiently full, a postponement until Friday was determined on, notwithstanding the general hostility to that day. She glided off in the most beautiful style, and her advent could not have been more propitious had it occurred on the most lucky day of the week. The new ship is a fine specimen of naval architecture, and is destined for the Mediterranean trade, under the command of Captain Chipman. Messrs. Jeanes & Co. have also a ship ('Wm. Chamberlain') of 900 tons on the stocks at the same yard, which is to be commanded by Captain Isaac Jennings. The contract for a third ship ('Bridgewater,' Captain E. W. Barstow), of between 1,600 and 1,700 tons, for the same firm, has been taken by Mr. Cramp."

The "Isaac Jeanes" made nine voyages before her sale in New York in July, 1862, when she was altered into a barque, and finally went ashore inside South Head below San Francisco, where she went to pieces March 9, 1876.

Her fourth voyage, from Philadelphia to San Francisco, was made in 108 days. She was considered a smart and handsome ship.

It was on her seventh voyage—New York to Baltimore, in ballast, from Baltimore to Marseilles, from there to Trapani, from thence to New Orleans—that she made one of the two American ships, the other being the "J. P. Whitney," that were lying here at Trapani.

CHAPTER XVII
1859-1860

TAKING THE BLACK VEIL IN SICILY.—RETURN VOYAGE TO NEW ORLEANS.
TREMENDOUS ROLLS AND AN ANIMATED OMELETTE.—A WEDDING PARTY ON
SHIPBOARD

THE ship's hold was made ready for the cargo of salt purchased through the agency of Senor Luigi, who also acted in the capacity of salt agent for Captain Chipman. I went on board the "Isaac Jeanes" and made the acquaintance of the captain and his estimable wife, a most charming lady, quiet and reserved, yet bright and vivacious with her friends, bubbling over with good humor and a fine conversationalist. Captain Chipman was a gentleman of rare ability, and one whom I was more than pleased later to number among my friends.

In a few days there came another arrival, the ship "Edward Hymen," Captain Neal, belonging to the same owners as the "J. P. Whitney." Mrs. Neal, the captain's wife, being with him, a pleasant little party was made up for sightseeing. Together we visited the churches, monasteries, nunneries, and all places of interest in the city. Taking delightful drives into the country, we inspected the vineyards, now laden with great, rich clusters of delicious grapes, of which we could pick and eat, all as free as air.

One of these excursions was to the ancient ruins of Trapani on Mt. Julian. We noted a portion of a wall of an old church or temple that was almost covered with Saracen heads. The coloring looked as fresh as though recently put on, yet many hundred years had passed since the artist had finished his work. He had gone to dust ages ago, yet his work remained, and the process that preserved the coloring in such a state of perfection has become one of the lost arts. The Baths of Venus were also very interesting.

While our dinner was being prepared at a Sicilian cafe, we sat in a room on the second floor with the wide open windows that extended to the floor admitting the soft balmy breezes, while directly opposite were the windows and gray walls of a richly endowed convent, which were built out beyond the walls with arched gratings, so that the nuns, or sisters, could sit in them, veiled, and take the air. Shortly two appeared, heavily veiled, and seating themselves, seemed to be conversing together. We, especially the ladies, watched them with great interest, and their conversation, by their animated gestures, seemed to be of anything but a very solemn nature. The ladies said they were laughing heartily, perhaps at us, for Captain Neal was doing his best to attract their attention, but they gave no sign of seeing us. Changing her position, one slightly disarranged her veil, showing just a glimpse of a sweet face, young and beautiful, not over two or three and twenty, the ladies said. In a few moments more, both vanished from our sight within the convent walls.

When dinner was ready all Sicilian dishes were served. The menu was composed of spaghetti, stews, macaroni, tomatoes and peppers, chicken fricasseed with tomatoes, sweets, light wines with fruit, black coffee and bread.

All thoroughly enjoyed the spread, after which the gentlemen lit their cigars, and while smoking admired the view. From where we sat, the bright blue waters of the Mediterranean were spread before us dotted with beautiful islands. A few miles away lay Marsala, with its glittering mounds of snow-white salt, appearing like a small piece of the frozen north drifted into summer seas. Taking carriages, we commenced our descent, and part way down we stopped at a monastery of Gray Friars, receiving a cordial welcome, with permission to look over the buildings. Everything wore a sombre hue, nothing to soften or light up the stern, austere aspect of the rooms or cells. In one large room were the skeletons of friars who had passed away, piled up in tiers, each one tagged, stating who he was, when he died, and perhaps a few remarks on his life-work. Some were in open caskets, while in the centre and at the ends of the room were piled artistically great mounds of skulls, thigh bones, and other portions of the human anatomy, presenting a most lugubrious appearance.

The friars themselves were garbed in the plainest and most severe style. A coarse robe and cowl, and a hair-rope girdle tied around their waists, with the ends hanging down in front, completed their costume.

We thanked the brethren for their courtesy, and contributing a small sum for the benefit of the Order, we took our carriage and commenced the descent, which having been accomplished, we drove to Luigi's office. As we were in the act of alighting a bell struck, and instantly all business stopped. Pedestrians, carriage drivers, each and every one dropped on their knees, crossing themselves, repeating their prayers and Ave Marias in the most solemn and devout manner. This continued for a few moments, when all arose, and business went on as if there had been no interruption.

The thirty thousand inhabitants of Trapani included ten thousand priests.

A few days after the visit to old Trapani, Mr. Luigi, our salt agent, asked me if I had ever seen the act of taking the black veil, adding that the daughter of a family with whom he was intimate was about to do so, and giving me a cordial invitation to attend the church with him and witness the ceremony, which offer was quickly accepted, with thanks.

On the appointed day we were early on hand at the church, which was well filled with the friends of the family. Shortly, a procession of maidens, with the young lady at their head, profusely decorated with flowers, all being dressed in white, wended their way up the hill and entered the church doors. All knelt, while the service went on, and she took upon herself the holy vows. Adjoining the body of the church, which was of vast dimensions, was the convent or nunnery, with grated windows, or rather openings, through which the sisterhood could see and hear all that was going on, without being themselves seen.

At the conclusion of this part of the service a priest appeared, and let down her luxuriant hair, which fell in waves about her shoulders, rippling down to the floor. With a pair of shears, he severed it close to her head, and taking it in her hands, she went around among her weeping relatives and friends, and giving each a tress with a few words of cheer and comfort, she smilingly returned to the priest, when the

199

black veil was thrown over her head, and taking her hand, he led her back of the altar, both vanishing from sight.

Then arose a strain of music mingled with the voices of the nuns from the grated openings, low and soft, gradually swelling in volume, yet thrillingly sweet and clear. Higher and higher it mounted, until in one grand burst of melody it rang among the fretted arches of the roof, seeming to fill that old sanctuary with one paean of triumph at the rescue of a soul from sin, and a fitting welcome into the portals of Paradise. It was to me one of the most impressive sights, and still lingers in my memory. The young lady herself was very beautiful. I was told by my agent that the young girls are all educated in the convents, during which time they wear the white veil. After receiving their education, and mingling with the world, their great aim is to form a suitable matrimonial alliance. They will not marry below their station, and as the wealthy, eligible young ladies far outnumber the young men who are up to their standard, and as it is a disgrace to remain single after a certain age, if they receive no suitable offer by the time they are three or four and twenty, they will generally renounce the world, enter the convent, and taking the black veil, spend the remainder of their lives within its walls, devoting their service and wealth to the church.

In Trapani, chickens, fowls and eggs cost but very little, so little that besides live stock three beef barrels were filled with eggs and laid down in salt for the homeward voyage. Two of the barrels were placed against the bulkhead of the inner or ladies' cabin, and by running a plank from

200

the mizzenmast to the side of the cabin they were deemed perfectly secure against any mishap on account of the weather.

Our salt in, and Luigi the agent settled with, our anchor was weighed and sail made, and with a fine easterly breeze we said good-by to Trapani, having passed a most pleasant three weeks in its waters.

We had a quick run to Gibraltar and through the straits, where, some ninety or a hundred miles west of Cape Spartel, we encountered a hard gale from west northwest that blew with great violence, the ship being hove to under a close-reefed main topsail, and foretopmast staysail for twelve hours, with a high sea running, the ship making good weather, except when she would fall off in the trough of the sea, causing her to roll heavily.

Breakfast had been announced by the steward, and I was seated in an armchair at the head of the table, with Mr. Connor, the first officer, on a settee at my right. The steward was having his hands full keeping the dishes on the table, for they evinced an unaccountable desire to jump over the storm-racks. The forward dining-cabin had an oilcloth carpet, which when wet was very slippery. The table, settees, and chairs, of course, were secured.

Coffee had been served, and we were in the act of lifting our first cup, when the ship gave several tremendous rolls. We were holding on to the table, when suddenly the lashings gave way, or rather the staples drew out of the deck, and over went the table, with all the breakfast and dishes, and before we could rise from our seats, the two barrels of eggs broke adrift, and in less time than it takes to tell it, every egg was smashed, and a sea of yolks and whites of eggs, mingled with the debris of the breakfast, was sweeping across the oilcloth with every roll of the ship.

Both mate and steward had gone down in the mass, and it was simply impossible to recover their footing, while with every lurch they would be swept from side to side, threatening to stave in the panels of the stateroom doors with their heads. My chair fortunately did not turn over, but with me in it, with feet drawn up, was dashed from side to side, until I grasped a door-knob, holding on for dear life, at the same time calling for the second mate. The scene in the cabin was indescribable. A snap-shot taken at the psychological moment would have been a bonanza to a photographer.

The second officer, in response to my summons, appeared at the cabin door, and taking in the situation, called in three or four of the watch. Life-lines were thrown in, and Mr. Connor, the steward and myself, were dragged out of our ridiculous, as well as most uncomfortable position. A few buckets of water made both the mate and steward look a little less like animated omelettes.

The work of cleaning up the mess with buckets, swabs, and brooms took about all the forenoon, but beyond the loss of the eggs, and the bruises and "barkings" of legs and arms, no damage was done.

The gale moderating and the wind hauling northerly, sail was again made, and a week later saw us within the region of the trade belt, with all the canvas that could be piled on, making good headway towards our destination. Delightful weather and favoring winds made the passage to

202

the Windward Islands a very pleasant one, and carrying the same steady winds through the Caribbean Sea and Gulf of Mexico, the "J. P. Whitney" arrived off the Southwest Pass forty-five days from Trapani, and taking a towboat, in due course made fast at the levee in New Orleans and commenced the discharge of our salt.

During my absence, Mrs. Whiting, who was an owner of three-eighths of the ship, sold her interest to Captain George T. Avery to take command, which he now did, and I turned the ship over to him, receiving orders to wait for another ship, then on her way from Liverpool to New Orleans, in the meantime settling down on shore to await the "R. B. Sumner's" arrival.

The photograph of the "J. P. Whitney" incorporated in this work is from a painting made at Malta in 1864. She was built at Castine, Maine. She was dismasted off the mouth of the Hoogly River to avoid being driven ashore, and afterwards refitted at Calcutta, sailed for Mauritius, and foundered with nearly all on board during a typhoon in the Indian Ocean.

Captain George T. Avery, to whom I turned over the command of the "J. P. Whitney" at New Orleans, was born at Castine, Maine, Feb. 9, 1825, and died at Newburyport, Mass., Sept. 20, 1884. He followed the sea as a calling for over forty years, commanding during that time many of the finest ships of our merchant marine in the days of the old sailing ships; among them the "Daniel I. Tenney," the "Importer," and the "J. P. Whitney." He was a typical New England representative of our old-time shipmasters. Honest, fearless in the discharge of his duty, self-reliant,

203

he won the esteem and respect, not only of his employers, but of all with whom he came in contact. Genial and courteous in his social relations, and upright in all his dealings, he passed through life a useful member of society and an ornament to his chosen profession. In his death he was truly mourned by all who knew him.

The photographs of the ships here mentioned were tendered through the courtesy of Captain Avery's son, Mr. Edward W. Avery of Melrose, Mass., who was born on the ship "J. P. Whitney," off Bermuda, and the ship was his home for the first three years of his life.

The illustration shows the "Daniel I. Tenney" passing Pier Head, Havre, France, outward bound. She was built in Newburyport, Mass., registered tonnage 1,727, and was a very deep ship, having three full decks. The upper deck was flush fore and aft. The crew's and officers' quarters being below decks made her easily handled in tacking or wearing ship. Although not a sharp built ship, she once outsailed the clipper ship "Seminole," and made a record of 324 miles in twenty-four hours. She was a big carrier, once having 2,576 tons of coal and 30,000 feet of lumber in her hold. She was sold and converted into a coal barge, and was lost with all hands off Cape Cod, the same night the steamship "Portland" went down with all on board.

The time passed pleasantly until the "R. B. Sumner" was reported at the bar,—a fine ship, somewhat larger than the "Whitney," but I was disappointed about taking the command.

Captain Elisha Dyer was an owner of one-quarter interest, and fully intended staying on shore that trip, and had so notified the firm, but he had been recently married, and his wife took a notion she would like to make a sea voyage with her husband. As a consequence he concluded to hold on to the command for another trip, and as there was not another vacancy in the fleet, like Micawber, I "waited for something to turn up."

I engaged rooms at a nice boarding-house on Julia Street, close to Magazine, where the family of Captain Gray, former captain of the "J. P. Whitney," had theirs, the rest of the boarders being young men, mostly clerks and bookkeepers in the mercantile and cotton houses of the city. Mrs. Conklin, a widow, who kept the house, had three grown up daughters, and a son who was in business in the city; a very fine family, the girls being pretty, bright, intelligent, and fond of music, while Mary, the eldest, was a fine harpist, and an accomplished pianist.

It was the early winter, and the city was in gala attire. Balls, theatre parties, and the opera were the regular thing, while evening parties at the house, *musicales* and oyster suppers constituted a round of gaiety that was very fascinating to a young man.

About this time my old friend and schoolmate, Captain Eben Graves, arrived in port in command of the barque "Panama." Not having seen each other for years, the meeting was a most pleasurable one for both, and our house being full, I gave him a cordial invitation to come up and share my rooms, which he gladly accepted. I introduced him to Mrs. Conklin and the girls, and it was not long before he was like a member of the family. Instead of going out in the evenings, he preferred to spend them at home, and I soon saw that between him and Miss Mary it was a case of love at first sight. As his stay was limited, matters had to arrange themselves quickly, and one evening after I had retired he awakened me to tell me the deed was done, Miss Mary had accepted him, and Mrs. Conklin had given her consent. The wedding was fixed for Saturday of the coming week, at 9 o'clock in the morning. After the wedding breakfast Captain Graves was to take his bride, with her family, servants and all, on board the barque. I, as best man, was to stand up with the captain, and accompany the wedding party to the barque, being placed in command pro tern, to take her down river to the lower levee to make up the tow, while the captain attended to his affairs up town, and I was given *carte blanche* to provide dinner. At eight P. M. the good-bys would be said, and Captain Graves and his bride would leave for New York, while our carriages would take us all back to the house. This was the programme as laid out by the captain that night in my room.

Extending my warmest congratulations to my old friend, I suggested the advisability of getting a little sleep, as it was then one o'clock, but Graves was not sleepy, and nearly two hours passed before I succeeded in closing my eyes.

From that time on, all was bustle and preparation; the invitations were issued, and the hundred and one things had to be attended to, that precede a wedding. The sisters were in a whirl of excitement, while I, having no special business of my own, took a hand in all that was going on. The week passed quickly, and the wedding morn ushered in, with bright sunshine, a most lovely day.

The guests gathered in the parlors, which had been prettily decorated, and just before nine o'clock the wedding party descended the stairs, and took their places, Miss Eva Lovering, a dear friend of Miss Mary, and a most charming young lady, being bridesmaid.

They were married with the Episcopal service. The words that bound them together for life were uttered, the signatures were made, congratulations were extended to the newly married pair, not forgetting the kiss to the bride, who, blushing, looked prettier than ever. The bridal party then descended to the breakfast room, under the guidance of brother "Tom," who, as master of ceremonies, filled the position most gracefully. Here for an hour mirth and jollity reigned, after which the ladies retired to change their costumes, and carriages were taken by Mrs. Captain Graves and family for the ship.

After seeing the party on board the captain left for up town, and at noon a towboat took the barque to the lower levee, where the tow was made up, the "Panama" being the outside ship.

After dinner had been served, the family party sat under the awnings inspecting the shipping, and asking all manner of questions. Not having ever been on a vessel of any kind before, it was a novel experience for them. By five o'clock, the captain came on board, and ordered tea, but no one seemed inclined to eat anything more, and as time drew near for parting with their sister the girls grew silent, a tear would glisten, an eyelash quiver, while they would laugh and try not to show it.

At last the whistle of the boat sounded warning, "All ashore that's going ashore!" and with a final embrace, a hearty handshake, and a fervent "God bless you," the ladies were assisted across the shipping to the levee, where entering the carriages, we drove home, more silent than in the morning. Arrived at the house, an hour was spent in conversation, the topic being "the captain and Mary."

"What kind of a voyage will she have?" "Will she be likely to be seasick?" and lots of other questions were addressed to me, to all of which I gave consoling replies.

CHAPTER XVIII
1860-1861

BUYING INTO THE "C. H. JORDAN."—A PROTRACTED CALM IN THE TROPICS.—
THE SALADERO DE LA FONDA, MONTEVIDEO.—THE EFFECT OF THE WAR
ON FOREIGN TRADE

THE next few days were spent in writing and sending notices to all friends, north and south, after which everything settled down into the regular routine, and I remained in New Orleans until the early spring, then taking passage for Boston, I purchased a quarter interest in a full-rigged brig, between four and five hundred tons burthen, that had been condemned by the United States government as a slaver engaged in the slave trade between the coast of Africa and Cuba.

This vessel had a history that I afterwards found out, but at the time I knew nothing more than that she had been picked up derelict off St. Thomas by a Provincetown whaler and brought into Provincetown. She had no flag, nor papers. Everything by which she could be identified had been destroyed. There were slave-shackles on board, and lumber for slave-decks, a large number of water casks, and all the fittings of a slave-ship; she was taken and condemned as such by the government, and sold at auction to Mr. Charles W. Adams of Boston. He in turn sold one quarter interest to me, to take command.

She was placed in Kelley's dry dock, East Boston. Her cabin, which was below decks, was torn out and a deck-house was put on for cabin accommodations; also a new galley in the place of the old iron caboose. Her heavy copper was stripped off and replaced by yellow metal, and about 1,500 through locust treenails driven, to strengthen her. Altogether she was a queer-looking craft. Her cabin, which had extended to the mainmast, was finished in mahogany and boxwood, with staterooms on each side. In the panels of the staterooms were imbedded bullets that had been fired from the skylight,—at the captain, probably,—while on the deck, in front of one of the rooms, was a large stain of blood.

Spanish built, with bluff bows above water, below she was very sharp, and from her mainmast aft she fell away, carrying nothing under the cabin deck but pig iron ballast. Above the between-deck beams she widened out, her greatest beam being at the fore rigging; from that she fell away aft, being very narrow at the stern, and steered with a big, long mahogany tiller, which was taken off, and a wheel substituted.

Having bought her from the government, an American register was obtained with some difficulty on account of her being of foreign build. The name given her by the purchaser was "Charles W. Jordan." Her spars were heavy, and of great spread, while from topmast, to'gallant and royalmast heads hung heavy preventer backstays, to which tackles could be hooked, and set up to heavy eye-bolts through the deck-beam on either side, the brig having every facility for carrying sail to the limit, if necessary.

Having shipped a crew, the "Jordan" sailed for Machias, Maine, to load lumber for Rio Janeiro, and the run from Boston to that port showing her sailing capabilities, I felt that nothing that did not use steam was to be feared. At Machias we took on our lumber, including deck-load even with the rails, and at the close of a dark, lowering day took our leave of Machias port, and the gale increasing, by midnight we were scudding under close reefs, headed south for the Gulf Stream.

At the time of sailing, the whole country was watching for the impending conflict between the North and South, although hostilities had not actually commenced.

Seeing few vessels and speaking none, our passage to the equator was made in exceptionally quick time, the N. E. trades being, up to 10° north, quite strong, and from this point falling off, but continuing of moderate strength to 5° north, when they failed altogether, and a calm of a week's duration succeeded.

There is scarcely anything more annoying than a protracted calm at sea, especially after having made a good passage up to a given point. As far as the eye can reach, bounded only by the horizon, lies a glassy unbroken surface, perhaps a slight, undulating ocean swell, on which the vessel lazily rolls from side to side, or lies motionless, the sails hanging limp or clewed up to prevent slatting and chafing. The sun, like a ball of fire, beats down upon the deck, causing the pitch and tar to bubble out of the seams, while the deck is like a furnace. Awnings are spread, but the men go about their work in a listless, half-hearted way, while the captain gazes eagerly around, whistling softly for a breeze, so the day wears on. Old Sol is getting lower and lower, until like a fiery globe he sinks below the horizon's edge. The shadows deepen and night creeps o'er the sea, and the stars come out, while a delicious coolness, in contrast with the fierce heat of the day, is felt. There is no sign of a wind. So passes the night, and almost before the stars have faded, the watch is turned to, decks are washed down and scrubbed, while every bit of woodwork, outside and in, receives its baptism of ocean water.

Meanwhile another day draws on apace and

> "Noiselessly as the daylight
> Comes when the night is done,
> And the crimson streak
> On ocean's cheek,
> Grows into the great sun."

Still no darkening shadow of a coming breeze, and we lie

> "As idle as a painted ship
> Upon a painted ocean."

Day after day, and sometimes week after week, passes, and still no wind. One can imagine the horrors of the "middle passage" (from the coast of Africa to Cuba) on a slave-ship in the old slave-carrying days, with such a calm. But relief is at hand. Afar off on the horizon a few small clouds are seen, while along the edge appears a dark shadow, gradually spreading and rapidly advancing. No squall that, but a steady wind, the first welcome breath of the S. E. trades, and we know the calm is a thing of the past.

With every stitch spread, and every sail trimmed to meet it, the good brig heels gently over, the white foam thrown from her bows, and once more endowed with life, she crosses the line, with yards braced sharp, continuing her way along the Brazilian coast.

We sighted Cape Frio, and bearing away to the westward, the following morning entered the beautiful bay of Rio Janeiro.

The brig having a clean bill of health, the doctor's visit was soon over, and the ship-chandler's boat pulled alongside. He wished to know if I wanted to go on shore, but as it was between four and five P. M. I concluded to wait until morning. He chanced, however, in naming over the American vessels in port, to mention the barque "Panama," Captain Graves. This altered the case, and I told him I believed I would go, after all, and having been taken alongside the barque, I ascended the gangway and stepped on deck, where the first officer, who was a stranger, received me. On inquiring for the captain I was told he had not yet come off from shore.

"Is Mrs. Graves on board?"

"Yes, sir, would you like to see her?"

"Why, yes, as the captain is not on board.' "

He ushered me on to the quarter-deck abaft the house, where Mrs. Graves sat in a rocker, and started to announce me, when, with one look and a scream of delight, she sprang from her chair, warmly greeting me, and seating ourselves, we commenced a review of the time since we parted. I answered all questions about the family, but we had not proceeded far, when she suddenly exclaimed, as a boat pulled towards us:

"There comes Eb.; we'll give him a surprise!"

Then she hustled me into a stateroom, where from my retirement I could hear Captain Graves say as he came aft:

213

"What! all alone, Mary? I saw some one here as I came aboard! Where is he?"

After keeping him wondering awhile, she pointed towards the door of the stateroom where I was, and opening it, we stood face to face!

With a shout he recognized me, and a hearty welcome and handshake followed.

We had so much to talk about that they insisted upon my taking up my quarters with them while in port, to which I gladly assented, going on board the brig daily, and returning at night to the "Panama."

At the request of my consignee I rechartered the "Jordan" to take the cargo on to Montevideo, instead of discharging at Rio, lumber being more in demand there, and a week later, bidding good-by to Captain Graves and wife, with the wish that I might see them on my return, the "C. H. Jordan" got under way, and running out past the fort and Sugar Loaf, with a fine breeze was soon bowling along towards Cape St. Mary, and nothing of note occurring, in a week we dropped anchor in the harbor of Montevideo. Uruguay is the smallest of the South American republics, covering an area of but seventy-two thousand square miles, while its capital Montevideo is the chief commercial center, having a population of about two hundred and fifty thousand inhabitants. All fruits and vegetables grown in Europe can be successfully raised there, the hot season holding sway from November to April, and the cold season from May to October. The chief industries are the raising of cattle and sheep, and other agricultural pursuits. The value of its animal products exported in 1897 was nearly twenty-seven million dollars, that of jerked beef alone amounting to about four and one half-millions.

Quite a number of vessels were in port, among them several American, including the United States frigate "Congress." (The sailing frigate "Congress," 50 guns, sunk in Hampton Roads, Va., March 8, 1862, after having been disabled while fast aground, by the Confederate ironclad steam-battery "Virginia," rebuilt on the hull of the U. S. steam frigate "Merrimac." This battle was the introduction of steel and steam into the navy.)

I was ordered by the consignees of our lumber to discharge at once, and recharter to take a cargo of jerked beef back to Rio Janeiro, and while making arrangements with Mr. Evans,—mentioned in a former chapter in connection with the death of Captain Smiley,—ship-chandler and provision dealer, who supplied about all the shipping with beef and vegetables, I formed the acquaintance of the different shipmasters, who made their headquarters at Evans's store, getting the news there, etc., etc.

Evans was a sharp, shrewd Englishman without much education, but keen at a trade, bluff and jolly, though at times very emphatic in his language. His business and books were superintended and kept by Captain Joseph W. Clapp, a genuine Nantucketer, who was the most original of men. Honest, attentive to business, with an eye always to his employer's interest, he displayed a rare tact in dealing with customers, that was invaluable to Mr. Evans, who was, at times, inclined to be irritable when anything went wrong, and many took exception to his language; but a witty remark or a funny story from "Joe" would straighten matters out, and I think Evans owed his success in business, in a great measure, to Clapp's ability, honesty and faithfulness. In society he was a general favorite; full of humor, and witty in conversation, he possessed a fund of stories of his island home and its inhabitants, that he could draw upon at will.

Horseback riding was freely indulged in, as at Buenos Ayres, and many a gallop I enjoyed to the other side of the bay, where was located the "Saladero de la Fonda," an immense establishment for the slaughtering of cattle and the curing and putting up of the "Carne Tasaga," or jerked beef of commerce, that was exported to Brazil and France in immense quantities. This was a place well worth visiting, and a goodly number of rides were taken around the bay to see the process of converting the steer into jerked beef.

There was a very large one-story building, or more properly shed, open at the sides, with a stone flooring, and gutters to carry off the blood that literally ran in rivers during the killing process, while along its entire length was a double track terminating at one end in a corral, or enclosure, which was built with an inclined plane towards the end nearest the shed, narrowing down to the width of a broad platform car, that during the killing was introduced under the bars of an enclosure between the shed and the end of the corral. This corral would contain three or four hundred steers, and had an opening into a large one that held many thousands. The walls of the smaller corral were broad enough for a man to walk on them around it, and throw the lasso over the cattle's heads, when they were jerked down on to the platform car standing ready to receive them; the other end of the lasso being carried through a pulley into a *patio*, or yard outside, where it was attached to a horse ridden by a *gaucho*, who, on the call from the lassoer, spurred up and yanked the animal out from among the others down the incline on to the car.

On a small platform, close to the bars, stood the man who did the killing, and who, by reaching over, could strike the animal just back of the horns in the neck with a knife, severing the spinal cord, when the steer would drop, as though shot, on to the car, and, the bars being drawn, it would shoot out along the track, which was lined with men about five or six feet apart, who tumbled them off the car, and in less than two minutes they were dissected. They took off the hide with a few sweeps of the long, sharp knives, two more removed the flesh from the ribs, while in less time than it takes to write it, the hide was going in one direction, the beef to vats for the soaking previous to pressing out and the curing in the sun,—during which time no rain was allowed to fall upon it,—making the jerked beef of commerce, while the bones, hoofs and horns were taken to the rendering house. There were separate establishments for all these purposes, and the entire works covered many acres, to say nothing of the great corral capable of holding ten thousand head of cattle.

A funny incident occurred during one of my visits, although for a short time it seemed to me to possess more of the tragic element. One fine morning, I had ridden over alone, fastened my horse, and entered

217

the shed that was supported by iron columns, not over clean, and was standing near the bars, watch in hand, timing a man as to the length of time he took to skin and dismember a steer; this work being so rapid as to excite wonder.

Sometimes when the bars would be dropped to let the car out, the killer having missed his aim, the car would come out with the steer alive and unhurt, in which case there would be fun for a few moments before the animal was killed.

This was the case on this particular morning. A shout called my attention from the man I was watching, and looking around, I caught sight of an infuriated bull, with tail in air, and lowered head, making for me. Regardless of clothing, I made a spring for a column and, climbing it, was just in time to escape his onrush, which was a fierce one. Turning from me, he attacked a pile of beef, which flew in all directions. The workman had taken refuge in the rear of the columns, from behind one of which a man, as the animal passed, sprang out, knife in hand, and hamstringing him, the excitement was over. These fellows did not mind it; a loose wild bull, being an affair of almost daily occurrence, had no terrors for them.

Meeting on shore daily the officers from the men-of-war in port, as well as the merchant captains, I listened with interest to the animated discussions on the prospects of a civil war, and the probable result from the same. Among the officers, many of whom were Southern men, the feeling was intense, and news was anxiously awaited with every mail.

Captains gathered each day at Evans's, and the situation was the all-absorbing topic of conversation.

The lumber discharged, the hold of the "C. H. Jordan "was made ready, by being matted, for the return cargo of jerked beef, not an inviting article to look at, but when washed and made into a savory stew better than it looked. Our lading completed and anchor weighed, we rounded the point, passing Lobos Island and Cape St. Mary, headed north for Rio.

With the exception of a little brush off the Rio Grande, our passage was a fair one, and in nine days, the brig again passed the Sugar Loaf, and came to anchor in the bay off the landing mole. The next day we hauled into what was called the "jerked beef tier," a line of small vessels that were moored, head and stern, off the city front, extending from the mole to Cobras Island, and having only cargoes of jerked beef on board, which were retailed from the vessel. Between the water front and this line was a passage for boats and small steamers.

As the shore people attended to the sale and delivery of the cargo, and I had sixty lay days to deliver the same, there was nothing to do but take it easy.

On shore among the shipping fraternity the war excitement was at fever heat. The news of the firing on Fort Sumter and the breaking out of the civil war had been received, and all knew what that meant. Besides the vessels hailing from northern ports, there were a very large number of barques and brigs hailing from Richmond, Virginia, and other southern ports, all engaged in the coffee trade. These were in a dilemma indeed. Once outside the shelter of the Bay of Rio Janeiro, they were liable to seizure as prizes by any American man-of-war that happened along. On the other hand, there was the choice of staying in port while the war lasted, and that might be for years, and Rio, though a beautiful spot to visit, was not just the place where one would choose to remain the year round indefinitely, or, as Jack would say, "until the vessel grounded on her beef bones."

"Curses both loud and deep" were frequent, while heated arguments in favor of the North or the South, as the case might be, were freely indulged in by the numerous captains. It was not only the Southerners who were troubled in mind; the flag was shut down on, and freights were not obtainable for Yankee bottoms without great difficulty. Visions of Southern privateers, loss of ship, and a sojourn in a Southern port or prison loomed up in the mind of the Northern captain, while many were not only anxious to get home, but also to enroll themselves in the army or navy as defenders of the constitution and the right.

To my great joy, I found the "Panama" still in port under orders to wait for coffee, but the consignees had not deemed it best to load her, as yet, and going on board I found an addition to the Graves family of a beautiful little daughter, and the captain was a very happy man.

CHAPTER XIX
1861-1862

THE FIASCO OF PROFESSOR LOVE.—THE DOM PEDRO RAILROAD. BRAZILIAN FORESTS.—RIO JANEIRO TO ST. THOMAS

A MONTH later, the cargo being all out, and not seeing any prospect of a freight north, feeling that as at this distance there was not much to fear from privateers,—it would be better to engage in that trade than to lie idle waiting for a freight to be offered north,—I chartered the brig to a Brazilian firm for six months to bring *carne tasaga*, or jerked beef, from Montevideo to Rio, and bade good-by to Captain Graves and his wife, whom I did not expect to see on my return, as he was about to commence the taking in of his coffee.

The day before sailing I was asked if I could take a passenger, and on my answering in the affirmative the passage money was handed me, with the understanding that he was to be aboard before daylight. A tug having been engaged, the brig was towed to sea very early, the towboat dropping us outside the islands, where taking the sea breeze, by nine o'clock we were once again on our way to the river. Shortly after leaving, the main topsail yard was carried away in the slings, but having a spare spar on board it was quickly replaced, and in two hours the "Jordan" was all right again. It was a wonder that the old spar lasted as long as it did, for on examination it was found to be decayed at heart.

Our passenger, whose name was Love, was a magician by profession, and claimed to be a son of the great English magician of that name, but in reality he was a fraud of the first water. I afterwards found out that he was leaving Rio "under the rose" and that there were many who were anxiously looking after him. I knew nothing of him at the time. He seemed to be a genial chap, who at times would give an exhibition of his skill at juggling which appeared to us very mysterious, and we were inclined to look upon him as one likely to draw a crowd.

His intention was to give an exhibition at the Mount and then go on to Buenos Ayres.

With fine breezes and good weather, in eight days we again passed Lobos Island, and let go our anchor in the harbor of Montevideo. On landing I introduced Mr. Love to Mr. Evans and Captain Clapp, bespeaking their good offices for him, also making him acquainted with the captains, telling them his profession, and booming him with a good word whenever I had the opportunity.

While we were making ready for another cargo of jerked beef, the time was passed when on shore mostly at Evans's discussing the war and the eventual outcome. Meanwhile Mr. Love had been busy.

The Grand Opera House had been engaged for one night only, his numerous engagements precluding a longer stay, and Montevideo was placarded with gaudy posters setting forth the accomplishments of the great Professor Love, a wizard of the highest order and son of the late eminent English magician of the same name. Never was anything better advertised. Montevideo was on the qui vive. The nerve of that fellow has been a wonder to me ever since!

The eventful night arrived, and the immense auditorium was packed from pit to dome, Captain Clapp and myself occupying seats in the dress circle.

There was no orchestra, so the great audience was thrown upon its own resources until the raising of the curtain, and after a delay of half an hour the throng began to exhibit signs of impatience.

At last, up went the curtain, showing the dimly lighted stage, a table here and there, and one or two rows of wax candles, with a few tawdry figures scattered about. There was an ominous silence. Presently the professor appeared from the wings, dressed in a tinsel robe covered with Egyptian characters and hieroglyphics, and bowing to the floor, first to the east, and then in succession to the three other cardinal points of the compass, assumed different postures occupying about five or ten minutes, while the audience sat in wondering silence. Then going behind the scene, he reappeared in a moment, and performed some simple tricks that probably every one had seen many times, also attempting some more delicate work with an assistant, but the whole performance was so flimsy and palpable as to be seen through by the veriest child.

Directly a murmur arose, then a hiss, then more hisses, until an uproar of indignation filled every part of the house. The professor, who had at first retired from the stage, now came to the front and attempted to speak, but the uproar was such that he could not be heard. Then came a shower of missiles,—cabbages, turnips, potatoes, eggs. He stood his ground until an iron crown that some one had torn from the

223

decorations came whizzing by his head, just missing it. Then he turned and fled. His assailants jumped on the stage in pursuit, but failed to catch him, as he had made good his escape from the rear of the theatre. He took with him the best part of the receipts, and getting on a steamer just leaving for Buenos Ayres, was seen no more.

The audience vented their rage on all his stage fittings.

"Well" said Captain Clapp, or "Joe" as I used to call him, as we came out of the Opera House together, "I'm blowed if that don't beat all. What if that iron crown had gone four inches more to the right?"

Love's fiasco formed the topic of conversation for many days after.

It was on this trip that I obtained in Montevideo full information relative to the history of the brig "Charles H. Jordan," former slaver. I had occasion to employ some men from shore, and one, on coming aboard, looked around and exclaimed:

"Why, I know this craft, only she's been altered!"

Overhearing the remark, I called the man aft, and questioned him. He said he had made two voyages in her to the coast of Africa, bringing slaves to Cuba and landing them on the south side of the island near the Isle of Pines. Both trips had been successful, and the brig being very fast, and a great favorite, was not destroyed after landing the darkies, as was often the case, to remove evidence. He said she was a very old vessel, built originally in and belonging to Barcelona, Spain, and being in great favor with her owners, she had been rebuilt on the same lines, and sent to Havana, where she was bought for the slave-trade. At the end of the second run he left her, and on the third trip to the African

224

coast, having about $30,000 in specie on board, the crew mutinied after reaching the coast, captured the brig and killed the captain and other officers, shooting the captain from the skylight in front of his stateroom. Running the brig down across the trades until in the vicinity of St. Thomas, they destroyed everything on board by which she could be identified, and taking to the boats, landed at that port, giving out that their vessel had sunk. From St. Thomas they proceeded to Havana, and having plenty of money, while "in their cups "they betrayed their secret and were arrested. Two of the crew turned state's evidence, and the rest were tried, convicted, and garroted. The brig was picked up by a whaler as before stated.

Having taken our cargo of jerked beef on board, we again took our departure for Rio, where we arrived safely and entered our berth in the tier for the sale of the cargo.

I spent most of the time on shore, daily looking for letters and news of the war, our place of rendezvous being at the ship-chandlery of George Essling, opposite Palace Square.

About this time I made the acquaintance of an engineer of the name of Moore, a Virginian, and one of the contractors for the building of the Dom Pedro Railroad, a road that was being built from Rio across the Sierras, into the table-lands of Brazil, to bring the products of the interior to the seaboard. At that time mules were the only means for transportation. During the rainy season, for almost six months of the year the roads were nearly impassable. It was impossible to get the products to a shipping point, and even in the dry season the rates of freight were enormous. To obviate this, the Dom Pedro Railroad was being built by the Brazilian government. Mr. Moore had a section of the road to build beyond the mountain near the Parahiba River, and being in the city for supplies, gave Captain William Hobbs, of the ship "Morning Glory," and myself an invitation to make him a two weeks' visit. At the end of that time he would be coming to the city again and would return with us. We gladly accepted, for this was an opportunity to see something of the country outside the limits of the port that was not to be slighted, and as there was nothing to keep us in the city, we made our preparations without delay, and one beautiful morning took the train for Bellaine, a station some twenty-five or thirty miles from Rio, thence to the village of Macawcos, a little place at the foot-hills, the terminus of the railroad. On leaving the train, we found a party of four or five of Moore's men with mules, and one horse belonging to Moore. Also awaiting our arrival were the pack animals to carry the supplies we had brought along. I not being accustomed to riding a mule, Moore gave up his horse to me, and the freight having been carefully packed on the animals, we mounted and started on our journey across the range of mountains. A fair road wound around hill and crag, sometimes doubling on itself. Upward, and still upward we climbed, until at night we drew rein at the little hamlet of Brandon, located on the summit of the mountain and the highest part of the road, where the main shaft of the tunnel had been sunk.

Moore had ordered our entertainment ahead, and alighting from our tired animals, hungry as bears, we entered a house where a good supper awaited us, to which we did ample justice. After supper, at the invitation of the section superintendent, we went down the shaft, upwards of a thousand feet in depth, in a bucket. There was little timbering, and it seemed a long time descending through the walls of solid rock. The headings were from eight hundred to twelve hundred feet from the shaft, and the workmen looked like spectres, flitting about in the gloom. I was told the tunnel had three shafts in which the work went on, as well as at the ends. It appeared to be a stupendous undertaking. Again entering the bucket, we were drawn slowly to the surface, and thanking the superintendent for his courtesy, we entered the house and shortly retired.

The temperature at this height was a marked contrast with that of Rio. When we left that city it was intensely hot, while here, blankets and spreads on the beds were not uncomfortable. After a sound sleep we awoke refreshed. Outside the scenery was fine, the hills and mountains showing up grandly, the peaks tinted with the light of the coming day, while lower down the valley the mist, not having lifted, still shrouded the view.

We partook of a hurried breakfast, and again mounting, commenced our descent adown the western slope, and reaching the foot-hills safely, made our way through heavily wooded districts, along ravines and over hills, until about four P. M. we entered Moore's section of the road and proceeded to his hut, which was the largest of a number. It was used for general dining purposes, while the cooking was done in a smaller building adjoining. Here we dismounted, all glad to rest, the section-hands gathering at the big hut to hear the news, and after a hearty supper pipes were lighted and the evening was given over to a general jollification.

"Early to bed and early to rise," was here the rule, and by nine o'clock the visitors from other sections got astride their mules, and with a "whoop, la!" galloped off in the darkness, our men seeking their shake-downs, and by ten the camp was still, all hands wrapped in

"Tired nature's sweet restorer, balmy sleep."

Gil Bias makes "Sancho" in "Don Quixote" say, "God bless the man who first invented sleep," and I think all, that night, would have echoed the prayer.

Arising with the daylight, and performing our ablutions in a big tin basin, we strolled out to take a look at our surroundings before breakfast. These were, a large cleared space in front of which was the virgin forest, a clear stream of water a couple of hundred feet from the house, and the woods alive with birds of every hue, parrots and paroquets screaming and chattering, their green plumage mingling with the most gorgeous hues of every color of the rainbow, but no song-birds such as we hear in our New England woods. About a quarter of a mile distant in the rear of the hut was a ravine, leading up among the hills, from which day and night issued a noise like distant thunder. I asked Moore what it was, and he replied, "Monkeys." The ravine, which was heavily wooded, contained tens of thousands of monkeys, who kept up an incessant roaring resembling thunder.

228

At the sounding of the horn, all hands filed in for breakfast, which consisted of flapjacks, bacon, sweet potatoes, stewed black beans and farina; the last two being the standard dish in Brazil among the working classes. Having made a hearty meal, the cook attended to the dishes, the hands went to their work, and Hobbs and myself had a great desire to go up the ravine, but Moore assured us it would not be safe, as many of the monkeys were of very large size and would attack a man very quickly if angry, and that there were so many of them, one would stand little show even if armed. So reluctantly we gave it up, and spent our time watching the men at work, strolling in the forest gun in hand but seeing little to shoot at, collecting leaves and ferns for specimens, watching the many-hued feathered tribe, and listening to the monkeys conversing; thus passed the two weeks very pleasantly and quickly.

Taking leave of the section-hands the last morning, we mounted our mules, this time leaving the horse behind, as we were going over the line of railroad, and mules were reckoned to be more sure-footed than a horse, and what a ride that return trip was! Along ledges, the path, in some places, not over a few feet wide, where one looked straight down one or two thousand feet; chasms across which a few trees were thrown, and you could look on the tree-tops a thousand feet below! We scaled rocks where it was necessary to dismount and clamber up after the mules as best we could, and following their example, bracing ourselves on banks of loose earth, we would shoot like an arrow to the bottom of a valley eight hundred feet deep! We forded streams, and at one time narrowly avoided a dangerous quicksand, and I mentally resolved, that, when built, there was not money enough in Brazil to tempt me to become a conductor or engineer on the Dom Pedro Railroad.

But all things have an end; so it was with our trip, and when over I would not have missed it.

When I arrived in Rio I found no chance of a freight and concluded to sail for home in ballast, taking the chances of privateers, and having received on board what few stores were required and cleared for St. Thomas, we said good-by to Rio Janeiro.

CHAPTER XX
1862

LIVELY CHASE BY A PRIVATEER.—IN COMMAND OF SHIP "DANUBE."—HEAVY
GALE.—CHINESE PIRATES.—THE "ARIEL" AT SHANGHAI

WE passed Cape Frio, and along the Brazil coast, with fine strong trades, Bahia and Pernambuco, and crossing the equator, were once more in the home waters of the north Atlantic. Up to this time we had seen very few vessels, and most of these showed no disposition to be neighborly, but edged off as far as possible. We, ourselves, looked upon every craft with suspicion; declining an intimate acquaintance until we were assured in our minds that she had no evil designs against us. All hands, fore and aft, were on the alert for a Southern privateer, but again, in this case, the old adage, "A watched pot, etc.," proved true, and one beautiful morning we sighted the island, and entered the cozy harbor of St. Thomas. On shore I found the flag was shut down on, and there were no available freights in the market for American bottoms, and having received the latest news of the war, we sailed for Boston.

All went well until we were north of Bermuda on the southern edge of the Gulf Stream, and coming on deck one morning, I noticed nearly in our wake a fore-and-aft schooner apparently pursued by an hermaphrodite brig. It had been blowing strong, with dirty looking weather the previous night, and the "Jordan" was under double-reefed topsails. Both the pursued and the pursuer were close-hauled on the port tack, with every inch of canvas that could be crowded on them. As they drew up on our weather beam it could be seen that the schooner was gaining on the brig and outwinding her, and evidently finding it was of no use, the pursuer bore away, and running down in my wake, was fast overhauling the "Jordan." I watched her with a glass, and from the number of men on her deck, I became suspicious, and calling all hands, the tackles were hooked on to the preventer backstays, while the order was given to shake out reefs and loose to'gallants. This work the boys sprang to with a will. Topsails were mastheaded and to'gallant sails set, as a squall that had been gathering to wind'ard came down upon us, and checking in the yards, and keeping her off two or three points, the old brig fairly flew through the water, reeling off fifteen or sixteen knots at least.

The squall lasted nearly two hours, settling down into a stiff blow, and we saw nothing more of our privateer, if such she was, and taking a pilot in the bay, we passed Boston Light, sailed up the harbor, and made fast alongside Battery Wharf.

I found the office on Doane Street closed when I went to see my co-owner Charles W. Adams, and upon going into Mr. Deshon's office on the floor below to make inquiries, I was informed that he had been engaged in running the blockade at Galveston, Texas, with his vessels, and had been arrested,—or, rather, had gone out of the back door as the United States marshal entered at the front, making his escape into Canada and from thence to England, where he was then residing.

On my return to the brig I was greeted by an officer who had been placed in charge during my absence, the "C. H. Jordan" having been seized by the government, *i. e.* Mr. Adams's part, and mine being indivisible could not be separated from his, and so was held as rebel property. This was a dilemma, but there was no help for it. The only thing to do was to get a power of attorney from Mr. Adams, which his brother finally succeeded in doing. We had her appraised and purchased her for the second time from the government, to whom I afterwards chartered her for six months to take naval stores to Port Royal (South Carolina), and placing Captain Knott Bray of Marblehead in command, I waited the arrival of the ship "Danube," then on her passage from Rio Janeiro to New York, and owned by my uncle, Mr. Thomas Appleton of Marblehead.

These were exciting times,—the spring of '62,—the dark and trying days of the Civil War. While the torch of patriotism glowed brightly, and the love of country kindled in the bosoms of the loyal North, still there were many who sought to extinguish it, by giving aid and succor to those who were doing their best to break up the republic, and trample upon the constitution. Troops were almost daily departing for the south, while the bulletin boards were constantly surrounded by eager throngs anxious for news from the front.

I had been recently married, and with the ship's arrival I took my departure, with my wife, for New York, to take command.

The "Danube" was a fine ship, of a thousand tons register, and had been chartered to load coal for Shanghai, China. She had been fitted out for eighteen months, and it was the intention of the owner to have her remain in the China seas, freighting, while the war lasted, there being a better show there than in home waters, with less chance of capture by privateers.

Taking leave of New York, and towing out past Sandy Hook, we bade good-by to Mr. Appleton and his wife, and other friends, who had accompanied us down the bay to see us off and return on the towboat. Sail was made quickly, fasts cast off from the tug, and the "Danube" was fairly entered upon her long voyage.

It was currently reported that Southern privateers were in the vicinity, including Semmes in the Confederate cruiser "Alabama," and a sharp lookout was kept day and night, but no sign of any craft bearing the "Bonnie Blue Flag" was sighted, and the "Danube" crossed the equator without making the acquaintance of friend or foe.

Good, strong S. E. trades swept us along the Brazil coast, when taking the fresh westerly gales, we were soon up with the Cape of Good Hope, and passed it with strong gales veering from southwest to west-northwest, and again entered the waters of the Indian Ocean. From this time on, strong, steady gales prevailed, with snow and hail storms, the "Danube" scudding under lower topsails, and reefed foresails, reeling off her two hundred and eighty to three hundred miles per day. This was, indeed, glorious sailing.

In the longitude of Mauritius we experienced a gale of more than usual severity. While not a revolving storm, it blew with hurricane force. The barometer had hung very low for twenty-four hours, and the sky had a wild look. It was blowing very heavily, with a high sea running, so I deemed it best to heave to before night, which was done,

234

the ship making good weather, shipping no water. At eleven P. M. (six bells) the sea seeming a little smoother, we kept her off on her course under two lower topsails. By eight bells (morning watch) it was blowing great guns, harder than ever.

Daylight broke, showing a wild scene. The wind was blowing with tremendous force, but the worst feature was the piling up of the seas, like huge mountains of water high above and threatening to sweep over the taffrail,—tumbling in at the waist as they rushed past, and flooding the main deck.

I regretted, then, that she had not remained hove to, for heaving to now was a serious matter!

By four bells, feeling that she must be brought to the wind or founder, I beckoned Mr. Broughton into the cabin companionway, where one could not be heard outside, and gave him his instructions.

I managed to get on the housetop holding on to the weather mizzen rigging.

Clewing up the weather side of the fore topsail, hauling spilling-lines well taut, leaving the lee clew still sheeted home, and bracing the head yards forward, the crew, with Mr. Broughton and the second and third officers, laid aft to the main braces.

Signing to the man at the wheel to ease down when there seemed a better chance of coming to without taking a sea aboard, giving at the same time a signal to ease off, and round in the main braces, slowly she swung into the wind, and had just brought the sea fairly abeam, when she gave two or three tremendous rolls that put her yard arms deep in the water.

Fortunately the coal that was between decks could not shift, having been looked after very carefully in New York, and stanchioned down with a view to just such an emergency, but it shifted at the ends, in the hold, giving her about four or five streaks list, which was carried the remainder of the passage.

Recovering, she came up to the sea, making fairly good weather, although falling off occasionally, but shipped no water to speak of, until about two bells in the first dog-watch, when a big wave broke on board, staving in the bulwarks aft, smashing the skylights, flooding the cabin, also staving the boats, and creating havoc generally; but the wind suddenly jumping into southwest, enabled the ship to come up, head to sea, when she lay more comfortably. With the change of wind, the gale began to abate, and by six bells (eleven P. M.) the "Danube" was again put upon her course. In due time we passed the islets of St. Paul and Amsterdam, when bearing away north, we took the trades, and shortly after sighted Java Head and entered Sunda Straits.

It was now the last of the southwest monsoon, and being anxious to get through the China seas before the northeast set in, we made no stop at Anger Point, but obtained our supplies of fruit, vegetables and live stock from the Malay trading-boats that boarded us before arriving off the point.

Leaving Anger, we crossed the Java Sea with a rattling breeze, entering Gaspar Strait, and were so fortunate as to get through before night, when the wind falling light, with a strong current, we brought the ship to anchor to await daylight. A sharp lookout with guns loaded and everything in readiness was kept during the night for pirate *proas*, should they make an attempt to board us. The "Danube" had a good armament, consisting of four large deck-guns, in the use of which the crew were well drilled; two of them being twelve-pounders, rifled, the other two smooth bores, a dozen and a half muskets, the same number of boarding-pikes, and pistols (large size), sabres, cutlasses, and a magazine with plenty of ammunition. This was necessary for a ship trading or freighting in these waters at this time, as the Chinese pirates were very numerous, the Chusan Archipelago being infested with them, as well as the southern coast. Pirating, among the Chinese, was a regularly organized business; their agents on shore kept them appraised of what would be profitable captures: junks with valuable cargoes or specie on board. While confining their depredations mostly to junks and smaller vessels, they were a formidable foe to European craft if they could catch them unawares. Theirs were fast-sailing junks, often with ten or twelve large guns,—stowed in the hold if they ran into port,—carrying a crew of from ninety to a hundred men. They were as cruel and bloodthirsty a set of scoundrels "as ever scuttled ship or cut a throat," showing no mercy when one was in their power, unless there was the chance of a big ransom being paid.

When at sea, their usual mode of procedure, on falling in with a vessel that they deemed safe to attack, was to get to wind'ard, keeping along in company, and gradually edging down upon her, but so slow and gradual as not to excite suspicion until very near. At the masthead of these piratical junks, if one looked closely, would be seen a package of glass or earthen jars; these contained the most villainous smelling compound, that only a Chinaman could stand, and not even he for long. Having approached near enough, one of their men would be seen shinning up the rigging, and when aloft the wheel would be put up and the junk run alongside, and the jars, or bottles, would be dashed down on the victim's decks. The fearful stench having driven all below deck, the pirates would spring from their concealment, and swarm on board, cutlass in hand, cutting down all who opposed them, and in a few moments the vessel would be in their possession, when the work of plundering and murdering went rapidly on.

These pirates have their regular haunts, villages and communities subject to their laws, governed by a chief, or head, who rules with a rod of iron; these being their places of rendezvous, from which they sally forth when advised by their agents, or for a piratical cruise. It was always considered a safe thing, when a junk was seen edging down upon one of our vessels, to get a gun or rifle ready, and when the Chinaman started to go aloft, to drop him before he got there. This accomplished, in ninety-nine cases out of a hundred they would haul off, and nothing further would be heard from them.

Meeting the northeast monsoon, the "Danube "passed outside of Formosa Island, now having a dead beat north of the Chusan Archipelago, to the Yangtse River, one of the great highways of the Celestial Empire.

A pilot was taken outside and we ascended the Yangtse to the mouth of the Woosung River, on which stands the city of Shanghai, the chief seaport of China, with a population of upwards of half a million, opened to foreign trade in 1842. It is one of the walled cities of China, and contains flourishing manufactories of silk, glass, and paper. Outside the city walls, on the banks of the Woosung, are the foreign concessions: French, German, English and American. They are all separate from each other, and contain the business houses, the various consulates, hotels, and residences of each particular country, also the centre of trade and commerce of the Chinese, who transact a large amount of business daily, while the streets are filled with bustling, hurrying throngs comprised of Chinese and representatives of almost every nation.

We sailed up the river with a strong flood-tide, and the "Danube" rounded to off the American quarter of the city, letting go her anchor one hundred and thirty-two days from New York. Shortly after anchoring, the tide, running very strong, caused the anchor chain to stretch out a long way ahead as taut as a harp-string. A large cargo-boat, laden, and under sail, attempted to cross our bow, but the tide proving too strong, she took the chain amidships. In an instant she capsized, her cargo of bales and boxes floating off, with her crew, up the stream! The river was full of boats and sampans belonging to the shipping, and the boatmen made a grand rush for the bales and boxes (loot), but not an effort from one to rescue the drowning men in the river. Our crew saved the big steering oar of the cargo-boat, and rescued

239

one poor fellow who clung to our chain, getting him on deck, where he stood shivering, the picture of woe, and I ordered "Sam," the sampan boatman, who had been one of the foremost in the race for loot, to take my involuntary passenger ashore with his steering oar.

This "Sam" did unwillingly, and on returning I noticed he still had the big steering oar, which he was getting on board.

"What are you doing with that oar, Sam? "I asked.

"Oh, that allee light, Cappee. Oar payee him passage ashore."

Thinking it a good opportunity to read "Sam "a moral lesson I said:

"You scamp, why did you not save those drowning brothers of yours, instead of stealing all you could lay your hands on?"

"Oh'ee, Cappee, can catchee one piecee box, long me, no time catchee China-man, no hab time, one, two, China-man drowned, no matter, more lice (rice) for China-man live."

My moral lesson was lost on "Sam "and I said no more.

A great river trade is carried on by steamers, mostly owned by American and English houses, trading between Shanghai and Hankeou, which had only been open to foreigners but a short time. Hauling in to the company's wharf to discharge our coal instead of into lighters, we were brought into contact with the land, and subjected to the poisonous miasma of the river's banks.

Until now my wife had most thoroughly enjoyed the sea life, her health was excellent, and she looked forward to the continuation of the voyage with a great deal of pleasure, but it was not to be.

Cholera, that dread scourge of the East, was raging at Shanghai, sweeping off hundreds daily, and in less than a week after arrival she was stricken down.

Everything was done, but, although she got over the disease, she had not strength to rally, and the sixth day she breathed her last, called home.

Her remains, after being embalmed, were sent home on the ship "Gamecock," Captain Clement Jayne, and interred at Marblehead.

After my wife's death I passed a large part of my time with my old friend and captain Edward Meacom,—formerly of the ship "Brutus,"—on board his ship the "Mermaid," while the coal having been discharged, a cargo of cotton was laden for Hongkong.

While at Shanghai I saw the "Ariel," the first ship I sailed in, serving as a hulk for storing opium, and except for the lack of her spars, she looked the same, bringing back memories of bygone days.

With a river pilot, the "Danube" took her departure from Shanghai, towing to Woosung.

CHAPTER XXI
1862-1863

FLYING THROUGH FORMOSA STRAITS.—IN SIGHT DAILY OF "MOUNTAIN WAVE" FROM MANILA TO MADAGASCAR.—FAREWELL TO OLD CAPE HORN.—SAN FRANCISCO AFTER FOURTEEN YEARS

To the northern end of Formosa the monsoon was light, but after dying away nearly calm, came out from N. N. E. in a furious squall, settling into a fresh gale, and sending the "Danube" through the Formosa Straits flying, under her two lower topsails. The night was dark as Erebus, and although a sharp lookout for Chinese fishing-boats was kept, it would have been impossible to have seen them, and in the event of meeting any, it would have been a case of "hardest fend off." The following morning being thick with fog, no land could be seen, but on its clearing at noon our course was shaped for the Lye-ee Moon Channel, the eastern entrance to the port of Hongkong.

Coming to anchor off the town of Victoria, the ship was at once surrounded by sampans containing artisans and washerwomen, all anxious to secure the ship's trade.

I was ordered by the consignee to discharge at once.

Hongkong, an island near the Canton River, was ceded to Great Britain in 1841, and with Kowluen on the opposite mainland, ceded in 1861, forms the British Crown Colony. Its area is twenty-nine square miles, and it is the centre of an extensive trade, largely through Hongkong, in Chinese silk and tea. Of the population of about 222,000, nine thousand of whom are white, about 137,000 are in Victoria, the capital.

A large number of craft of almost all nationalities lying at anchor in the harbor, included many junks, steamers, and men-of-war, and the bands of the latter, playing each afternoon about sunset, made the harbor very lively. From the top of the hill overlooking the town and harbor, the view is fine. The ships at that distance looked like toy boats.

The "Romance of the Seas," one of the famous clippers of the '50's, that lay loaded ready for sea, appeared, as one looked down on her from that height, like a beautiful yacht. This was her last trip. She was lost at sea with all hands.

While seated in the house of Messrs. Russell & Sturgis, our consignees, one forenoon, reading the latest home news, every one was suddenly startled by the entrance of a clerk, who announced that the P. & O. (Peninsular and Oriental) Company's steamer that had sailed early that morning was returning through the Lema Channel, with her signal set, "I am on fire!"

As she had chests of opium in her forehold, valued at $3,000,000, the excitement was intense, all leaving for the water front to see her enter the harbor, where she was beached on the Kowluen shore. She was scuttled by the men-of-war boats firing pointblank shots at her between wind and water, the fire being gradually extinguished, and although the damage was considerable, the opium was untouched.

Our cotton out and ship ballasted, the "Danube" sailed from Hongkong, seeking a freight, and my intention when leaving was to run around to Calcutta, touching at Singapore, in hopes of getting a good freight to the United States, or some port in Europe, but fairly outside, the "Danube's" course was shaped for Manila to try the market.

The fifth day out we passed the island of Corregidor at the entrance, and sailing up Manila Bay, dropped anchor off the city of Manila, the capital of the Philippine Islands, since made famous by the war with Spain.

The old city of Manila, situated on the western coast of the island of Luzon, where the Pasig River joins Manila Bay, six hundred and twenty-five miles from Hongkong, was founded by Spaniards in 1571, and was comparatively small. It was surrounded by a wall, and contained an old cathedral of the 17th century and other churches, the archbishop's palace, monasteries, convents, the governor's palace, and numerous government buildings. Binondo, the great commercial center, lies on the north bank of the Pasig; the retail trade was then in the hands of the Chinese, but the import and export trade was controlled by foreigners. In the native part, the houses of the Malays were mostly thatched huts, and a fire breaking out one night swept off some 1,500 in two or three hours, running from one house to another, which burned like tinder.

The ship was consigned to the house of Russell & Sturgis, of which Mr. Green (later the husband of Mrs. Hetty Green) was managing head, and I was offered a freight for Boston that footed up rising $22,000 in gold. There were no unchartered vessels in port, but knowing several were due, I accepted the offer, and the "Danube" was speedily made ready for loading.

Manila at this season (winter months) was charming. Residents and visitors alike appreciated the afternoon drives to Lunetta Park to listen to the exquisite music of the band and enjoy the cool breezes. The hotels were very poor, and it was more comfortable on shipboard, but I went on shore daily, returning at night.

The American merchant ships in port, besides the "Danube," were the "Mountain Wave," the "Galatea" and the "Cyclone;" also the "Wabash" an American war-ship. We now being homeward bound, and having far more provisions than could be used on the passage, I sold the surplus at good prices, and later made a few investments that paid well.

Cigars, at this time, were very cheap in Manila; the No. 1's were a very fine quality, costing but twelve dollars per thousand, packed and put on board, while a smaller cigar, No. 2's, only cost eight dollars. Thinking these figures could not again be duplicated, and being at that time an ardent lover of the weed, I purchased some thirty thousand, twenty thousand of them being No. 2's, the remainder No. 1's, and afterwards disposed of the same in Boston at seventy and thirty dollars per thousand, besides keeping five thousand for my own use.

I purchased some ten or twelve "pieces" of pina cloth, containing eighteen yards to the "piece," made from the fibre of the pineapple. This product of the fertile Philippines is cultivated principally for this fibre, which is woven into a most beautiful fabric for ladies' wear, extensively manufactured in Manila. It is of various colors, fine and delicate, but durable, just the material for the heated summer months. Eighteen yards was considered the proper quantity for a dress pattern.

In addition to these goods, I had, just before sailing from Shanghai, taken off the hands of one of the clerks of Russell & Sturgis, a complete invoice of Japanese curios, bric-à-brac, with two nests of fine camphor trunks. He had purchased them to take home with him, but his plans being changed to remain in Shanghai for an indefinite period, he offered me the entire lot at what he paid for them, a very low figure.

Previous to our sailing from New York, my aunt, wife of the owner at that time, Mr. Thomas Appleton of Marblehead, had asked me, if I saw anything pretty for house ornamentation, to get it for her, and this I considered a rare opportunity. Having no use for any of them now, myself, I gave her the lot on my arrival home, and they were highly appreciated. The pina cloth made up into nice summer dresses for the three girls, members of a most charming family with whom I passed many pleasant days when home from my voyages.

We sailed from Manila in company with the ship "Mountain Wave" and passed down the China Sea together, being in sight of each other daily all through the Indian Ocean until we were up with the south end of Madagascar. The wind then coming out ahead, we parted company, each going off on separate tacks, and we did not again fall in with each other. It was the most equal sailing I ever knew, on the part of two ships, for such a length of time and for so long a distance. The "Mountain Wave," however, arrived a week ahead of the "Danube."

Around the Cape of Good Hope, past St. Helena, Ascension Island, Fernando Norohna, and across the line (equator) the "Danube "steadily held her course, each night seeing us "a day's march (or sail) nearer home." Nothing of note outside the regular daily ship's work occurring from the time of leaving the Cape till we reached the equator,—not a sail had been sighted,— we almost began to feel as though we were alone on the waste of waters, but now, again in the north Atlantic, a sharp lookout was kept for steamers and sailing craft of suspicious appearance. All knew Semmes in the "Alabama" was abroad in these waters, seeking whom he could gather in, and the feeling that any day or hour we might run across him caused an uneasiness that was felt throughout the ship, but our fears were groundless.

Sighting few vessels and speaking none, the "Danube" passed Bermuda and the Gulf Stream, on the northern edge of which we experienced light southerly airs and foggy weather. Soundings indicated that we were to the southward and westward of Nantucket, and feeling our way, with the lead, around the great shoal, the fog being very dense, we finally struck channel soundings, when fanning along, with light southerly breezes, the "Danube" crept past Chatham on the elbow of Cape Cod, the Nauset three lights, the high sand-banks of the cape highlands, seeing nothing, but keeping the fog-horn sounding as a warning to other vessels, until we were north of the Highland Light with the bay open, when, the fog lifting, the most welcome sight of the lighthouse and sand-dunes of old Cape Cod came into view. Taking a pilot on board when half-way up the bay, we obtained all the news of the war, with the information that Mr. Horace Broughton, my first officer, had been drafted, and was liable to serve his country either in the army or navy, unless he paid $300 for a substitute. A tugboat which we took outside the light towed the ship up the harbor, docking at East Boston, one hundred and thirty days from Manila.

Our freight of $22,000, payable in gold, when gold was at a premium of two hundred and forty, caused the owners to smile and congratulate themselves.

The owners at that time were James Nesmith and Sons of New York, to whom, I had been informed by a letter from my uncle Mr. Appleton on my arrival at Shanghai, he had made over the ship. In future I was to take my instructions from them.

Discharging was at once commenced, and a week later saw the "Danube" in the market for a freight.

I was stopping at Marblehead, visiting the ship at Boston daily, and the time passed pleasantly. The war was the all-engrossing topic of the day, enlisting was constantly going on, and troops were leaving for the front almost daily. There was martial music in the air at almost every turn, while returning sick and disabled soldiers, worn down by the hardships and privations of the battlefields, were sad sights to witness, but there was no shrinking, no holding back among the loyal sons of the North. All did their duty, and a united country to-day is the result of their efforts.

During our six weeks' stay in port, Mr. Broughton, my first officer, concluded to put a substitute in the army, and embarked upon the matrimonial sea, taking for his wife a most estimable young lady of Marblehead.

Chartering the ship to load in Winsor's Line for San Francisco with general cargo, the "Danube" was laid on the berth for loading, and in thirty days was again ready for sea. With the crew on board the ship we hauled into the stream, and coming to an anchor, we took on board some five hundred kegs of gunpowder, which were stowed in the main hatch, after which the ship was ready for sea, and anchor weighed, we proceeded down the harbor. Dropping the pilot outside of Boston Light, we gave a farewell wave of the hand to the pilot-boat, and the "Danube," with all her canvas spread to a brisk westerly breeze, rounded the Highland Light, and passing out South Channel, again entered upon her 15,000 mile run.

I soon found the "Danube" was very logy and dull at sailing. She had taken in large quantities of iron that brought her very low in the water, and she seemed to have lost the springy feeling she had on her homeward voyage from Manila, but there was now no help for it, and it soon became apparent that the passage to San Francisco would be a long one, and two stiff southeasters before reaching the trade wind belt did not help matters. The trade winds were very light, and losing them entirely in the latitude of 8° north, we experienced nothing but light airs, squalls and calms, to the latitude of 2° north, where we took the S. E. trades, which were fairly strong, while gales with thunder and lightning were encountered off the River Plate (Rio de la Plata), and running down the Patagonian coast the ship was put in complete order to meet heavy weather off Cape Horn. Passing between the Falklands and the coast, we sighted the east end of Staten Land, but before we had rounded it and the "Danube" was pointed for Cape Horn, a howling gale from the W. S. W. struck us, accompanied with snow and sleet, and heaving to under a lower main topsail and foretopmast staysail, the ship buffeted the big Cape Horn seas for a week, when a favorable slant of wind enabled the ship to recover her lost ground; but it was short-lived,—gale succeeded gale, in rapid succession, and it was thirty days from the time of passing Staten Land ere we had gained enough westing to bear away north, but the change came at last. After blowing heavily from N. W. for several days, it veered into south-southwest.

Keeping her off to the north'ard and west'ard, under two lower topsails and reefed foresail, until the sea went down a little, the "Danube" made good progress towards better weather, while the wind holding steady from the southward, each day showed a marked change. It had been a long, hard experience off the stormy Cape, but we could congratulate ourselves on the ship sustaining no damage under all the heavy buffeting she had undergone in the past month.

Gradually our feathered companions, the albatross, the Cape pigeon, and "Mother Carey's chickens," that had kept us company around the Cape, having seen us safely through the most trying part of our passage, dropped off, as though feeling their escort was no longer needed and they could now bid us good-by.

The change to smooth seas and bright pleasant weather was rapid, and sail was gradually increased until the "Danube" was again covered with canvas and fast leaving Cape Horn in the background.

After being knocked about for four or five weeks in the high latitudes of the Cape, one is in the mood to enjoy and appreciate the delightful sailing through the trade winds of the south Pacific.

Crossing the equator, and taking the trades in the north Pacific, the "Danube" arrived off the heads of San Francisco, where taking a pilot on board, again I entered the bay, after an absence of nearly fourteen years.

What changes had occurred in that time! How vividly were the scenes and incidents recalled that passed in review before my mind's eye in connection with the fourteen years since I sailed out by these heads, as one of the crew of the barque "Zingari" bound for Valparaiso! What changes, since the early days, before California was admitted into the glorious sisterhood of States, when Oregon was a wilderness, and Portland, the capital, a city only in name! Now, under the march of progress, the country was well settled, with thriving towns, villages, and smiling farms. Portland, still the chief city, regularly laid out, had a large, bustling population, and a big steamship trade with San Francisco, and elsewhere.

San Francisco! The ship hauled in at the wharf at Clark's Point for discharging, but I should never have recognized it as the spot I landed at fourteen years before. Now there were wharves, with ships discharging their cargoes, a fine street leading over the hill lined with dwellings and stores,—no trace left of the shanty or "hotel" with "Delmonico's" over the entrance, or Mr. Benjamin Dixey's restaurant. Fine hotels and residences, big storehouses, and piers for shipping, streets and avenues handsomely laid out and thronged with busy multitudes, all told of the advancement made, and the growth of the "City of the Golden Gate," since the early days of '50.

On our way up the bay, the stevedore's boat pulled alongside, bringing the mail, and among the letters was one from the New York owners, containing a charter to proceed from San Francisco to Baker's Island and load guano for the North Sea, taking orders at Falmouth, England.

Consigning to the house of Charles W. Brooks & Co., Mr. Frank Ladd being the junior partner, we commenced the discharge of the cargo, which came out in good order, having sustained no damage.

I have, in a previous chapter, spoken of the large variety of cockroaches on board the ship "Brutus," Calcutta trader. Across the docks, opposite the "Danube," lay the ship "Guiding Star," Captain Small, just out from Boston, where she had discharged a Calcutta cargo. This ship was literally alive with roaches, but at the time I did not know it.

In the evening I went on board to make Captain Small a social call, and when, after passing a very pleasant hour, he invited me to spend the night with him, I accepted, and he gave me his stateroom, taking a spare room for himself.

Retiring about eleven o'clock, and pulling off my boots, I disrobed and turned in, sleeping soundly until morning, when I arose, and proceeding to dress, found nothing left of my boots but the soles and straps. All outside of these resembled a piece of brown tissue paper perforated with tiny holes. On asking Captain Small about it, he explained that he meant to have told me to put everything, including my boots, in the basket at the head of the bed, but he forgot it! The cockroaches had eaten them in the night, and the captain's forgetfulness cost me a new pair of boots. However, he was good enough to loan me a pair to put on.

The "Guiding Star's" cargo consisted largely of cases of boots and shoes, also carriages. The damage to these goods was, I understood, upwards of a hundred thousand dollars. As the cases were hoisted out of her hold and on to the dock, crowds of people gathered to look at the destruction, while the press teemed with the most extravagant nonsense regarding the pest, one paper stating that on taking out the large guns destined for Mare Island Navy Yard, it was found that the cockroaches had increased the bores from a half to three quarters of an inch in diameter. The damage was bad enough, and how it was settled I never knew.

Earthquakes were of frequent occurrence during our stay, some severe shocks being experienced, but no great amount of damage was done outside of giving the residents a scare.

Previous to my arrival home from Manila, I had been very much troubled with rheumatism, which had increased on the passage out, until now it became difficult to exercise my limbs or get my boots on in the morning. I consulted a specialist on rheumatism, and he was of the opinion that he could cure me, but it would take two and perhaps three months. Meanwhile I would have to go under special treatment, which, while not confining me to the house, would interfere with my going to sea. My consignees, knowing my physician well, advised me to stop and continue the treatment, assuring me he was very successful in cases like mine, so having communicated with the owners and obtained their sanction, the cargo being out and ship ballasted, I turned the command of the "Danube" over to my first officer, Mr. Broughton, who had been with me three years, and accompanying the ship outside the heads, with a hearty handshake, and wishing him a safe and prosperous voyage, I returned to San Francisco on the towboat. I was sorry to leave the ship, but I felt that in my state of health the voyage would probably use me up, and as the treatment was benefiting me, I made up my mind it would be better to stop and go through with it, a course I have never since regretted, for every particle of the disease was eradicated from my system, and I have never been troubled with it to any great extent since.

To be in San Francisco without a command was a novel experience for me, but I was not long unemployed. The "Eagle Wing," a sixteen-hundred-ton clipper ship, arrived in charge of the mate, Captain Linnell having been killed on the passage out, off the River Plate (Rio de la Plata) in a terrible manner.

The ship, while running free, was suddenly taken aback in a heavy squall, and the boom tackle parting, the heavy spanker-boom swept across the quarter-deck, the sheet catching Captain Linnell, and throwing him against the wheel, driving the spoke handles into his body, death resulting very shortly therefrom. For some reason, my consignees, who were friends of the owners of the ship, were not satisfied with the conduct of the mate, then in command, but could do nothing without a power of attorney from the owners. This they obtained, and sending for me, I was placed in command of the "Eagle Wing," to attend to her business until a captain could be sent out from New York. I stated to Messrs. Brooks & Co. that while I could attend to the ship's business in port, which would not interfere with my medical treatment, I would not go to sea in her, having just left my own ship. This was all settled, and they were to pay me $200 per month, gold, and my board at the Russ House.

My first act, after taking charge, was to give the mate and cook their discharge, for the reason that they were caught selling the ship's stores and sails, which I traced and was fortunate in recovering from the parties to whom they were sold. I retained the carpenter, who seemed an honest fellow; in fact, it was through him I first obtained my information of the rascality of the others.

Employing a good, reliable ship-keeper, I placed him on board, after the cargo was out, and taking in six hundred tons of ballast to keep her on her feet, I had her anchored in the stream to await the arrival of Captain George B. Kellum from New York.

I had now plenty of leisure, and one morning, I went with a party,— four making up our number, two city merchants, Captain Pendelton and myself,—for a drive to some medical springs, a health resort about twenty-five miles south of the city. We left at 6 A. M., seated in an open carriage, behind a spanking pair of grays. The drive in the open air, which was as bracing and exhilarating as champagne, through a beautiful country, over good roads, was one long to be remembered. I had often heard people speak of the glorious climate of California, but I had never realized fully, until that morning, what it meant.

Arriving at the Springs between nine and ten o'clock, breakfast was ordered, and we impatiently awaited its preparation, in the meanwhile strolling about the grounds, which were prettily laid out, and taking in long draughts of the purest air.

When breakfast was announced we filed into a cozy room decked with flowers, the open windows allowing the fresh air laden with the fragrance of the woods to sweep through. The table, with its snowy linen and silver service, was spread with the most tempting repast of fruit, fresh eggs and crisp bacon, tender steak done to a turn, and the crowning dish a large platter of fresh mountain trout, that, as the Irishman said, "were but a few hours before walking around their real estate, little thinking of the invitation they would receive to join four gentlemen at breakfast this morning!"

With keen appetites sharpened by the morning drive, we did ample justice to the bountiful spread, and at noon, leaving the Springs, and driving leisurely back to the city, we arrived in time for dinner at six, it being voted by all the most enjoyable trip of the season.

Messrs. Brooks and Ladd, upon whom I called daily, were engaged in a large sugar trade with the Sandwich Islands (Hawaii). Mr. Ladd had told me he had lived in Honolulu, and I asked him if he ever knew one Field, who was a shipmate of mine and left the ship at Honolulu, in '48, to go into the house of Charles Brewer & Co., merchants. "What was his first name?" he asked.

"Barnum," I replied, "Barnum W. Field."

"Why, yes," he answered, "I was brought up in his counting-room."

He then gave me a sketch of the career, to date, of Mr. Field, or "Barney" as we designated him on the "Tsar." He said Field went to California for Messrs. Brewer & Co. in the '50's and made a good deal of money for his house; later he went into business for himself in Honolulu, and Ladd had gone into his counting-room. Shortly after this Field left the island, and was then in New York, engaged in the western produce business on Broadway.

This information I was glad to get, as I had a desire to know what had become of him and how he had prospered.

The "Eagle Wing" was chartered to load for New York, and Captain Kellum having arrived, I turned over the command to him. Over two months had now elapsed, and I was feeling so much better I was anxious to be off, and two weeks later I was told by my doctor, giving me advice as to diet, etc., that it was safe for me to leave.

CHAPTER XXII
1863-1864

THE PILOT SERVICE IN '63.—PACIFIC MAIL STEAMSHIPS.—ACAPULCO.—
ISTHMUS OF PANAMA.—SUPERCARGO TO THE BAHAMA ISLANDS.—
SCHOONER "ELIZABETH"

AMONG my friends whom I bade good-by were a number of pilots. I had been of some service to them during my stay in port. An attempt had been made to do away with the pilot-boats, and have the pilots only on the towboats. These, of course, always carrying a pilot, would enable the captain to have his ship towed to sea in one tide, and it not being compulsory to take another pilot other than the one on the towboat, the regular pilotage outward would be saved.

This would enable the ship to get to sea, not only quickly, but cheaply, as the towing rates were not high, being kept down by the pilots, who were independent of the Towboat Association. This, at first glance, seemed a good thing for the shipping, but it would have operated disastrously for the pilot service, as without the ships to take to sea, they would have to give up their boats and go out of business, throwing the whole pilotage business into the hands of the towboat companies, who, I argued, would naturally put up their rates, and the shipping would be at their mercy. In short, it would establish a complete monopoly of the pilot and towage systems. This I worked against in favor of the pilot-boat system, taking the ground that it was entering a port a pilot was most needed, and that when a captain had brought his ship inside the Farralones from off a long passage, it blowing hard perhaps, and the land shrouded in thick fog, with the bar breaking a feather white, and a rock-ribbed coast close aboard, he felt a deal more comfortable with a pilot on board, and a pilot-boat would lie off under the islands, looking for him in bad weather,—as well as bright sunshine,—when no towboat was going to cross the bar and hunt around in the fog for his ship. He could do the best he could, and look after himself until the weather cleared, when, if he were near enough, a boat might run out and tow him to port. The whole matter was gone over and argued, pro and con, not only among the pilots, but by the captains in port. In the end the pilots came out ahead, and appreciating the part I had taken in the controversy, they presented me with a beautiful cane appropriately inscribed. It was of Mexican wood, dark, similar to rosewood, and a fine specimen of gold quartz was inserted in the head. This I treasure as a reminder of my last visit to San Francisco, nearly forty-four years ago, and the pleasant associations formed during my stay.

I engaged passage on the Pacific Mail Steamship "Constitution," for New York via Panama, and we steamed out of San Francisco Bay with a large passenger list,—between nine hundred and a thousand. There was ample accommodation on the big "Constitution," but with the much smaller boat on the Atlantic side, it was a problem where they would all be stowed. But the problem did not seem to disturb any one. We had a pleasant run down the coast, touching a few hours at Acapulco, Mexico, to land mails and passengers, during which time those of the through passengers who wished could go ashore, but it was so much pleasanter on board under the awnings than wandering around on shore in the hot sun, few availed themselves of the opportunity, and the whistle soon calling aboard all stragglers, with her prow pointing seaward, the "Constitution" bade good-by to Acapulco, while the gong sounded for dinner.

Commodore Watkins and his chief executive, Captain Caverly, were two of the most efficient officers in the service, genial and courteous to their passengers. The discipline of the ship was perfect, every officer and every man instantly at his station, at fire signals or emergency calls. One was made to feel an unusual sense of security on a steamship in charge of such men, and, as the result of close observation, I offer this slight tribute to their worth.

Arriving at Panama, we were transferred to the cars of the Panama Railroad Company, which after a four hours' ride, brought us to Aspinwall (Colon), where we embarked on the steamer "North Star" for New York. Once on board, the change was quickly noticed between the two boats. Staterooms were packed to the limit, while the remainder of the passengers slept on tables and under tables, on the cabin deck, in short anywhere they could find a resting-place without being trampled upon.

However, there was, generally speaking, no grumbling, all accepting the situation, and as long as the larder held out and a good table was set, everything was harmonious. Bright, pleasant weather and a smooth sea prevailed the entire passage.

A funny incident occurred which caused a great deal of amusement to those knowing the secret. The bar on the boat was not overstocked, and the bartender, not anticipating such a rush, had a scant supply of liquors, while two-thirds of the crowd were extremely bibulous. As a consequence the stock was quickly reduced until but one bottle of brandy remained. This bottle did service for nearly three days, and must have supplied some hundred and fifty to two hundred passengers with drinks at two bits (25 cents) each.

The bartender hated to close down, and as fast as a drink was called for it was replaced by the same amount of colored water. It grew to be comical to see a passenger walk up and call for a glass of brandy and the bottle passed out, and in five minutes one or two more saunter up and call for whiskey and the same bottle handed out. This was repeated until not the least odor of any kind of liquor remained. A man would deposit a quarter, fill his glass brimming full and drink it off, then turn away with a look of disgust, muttering something about the "blarsted" weakness of the spirits. It was of no use, though; twenty-four hours before arriving the barkeeper took down his sign and closed up. For nearly three days that could truly have been called a temperance bar.

On arrival and hauling in at the pier in New York, the passengers quickly scattered.

Walking up Broadway, my eye encountered a large sign reading "Barnum W. Field, Western Produce." I crossed quickly, and entering the store, which was large and well-filled, I walked to the rear, and asked one of the many clerks employed, if Mr. Field was in.

"Yes, but he is engaged for the moment," was the reply. "Shall I take your name?"

While we were talking, two gentlemen emerged from the private office and passed to the forward end of the store.

"Which is Mr. Field?" I asked. "The tall, large man," was the answer. Following and standing near them until the gentleman turned to go, I stepped up, and holding out my hand, said, "Good morning, Barney."

"You have the advantage of me," he said, looking sharply at me, and taking my hand. "Your face has a familiar look, but I can't place you."

"Yet we were shipmates and chums," I laughed.

"Where?" said he.

"On the ship 'Tsar,' " I replied.

A look of surprise crossed his features, and calling my name, he heartily shook hands, and invited me into his private office, where we sat an hour or more, comparing notes since the time we had left the ship in Honolulu, in '48; then bidding him good-by, and promising to see him when again in New York, I drove to—where the Grand Central Station is now, and took the train for Boston.

It had now been three years since the breaking out of the Civil War, and the end was not yet. American shipping, aside from our navy, was still at a discount, with very little moving, except under a foreign flag.

Mr. George Deshon asked me, one day when I had called into Mr. Deshon's office on Doane Street, if I would take a trip to the Bahamas, and when I inquired the nature of the business, and what he wished of me, he explained the situation. Owing to the war, Nassau had become

262

the headquarters of the blockade runners, and there was a great deal of money afloat among the inhabitants of the islands, chiefly a colored population. He believed that a good business could be done by trading, and selling to the blacks a miscellaneous cargo, made up of articles adapted to their needs, that could be disposed of at a great profit, adding that he and his brother had bought a schooner and were going to load her. He had a list of the cargo he was buying made and shown to me, and said he wanted a man to command her, whom he knew and in whom he could place confidence; to take entire charge and management not only of the schooner but of the cargo, and dispose of the latter among the darkies at the islands; also, to purchase a return cargo of fruit, or anything I thought would pay. He offered me satisfactory compensation, and I accepted the position, at once taking charge of the schooner lying at India Wharf, which I found to be the old fishing-schooner "Elizabeth," formerly of Marblehead, a staunch old craft, notwithstanding her age. Her cabin accommodations had been enlarged, all hands living aft, while the fo'c'sle, or forepeak, had been thrown into the hold. Sails and rigging were in good order, being comparatively new. She was not a fast sailer, but a fine sea-boat, as easy in a gale, hove to, as an old shoe.

On the following day the cargo began to come alongside, and I remained on the dock to receive and receipt for it. While thus engaged a party of seven men strolled down the wharf, looking at the different craft. Well knowing them to be seafaring men, there yet was something about them different from the fo'c'sle "Jack" that one sees about

263

wharves and along the water front. While I was watching them, trying to size them up, they finally stopped alongside the schooner, looking at her cargo of bales and boxes, and one of them, approaching me, asked where she was bound.

"To the Bahamas," I answered.

"Where?" he again asked.

"To the Bahama Islands, West Indies," I replied.

"Going to sail quickly?"

"As soon as loaded."

"Got your crew?"

"Not yet."

"Can we go on board and look her over?"

"Certainly," I said.

Presently he returned, and said they would all like to ship, asking what wages I was paying. "Fifty dollars per month, and sixty dollars to mate and cook," was the answer. This was satisfactory, and settling on one for mate and one for cook amongst themselves, they asked me if I would accept them as such. I told them I would if they knew their business. There was a mystery about them, but I was satisfied their motive in shipping was straight, and they were all able-bodied, bright, intelligent men, just what I wanted for the cruise, so giving them a note to the shipping-master, they were enrolled by him on the articles of the good schooner "Elizabeth" for a voyage to the Bahamas and a market, for a term not exceeding nine months. Returning to the schooner, they went to work, took in and stowed her cargo, got stores aboard, bent sails, filled water, and got the vessel ready for sea without my having to employ a man outside my crew.

We sailed with a fine, strong, westerly wind, having made arrangements with Mr. George Deshon to meet me at Harbor Island, a small island that makes the harbor of Eleuthera, my first port of call.

After getting outside Boston Light, we had occasion to jibe ship, and I noted the mate, or first hand, with the crew, knew much more about a schooner and her working than I did, for I was accustomed to square-riggers! No orders were necessary except to tell the mate what I wanted done, every man knowing what was required beforehand.

The wind hauling to the southward, and blowing a stiff gale, we hove to on the southeast part of Georges Bank, and putting the wheel alee in the becket, with one on deck for the lookout, all hands settled down to enjoy themselves in the cabin, where it was warm and comfortable. Green, my first hand, a big fellow from Castine, Maine, got out his fiddle, and being a good performer, made everything lively for a couple of hours.

It all came out that evening,—who my crew were. They were, every one of them, skippers of coasting schooners who had been drafted into the army, and having no desire to serve and no wish to hire or money to pay a substitute, they concluded to get out of the country in a body, and stay out until the war was over, and so came to Boston, and seeing an opportunity to get a berth with me for five or six months with good pay, had shipped on the "Elizabeth." Although not wishing to serve in the army, they were brim full of patriotism, as will be seen later on.

Altogether, they were a fine set of men, sober, industrious, implicitly obedient to orders, honest; feeling, each one, a responsibility to make the trading trip a success. Night or day they were always ready for a call, and not a word of grumbling.

The gale moderating, and wind hauling in the right quarter, the "Elizabeth" soon made Abaco, the most northern of the Bahama group, and passing Green Turtle Key and Abaco Light, we shortly sighted Harbor Island.

A fine landmark for the entrance on the east side was a row of cocoanut palms all inclined one way. A tongue of land overlapping the entrance to the harbor, it was not easy to distinguish unless close in, but the trees formed a capital guide to the entrance. There is another entrance on the north side through the reef. About all these islands, like those of the Pacific, are surrounded by a coral reef, with passages through in various places. Running down inshore, two of the islanders came off, one of whom piloted us safely into the harbor, where we dropped anchor and lay as though in a mill-pond.

The Bahama Islands, on the verge of the belt of trade winds, have the most delightful climate for a winter resort, neither too hot, nor too cold.

Nassau, on Providence Island, the capital, has fine hotel accommodations for the visitor wishing to escape the rigors of a northern winter, and one of the most enjoyable trips during his stay is a visit to the outlying islands and keys, the inhabitants of which are of the most sociable class, doing everything to make the visitor's time pass pleasantly. They are mostly colored, with a large sprinkling of whites.

As the sailing on these trips is all inside the keys and reefs, the water is smooth and there is no fear of seasickness while passing over reefs, which, seen through the clear water, with their wealth of sponges and sea-fans, coral, bright-waving marine foliage and myriads of fish of every hue, form a most interesting study for the student of life beneath the waves.

Here I was joined by Mr. George Deshon, who had come out by steamer, and had been waiting several days for my arrival, and disposing of some of our stock here, we ran around to a little settlement called the "Current," where we made some sales of furniture and provisions, sailing thence to Governor's Harbor and Rock Sound, ports of Eleuthera.

A MONTH, or more, had been occupied in coasting along the shores of the various islands and keys, stopping at every little settlement to barter, and we had but half disposed of our cargo. Sometimes we anchored off the beach, as at Cat Island, and went ashore to drum up trade, and having landed a lot of whatever we thought would be in demand, we held auctions on the beach. These occasions would be rare fun for the crew, as Green was a capital auctioneer, and the rest of the boys made it lively for the colored folks. Frequently, when there had been a good trade, and the bidding lively, we would announce a dance in the evening at one of their houses, for which they were always ready, and Green with his fiddle and Thomas with the accordion would open the ball.

This got noised around and helped trade amazingly, the populace being always glad to see us. Mr. Deshon always enjoyed these occasions, and entered heartily into the spirit of them.

Governor's Harbor, on the west side of Eleuthera, the shipping point for pineapples to the English market, was a town of considerable importance. At this time there were no steamers engaged in the fruit trade, but a beautiful class of clipper schooners, Clyde built, that congregated at Governor's Harbor, waiting for their cargoes of pines.

Only the sugar-loaf pines were carried, the scarlet or Spanish not being so much in favor with the English people. These pines were carried in the tree or shrub, and handled with great care; shrub, stalk and pineapples being shipped as growing. It took a great deal more room to ship them in this way, but the safe carriage of the fruit was insured, and the high price paid for pines in the English market warranted the extra expense.

Green turtle were also carried by these fruiters and brought a high price. A large corral was kept by the agent, who bought all that was brought in, paying regular market rates for them. It was enclosed with stakes that would hold a great number until time for shipment. Turtle of other kinds abounded in these waters; among them the loggerhead, an immense fellow, sometimes weighing from five hundred to six hundred pounds; also the hawksbill, a smaller turtle, prized for its shell. Frequent excursions were made to the beaches on the ocean side, on bright moonlight nights, to watch for, and capture turtle. Lying still and watching, we would see them emerge from the water and crawl up the beach above high-water mark, to lay their eggs, to be hatched out by the sun and the warmth of the sand. When well up the beach, a rush would be made upon them, and before they could turn to the water they would be thrown upon their backs, making their escape impossible, as they could not turn over on land. Some of the big fellows required the united strength of three or four men to turn them. Great care had to be taken to prevent their getting headed for the water, in which case it was almost impossible to stop them, for if you were in front of them they would bite most savagely, and in their rear one would be blinded by the shower of sand and small pebbles thrown out by their rear flippers. Their eggs are carefully covered when they are in the sand, but when the young turtle hatch out and make for the water, they have numerous enemies who are on the lookout for them, and between the birds of the air and the fish in the sea, the turtle family have a very hard time of it. Although there may be a hundred or more eggs hatched out, not a fifth of the brood survive. The eggs are round, about half the size of a hen's egg, yellow in appearance, and soft-shelled. They are very nice roasted, or made into an omelet. To find them in the sand, one goes around with a sharp pointed stick, and when a nest is found by punching, uncovers and removes the eggs.

Rock Sound is a deep bay on the southern end of Eleuthera, and a town of the same name lies at the head of the bay. A quarter of a mile inland is a natural curiosity called the "Ocean Hole," a perfectly round basin, having a circumference of about 5,000 feet, with walls of stone rising from the water perpendicular and smooth, to a height of 50 feet. There is only one place where one can descend to the water. It is surrounded by trees, and is not visible to one approaching it until he is close to it. In this basin the tide ebbs and flows and the water is as blue as the ocean water outside the reef, showing that it must have an ocean outlet. Salt-water fish are found in it, and in the centre there is apparently no soundings. Articles that have been thrown in have been found on the north end of the island, forty-five miles distant.

One evening we were about leaving Rock Sound, where our trade had been very good as well as at Governor's Harbor, and all hands went ashore. I was settling up business, intending to sail in the morning for a little place called the "Cove." Pulling on board just as a coasting schooner came to an anchor, we passed her boat with the crew pulling ashore, and on hailing them we learnt that she was from Nassau. To our inquiry for news of the war they replied that "that old scoundrel Lincoln had been shot."

Ordering the boat's head around for shore again, we landed with them to get particulars, which we obtained with so much denunciation of the administration of our government,—President Lincoln and all officials,—that the ire of Green and the rest of the crew was roused, and they responded in a manner that brought on a free-for-all fight. The chaps fought well, but were no match for our boys, and in a very short time they received the pounding of their lives, after which all our men went on board happy, having in their opinion aired their patriotism, and vindicated the honor of the old flag.

When we arrived at the Cove, Mr. Deshon left for Nassau to take the steamer for New York. I went down with him in a small boat, and we had with us the specie that we had taken on the trip. We arrived just in time for me to see him on board the steamer before she sailed. Returning to the schooner, I arranged for the sale of the remaining portion of the cargo, and putting on shore a part, returned to Governor's Harbor with the balance, which was landed, and taking on a small load of pines, we sailed for Boston, where we arrived without mishap, having been absent three months. The crew having been paid off, left for home, there being now little danger from the draft.

Mr. Deshon concluding not to make another venture, I was engaged by Mr. Joseph E. Manning to make one more trip as supercargo, and was in Nassau in company with a large number of the most famous blockade runners, all engaged in running cotton. This was a money-making business for those who engaged in it, if they escaped capture by the blockading fleet. The steamers, designed especially for speed, long, low, and very sharp, would come out from England, laden with a cargo destined for the South but shipped to Nassau, where, on arrival, the cargo was taken out and then hurriedly put on board again, when she was ready for her run. If successful, the captain received $5,000 in gold, and one or more bales of cotton, and all on board were pecuniarily interested. It was not, by all accounts, such a difficult matter to get into port, but the getting out, laden with cotton, was the problem to be worked out. Frequently, when having successfully run the gauntlet of the blockading fleet off the port, and thinking they were all clear and safe, they would find themselves at daylight close under the guns of a U. S. gunboat stationed on the offshore blockade. An amusing incident, as related by Captain William Swasey of Marblehead, acting master of one of the gunboats on the outer station, is a case in point.

One morning at daylight a steamer was sighted close aboard, and being covered by the guns of the gunboat, it was too late to escape. Heaving her to, Captain Swasey was ordered on board the blockade runner to bring the captain to the gunboat. Naturally he was chagrined to find himself caught in a trap, after supposing himself past all danger.

Ascending the gangway, Captain Swasey stepped on board. With an extended hand and in a cheerful, breezy manner, he greeted the runner's captain, who stood aft, bidding him good morning, and adding that he was very glad to see him.

"Are you?" said the captain of the captured vessel. "Well! It's a d—d sight more that I am to see you, this morning."

The men were taken out, a prize crew put on board, and the vessel with her cargo was sent to a northern port. The prize money from these captures was something enormous. This same acting master received some ten thousand dollars as his share in six months' time, while a captain who was formerly my second mate, and who was in the volunteer naval service, was so fortunate as to receive as his share from his prize money, upwards of eighty thousand dollars.

After making a cruise through the islands and returning to Nassau, we found there the ram "Stonewall Jackson," built for the Confederates and named for the Confederate General Thomas J. Jackson, nicknamed "Stonewall." It was a most formidable-looking craft, anchored outside the harbor. She was, however, too late to do any damage, as but a short time after came the news of the fall of the Confederacy. The news came like a thunderbolt to Nassau and its merchants. All were confident the war would last for a year and perhaps years longer, and merchants found a ready market at top prices for their goods. The inhabitants of the Bahamas were literally rolling in wealth; the labor of the blacks commanding from three to five dollars an hour on night work, and the work was going on night and day.

Nassau was the hot-bed of secession, and it was extremely unhealthy to show sympathy for the North within its borders. Orders were sent to England, limits taken off, and every warehouse was stuffed with goods, when the news came that the war was over!

Prices on everything dropped far below the zero mark. Every house, except two, went under, while goods of all descriptions were rushed out among the islands, to be sold at any price that could be obtained. Fine boots that were formerly sold at ten or twelve dollars a pair, were let go at fifty cents, and other things in like proportion. It was a great blow to Nassau, and one from which it took a long time to recover.

My invoice having been disposed of before the crash came, I chartered the schooner to a Nassau house, one of the two that withstood the shock, to load oranges at Andros Island for New York, and sending the captain off, I remained to settle up some business before taking the steamer for New York. Returning to Harbor Island, I remained there two weeks, when a schooner arrived with a delegation on board, including the candidates for election to the House of Assembly at Nassau. They were on a tour of the islands, holding meetings at all the principal points, canvassing for votes, and were a jolly lot.

I had business at Green Turtle Key, and on my mentioning it to the captain of the schooner, whom I knew very well, he gave me a most cordial invitation to join the party on board and make the trip with them. This invitation I was not slow to accept, as I had no way of getting over except by chartering a small craft to take me across, and that was expensive.

The general election for the members of the "Assembly,"—the legislative body in the Bahamas, which are governed by Great Britain,—was a great affair, participated in by every voter in the group; as much, or more, interest and party spirit being shown, as in our presidential election at home. Although no salary is attached to the office, it is deemed the highest honor to serve as a member of the "House" and be able to place "M. A." after the incumbent's name, while large sums, as with us, are expended in campaign expenses, and to influence votes. Our party, composed of gentlemen upon making whose acquaintance I found to be a most congenial set, was well supplied with spirited arguments, which, with the eatables, were carefully stowed in the schooner's hold, to be brought forth as occasion demanded, and the candidate making the best showing in this line and with good oratorical powers, was the one who generally won the prize.

Our first stop, after leaving Harbor Island, was at Cherry Harbor, a small settlement just inside the keys on the island of Abaco. Here we found our rival candidate, who was having things all his own way. He had addressed his constituents, sent out his henchmen, counted noses, and was so firm in the belief that he would be elected the following day at Cherry Harbor, that he had ordered a large pig killed to make a big pork pie or stew for the voters.

No sooner was our anchor dropped than a dozen or more colored gentlemen boarded us, knowing we had on board the rival candidate.

They were received with open arms and told us about all the proceedings on shore, of the pig being killed and so forth. They were talked to, the spirited arguments were brought forth, also the eatables, and in an hour they went ashore pledged to our party and to influence all their friends; in short, to invite the whole population to come on board and partake of the good things, after which the Hon. Mr. So and So, the candidate, and other distinguished guests, would address the citizens of Cherry Harbor on the issues at stake, and the welfare and prosperity of the Bahama Islands; also announcing that a dance would be held after the speaking, to which all were invited, and refreshments, with light wines for the ladies, would be provided through the liberality and courtesy of the Hon. Mr. So and So, our distinguished candidate.

The election came off, and it is needless to say our candidate was elected by a rousing majority. Our rival, scenting defeat, sent out word the following morning not to kill the pig, but he was assured it was not only killed but eaten!

Leaving Cherry Harbor for Green Turtle Key and passing Great Harbor until our return, we arrived in the evening, at once going ashore, where our constituents were awaiting us. Our advance agents reported everything in good form and victory certain.

Green Turtle Key, lying northeast of Abaco is a thriving settlement, having a mixed population of whites and colored about equally divided. They live by fishing, orange culture, and the cultivation of the land for raising their own vegetables, wrecking, or any employment that offers. They are a most hospitable class, their doors always open to strangers.

The following day, being election, was observed as a holiday. Turtle was served up, in every style, to the voters, and, in fact, to any one who would partake. Speeches were made, and after the votes were counted, and it was announced that our candidate was the one elected, a general jollification was held, which lasted into the early morning hours.

Continuing on to Great Harbor, I there took leave of my hospitable host, I wishing to go to Nassau, while they were bound for Long Island and Rum Key. A small craft, bound over, suiting my convenience, I reached Nassau safely, in time for the New York steamer, and two days later, bidding adieu to the Bahamas, a pleasant run of four days brought us to the pier in North River.

CHAPTER XXIV
1866-1867

THE BARQUE "KEYSTONE"—WAR SCENES AT RICHMOND AND PETERSBURG.—
RIVER GIRONDE AND BORDEAUX.—HAPPY OCEAN LIFE IN OLD SAILING
SHIP DAYS

THE war had closed, but all business was in a most unsettled state. Wounded and disabled troops were constantly returning to the headquarters of the several States to be mustered out, and although there was joy at the ending of the war and the preservation of the Union, sad scenes were daily witnessed. Many households were in sorrow, throughout the land, mourning for fathers, husbands and sons, who had gone forth to battle, laying down their lives for their country and to preserve the Union and the honor of the flag.

The next eight months I spent on shore, constantly on the watch for a vessel I could buy into that would be suitable. I had contracted a second marriage, and intended to take my wife with me on the voyage, and getting the refusal of a new barque of eight hundred tons, then on her first voyage from Havana to New York, to command if satisfactory, I awaited her arrival at the latter port with some degree of impatience.

Upon her arrival I inspected her, and at once closed the purchase and took charge. The "Keystone" was a fine vessel, having good carrying capacity. She was fairly sharp, had fine sailing qualities and nice accommodations, consisting of a roomy main cabin with a cozy after, or ladies' cabin; just the craft in which to make a lady comfortable, and a captain taking his wife to sea with him would have a very pleasant home.

I obtained a charter to load tobacco at City Point, Va., for Bordeaux, and the barque was fitted out for six months, expecting to return to New York from Europe.

My first officer, Mr. Charles B. Nelson, was a stranger to me, but highly recommended, while my second officer, Mr. Edwin H. Lovett, had formerly served with me in the same position on the ship "J. P. Whitney."

I returned to Boston for my wife and to settle a few business matters, and took the train back to New York, arriving at 10 P. M. and putting up at a hotel until ready for sea. My wife's brother accompanied us, to spend a few days with his sister and see her off. This made it very pleasant, for he could escort her around shopping or sightseeing, while I was busy, attending to the business of the barque.

When everything was in readiness for sailing, we embarked, Brother George going down the bay with us to return on the towboat from Sandy Hook.

Hauling into the stream, the tug came alongside, and making fast, we proceeded down the harbor, bidding good-by to New York on as bright and beautiful a July morning as one could ever witness, little thinking that three years would roll around, and great changes occur, ere we again saw it.

Arriving at Sandy Hook, sail was made, after which George took a final leave of his sister and went on board the tug; fasts were cast off, and with a "good-by and pleasant voyage" from the towboat captain, we parted company, the tug returning to New York, while the "Keystone" continued her voyage south.

Looking over our crew to see who we had on board, the result was entirely satisfactory. The crew were mostly Swedes and Norwegians, with a Finn and two Germans, all able-bodied men, and good sailors, as afterwards proved; a carpenter, my old Chinese steward that I was fortunate enough to run across in New York, a Malay cook, Mrs. Whidden and myself, made up the barque's complement of sixteen, all told.

A quick run brought us to Fortress Monroe, where, taking a pilot, we sailed up the James River to City Point, and made fast to the wharf to await our cargo of tobacco, which was to be sent down from Richmond in lighters.

The trip up the river was of more than usual interest. It was so soon after the close of the war, that almost every foot of ground and point of land had a history, and the pilot pointed out to us where some of the most thrilling scenes were enacted.

As it would be a week before our cargo would begin to arrive, we improved the time by visiting Richmond, and for a few days made our headquarters at the Spotswood Hotel. Although the war was ended, the old spirit of secession was still strong in the hearts of the South. In Richmond, the capital of the Confederacy, the feeling of rancor and bitterness towards the North was still apparent, and cropped out when conversing with the citizens, the old residents particularly, and it was

280

not to be wondered at; the wound was so recent, that any reference to the struggle between the North and South was sure to bring out an expression of opinion favorable to the latter. For this reason, we carefully avoided the subject of the war, unless sure of our ground; being desirous of information, we did not wish to antagonize any one. Returning to City Point, we took the train for Petersburg, and visited the battlefields, in front of the town, where occurred some of the hardest fighting of the war; the crater, of the mine designed by the Union forces to undermine a Confederate fort, and the blowing up of the same, July 30, 1864; the rifle pits and trenches where the sharpshooters of both armies lay entrenched almost within a stone's throw of one another, each seeking to pick off his opponent if he exposed himself to fire; each and every spot being pointed out by our guide, who was an ex-Confederate soldier, and an active participant in the struggle before Petersburg.

Relics of the fight were to be picked up on every side,—bullets, broken gun-stocks and ramrods, army buttons,—and we could imagine the tide of battle that surged around this spot, which now the sun shone down upon so peacefully and bright, but the most vivid imagining would fall far short of the reality.

In the evening, at the hotel we listened to thrilling stories of the fighting before Petersburg "in the days that tried men's souls," and taking our train the following morning for City Point, we bade adieu to these historic scenes, feeling well repaid for our visit.

We made some very pleasant acquaintances at City Point, and our time passed quickly in a round of visiting and sightseeing, until, our lading completed, we bade good-by to our shore friends, and taking a pilot on board, proceeded down river in tow of a tugboat. Arriving at Fortress Monroe, we came to anchor for the night, and early next morning, got under way, and proceeded to sea.

A heavy swell from the south'ard and a fall in the barometer indicated a blow from that quarter, but the wind being fair, strong west, the "Keystone" was kept due east to cross the Gulf Stream, and if the storm proved to be a hurricane, as I suspected by the great swell, I expected to escape it, or the worst part of it, by pushing her across its path before it reached our latitude. This was most fortunate, for, as we learned later, a furious hurricane, that followed the course of the Gulf Stream, swept across our wake twelve to fifteen hours after we had passed, doing immense damage to shipping caught in its path, and along the coast; while we carried our fair wind and smooth sea the entire passage to the mouth of the River Gironde, not even having occasion to hand a royal, and making the run in twenty-one days from Hampton Roads.

This was my wife's first ocean experience, barring the short run from New York to City Point, and there was not a day's sickness to mar her pleasure, and no rough weather.

We entered the river, and having passed the high lighthouse of Cordouan, a pilot came aboard, and we proceeded up-stream and taking a tug a little below the city of Bordeaux, and towing past the tiers of

282

shipping, the "Keystone" was moored but a short distance from the banks that rise at quite a steep incline from the water.

I found, on calling upon my consignees, that tobacco cargoes were discharged singly, and we would have to await our turn, although we were ready for discharging. There were two ships ahead of us. We had thirty-five lay days and were obliged to wait. This was bad, but there was no help for it.

The city of Bordeaux, on the banks of the Gironde River, is the centre of the wine export trade. Many American vessels were in port, and quite a number of captains had their wives or families with them, among whom there was frequent visiting, dinner parties, rides, shopping and shore excursions, all of which served to pass the time in a most enjoyable manner, making it very pleasant for the ladies.

The city is well laid out, the streets are broad and clean, there are handsome public squares with fountains, and many beautiful public buildings.

Among the many places of interest which we visited was the Basilique St. Andre (Cathedral of St. Andrew), a very ancient building erected more than twelve hundred years ago. It is very quaint and massive, and of great interest to the student of architecture. Some years back, in excavating for repairs, the workmen had discovered and unearthed between two hundred and three hundred bodies that had been interred within its walls. There was no record of them, or how long they had been buried, but it must have been centuries; yet there was little evidence of decay, save that the skin was dark and resembled leather. They had long dark hair, and the features of some were almost perfect. We were told that their preservation was owing to the peculiar nature of the earth in which they were buried. They were ranged, standing with no glass between them and the observer, around a large room, or crypt, under one corner of the edifice, and were objects of great curiosity to all visitors.

The cathedral was open at all hours, and service almost constantly going on.

Notre Dame was another fine old church,—or new beside St. Andre, being but three hundred years old. This was the English church, where services were held daily.

At the upper end of the city are beautiful gardens, facing the river and the Quai Louis XVIII. On each side of the entrance stand two high light-towers, which act as a river guide at night. These gardens are great pleasure resorts. Public and private fairs and fetes are held there, and games of all kinds. In company with others we visited them many times, always finding something interesting and amusing.

Our visits to the great canning establishments, where fish, flesh and fowl, fruits, and every kind of vegetable, were put up in cans for export to every part of the world, were most interesting and instructive. The great kitchens where everything was prepared, the immense caldrons and cooking apparatus, the canning and sealing department, and great storehouses, all came under our inspection, and throughout the whole great establishment everything was cleanliness itself,—not a speck of dirt or dust to be seen,—and in after days we relished our stock of canned goods much more from having witnessed the perfect *modus operandi*.

We chartered the "Keystone" for Buenos Ayres, to load wines and liquors, and having got rid of our tobacco, we commenced our lading, and in sixty-five days from entering the port of Bordeaux were again ready for sea.

All stores on board, taking a river pilot, we proceeded down river in tow of a tug, in company with the barque "White Cloud," Captain Ames, who was bound for New Orleans. Discharging our pilot at Pauillac, all sail was made, and with a fine rattling breeze, we were soon clear of the Bay of Biscay, and heading south for the trade winds; obtaining a fine view of Madeira in passing, also the Peak of Teneriffe (Canary Islands), towering among the clouds. The wind gradually hauling to the eastward, the trade clouds began to appear hanging around the horizon, with shoals of flying-fish, and fields of gulfweed, in that soft, balmy atmosphere inseparable from the region of the trade winds. Night after night we remained on deck until nearly the close of the first watch, admiring the glory of the heavens spangled with stars, and resplendent with the constellations of our northern hemisphere, watching them each night sink lower and lower in the northern quarter, while in the south new ones took their places.

Our crew were quite musical, and in addition to fine voices, a number of them were possessed of several instruments, including a violin, flute, an accordion and a cornet, their owners being good performers on each. The second dog-watch, in good weather, was generally devoted to a concert forward, both vocal and instrumental, and frequently it would be two bells (9 P. M.) before they would go below. Their selections were good, and we thoroughly enjoyed their music.

My wife, to whom all this was new, was in love with the sea, and up to the present time she had not seen a gale or experienced any rough weather. While at Bordeaux I had the opportunity of buying a fine upright piano at a very low figure. Mrs. Whidden being a good performer, I thought it would serve to while away many hours that otherwise might be weary for her, and I never regretted the purchase. In the roomy after, or ladies', cabin there was ample space for it, and it made our quarters decidedly homelike. A good stock of sheet music, in addition to all the popular airs of the day, with her hymns and church music, completed the outfit. The purchase of this piano was a good investment aside from the pleasure derived from it, as will be seen later.

The work of the barque went smoothly on, the crew being most efficient, quick to obey orders, quiet and respectful, while the officers were all that could be desired. There was no noise, or profanity, but a firm, steady course of discipline, that invariably commanded respect. Meanwhile, we were rapidly approaching the equator.

FOUR MONTHS AT FEVER STRICKEN BUENOS AYRES.—THREE HUNDRED SAIL IN PORT. THE BOTANICAL GARDENS OF RIO JANEIRO.—A WEIRD NIGHT AT BOTOFOGO

CROSSING the parallel of 6° north, the wind growing lighter, we finally took leave of the northeast trade winds ere we had made a further degree of southing; ending them with a squall of wind and rain accompanied by heavy thunder and vivid lightning, succeeded by calms and sunshine varied by squalls of wind and torrential rains which continued for nearly a week. In latitude 1° north, we caught the welcome southeast trades, and, with a taut bowline crossed the line, and sighting Fernando Norohna, the "Keystone" ran past Pernambuco, Bahia and the Abrolhos Islands, and Cape Frio, and as we drew south, the wind gradually hauled to the west'ard by the northern quarter. Beautiful weather still continued, the nights glorious with the constellations of the southern heavens; among many others nightly visible in their beauty the "Magellan clouds" and "Southern Cross."

Moonlight on the water. Can anything be more beautiful than a ship on the water at night, under the soft light of a full moon, in the region of the trade winds? There is a fine, steady breeze filling every sail, with the canvas asleep and showing snow-white in its beams, each sail and spar and rope standing out in bold relief, and while a portion of the ship hidden from its rays makes of the whole a perfect picture of lights and shadows, the ship glides noiselessly on; no sound, save the striking of the bell that tells the passing hours of the night, and an occasional order from the officer of the deck.

Many such nights we remained on deck till past the midnight hour when the scene was too beautiful for us to leave and go below.

"Land ho!" rang out on the morning of the forty-eighth day from Bordeaux, and Cape St. Mary, the northern cape to the entrance of the Rio de la Plata, could in a short time be plainly seen from the deck. Getting chain cables up and anchors on the bow, we stood in for Lobos Island, passed it and dropping anchor off the point of Montevideo, set a signal for a river pilot to take us up the river to Buenos Ayres, and early next morning one came one board, bringing a quarter of fresh beef and some vegetables, which were very acceptable after our voyage, but at the same time he was the bearer of news not of a cheerful nature.

Cholera and yellow fever were raging at Buenos Ayres, hundreds dying daily, with from three hundred to four hundred vessels in port. It was almost impossible to get labor or lighters, and some of them had been there between two and three months before breaking bulk. As our cargo was one that could only go in the Custom House deposits, the outlook for getting away in quick time was not brilliant.

For myself I had no fear; never having been attacked by epidemics, I considered myself immune, but I trembled for my wife, and Helen's death from cholera in Shanghai came vividly before me, but there was nothing to do but face the music. I did not let her know my fears, but made light of it as much as possible.

We anchored in the outer roadstead, some ten miles from the city, among a large fleet of shipping, but so far from land that only the spires of the city churches could be seen through the glass from the barque's deck, and it seemed, except for the turbid water and the adjacent shipping, like being at sea.

When I went ashore to see my consignees, I found the chances of discharging at an early day were slight indeed. I also learned that the victims of cholera were largely among the natives and Italian population, no American captains or their families having been taken down. Care in diet and mode of living seemed to have a great deal to do with the preservation of health. The shipping had been very free from cholera or fever, so far.

I engaged rooms and board at my old quarters, Mrs. Bradley's, and went back on board the barque, but the next morning we took up our quarters on terra firma. A number of captains' wives were guests of Mrs. Bradley, who, with her three daughters, made the house very pleasant and homelike; a good piano with the girls' fine voices added much to the pleasure of our stay, and a jolly company of captains kept all thought of cholera and yellow fever from our minds. If any one gave it a thought, he never expressed it. There was, it is true, not so much shopping and visiting, or riding into the country, as there otherwise would have been, but the ladies were not confined indoors, our house having two large *patios*, or enclosures, into which the doors of each room opened; so the guests only had to step from their rooms into the open air of the patio. Occasional visits on shipboard, for a few days or a week, helped to break the monotony.

Sixty days passed before we could commence the discharging of our cargo, and it was four months from our arrival ere the last cask was taken on shore, it having been impossible to obtain lighters. All our lay days were used up, and we were a long time on demurrage, but it was not enough to pay for the delay.

But all things have an end, and with thankful hearts that no one had been stricken down with cholera or fever, we hove up our anchors one morning, and said good-by to Buenos Ayres with no regrets, and with a fair wind took our departure for Rio Janeiro in search of a freight.

Landing our pilot at Montevideo, familiarly called the "Mount," the "Keystone" proceeded to sea, and never did blue water and ocean breezes seem so grateful as after our four months' stay in fever-stricken Buenos Ayres.

Brisk southerly winds soon brought us in sight of the high land at the entrance to Rio, with nothing of note having occurred after leaving the Mount.

Rio Janeiro was familiar to me, but to my wife scenery of this kind was a new experience. The peaks of the mountains of Gabia and Corcovada and Sugar Loaf Hill, forming the contour of an immense man lying on his back, was a wonder to her, and as we drew in with the land, passing the islands of Pai and Mai, the great bay opening before us, entering the narrow passage between the high bluff on the right where the guns of Fort Santa Cruz frowned down upon us, and the Sugar Loaf

Hill with its high conical peak on the left, the bright sparkling waters of the great bay extending inland sixteen miles, dotted with beautiful islands and covering upwards of fifty square miles of anchorage, her delight was unbounded.

As we sailed on, the entrance to Botofogo Bay, extending inland back of the Sugar Loaf, and Gloria Hill, with its lovely dwellings and white church where the Emperor Dom Pedro attended divine service with his family, the ranges of hills and mountains in the background, all clothed in luxuriant tropical foliage, brought forth exclamations of rapture, appearing to her, as one writer declares, "like entering the gate of a tropical paradise."

We came to anchor off the city below Cobras Island, and after the doctor's visit, obtained permission to go ashore, and on landing I met my old broker, Mr. Machado, who offered me a charter to go to Bahia to load sugar for Liverpool, England. The rate was fair, the only objection being in the number of lay days wanted by the charterers, but after dickering awhile I got them reduced to two-thirds the number, when I accepted and signed the charter-party.

Our stay now being limited, we wished to take in all we could in the short time allotted to us.

We were not long in noting that different streets were devoted to each line of goods; for instance, in the Rue de Ouvidor (Gold Street) one finds no class of goods but jewelry, so it was not hard to find when we desired to visit the jewelers' establishments, and the same with those of the dealers in millinery and dry goods.

After a short season of shopping and admiring the many beautiful things to be seen, we drove to the Botanical Gardens, justly famed throughout the world, a lovely feature of these gardens being a magnificent straight avenue of majestic palms. The road to this botanical park is a continuous garden in itself, abounding in every variety of tropical fruit, and flowers of rare beauty which greet the eye on every side and fill the air with a delicious fragrance. Trees of every description are here seen in all their beauty, while the culture of the tea plant is an attraction. One could remain here months, and then not tire of the beauty of these gardens.

Mount Corcovada, three thousand feet in height, towers above this lovely park; its copious springs of clear water, that form the principal supply of the city, being conveyed to the numerous reservoirs and fountains by means of an aqueduct twelve miles long, built more than a century ago, which crosses a valley ninety feet deep on two great tiers of arches.

In the afternoon we drove to Botofogo, a summer resort of the wealthy class during the heated term, who drive out from the city each afternoon and return in the morning to attend to business. An ideal spot is Botofogo. Its shores form a beautiful crescent-shaped bay of the waters that flow in from the sea back of the Sugar Loaf Mountain, pure, bright, and sparkling as crystal.

Hard, smooth beaches, with light yellow sand, afford incomparable bathing facilities, and around this bay a smooth, broad road stretches away for miles, making a fine driveway, where may be seen every afternoon, as the sun sinks behind the peaks of Gabia and Corcovada, the elegant equipages of the elite of the capital, filled with gay, laughing groups of ladies and gentlemen, out for their evening drive. The rich dresses and bright colors of the ladies, blending with the plain conventional black of their male companions, make a pretty picture.

Surrounding the bay on the hillsides stand beautiful cottages, the summer homes of Rio's prosperous citizens, while interspersed, rising from their own spacious grounds amid towering palms, stately mangoes, and a wealth of flowers, are the magnificent hotels, one of which was the scene of a ludicrous incident, heartily laughed at afterwards, but at the time fraught with terror to Mrs. Whidden.

These hotels were always well filled with guests both transient and permanent.

We engaged a room for a night without going to it, and strolled out sightseeing.

As the sun sank, the short twilight deepened into night, the stars appeared, lights twinkled from the cottages, the evening breeze swept, cool, across the bay, while soft, delicious music, low and sweet, from the band at one of the hotels, was wafted to our ears, inducing a dreamy, restful feeling. From a cottage on the hill we listened to sweet voices mingling in a love song, accompanied by the music of harp or guitar. Numerous pleasure yachts were filled with a gay throng enjoying an evening on the water; their songs and laughter mingled with strains of music could be distinctly heard, borne on the evening breeze. From behind the crest of Sugar Loaf the moon appeared, flooding the entire bay with a sheen of silver, completing a picture of exquisite beauty.

As the evening waned we sought our hotel, tired, but having passed a most enjoyable day, and after partaking of a light supper, we were shown to our apartment. The sleeping-rooms, containing four-poster beds with enormous canopies overhead, were on each side of the entrance to a large, roomy sitting-room at the end of a long, gloomy hall or passage at the rear end of the house, and evidently little used. Three windows in the sitting-room, extending nearly to the floor on one side, looked out upon the grounds. Palms, and other trees came close to the windows, their branches brushing the screens as they waved in the night air. A massive, round mahogany table occupied the centre of the room, above which hung the gas chandelier. Dark mahogany and ebony furniture, with an uncarpeted floor nearly black; and highly polished, gave to the surroundings a gloomy, sombre appearance,—which was not improved by lighting up, the gas being so poor as only to render the darkness more visible,—and an uncanny look to the room, producing a most depressing effect, equal to a nightmare, on the feelings of a nervous person. Although not inclined to nervousness myself, my wife was, to the extreme. A slight alarm would cause her to jump and scream, while voices at night, unaccounted for, would keep her awake imagining things until she had worked herself into a state of absolute terror.

With nothing to read, and not caring to attempt writing in the poor light, we sat talking of what we had seen during the day, but I could see my wife took little interest in the conversation, her eye wandering to the dark recesses of the room and starting at the grazing of the screens by the branches of the trees, until finding it was becoming irksome, we gave it up and retired.

Being very tired, I quickly dropped into a doze, but not for long. I felt a slight shake and a low whisper in my ear:

"There's some one in the room, John. Don't you hear them?"

Raising my head, I listened. Yes. In a moment I heard a noise as of some one moving lightly across the floor. The fact of having a considerable sum of money with me, which I had been too late to deposit, perhaps made me more nervous. Whispering to my wife to keep quiet, and reaching for a revolver under my pillow, I struck a light, and walked softly into the large room.

All was quiet. No appearance of any intruder; the noise having ceased with the scratching of the match. Satisfying myself that there was no cause for alarm, I assured my wife that her fears were groundless, and sank into an uneasy slumber, only to be awakened by a pinch and a tremulous whisper:

"There's certainly some one in that room, John. I can hear them plainly."

Again I listened. Yes, I could plainly hear some one creeping across the room, and a rustling noise as though the windows were being tampered with,—which, by the way, were all open.

Again, pistol in one hand, and a match in the other, I crept to the chandelier and turned on the light, at the same time glancing keenly

295

around the room. Still there was nothing disturbed; the noise had ceased, and for this I could not account. Examining the windows, also the other sleeping-room carefully, and finding all right, I began to wonder, although not a believer in ghosts or the supernatural, if the chamber was haunted. Leaving the gas burning at my wife's suggestion, I lay awake awhile, and hearing nothing further, was just losing myself, when a horrified whisper in my ear brought my eyes again wide open.

"Look overhead at the canopy. Isn't it much lower?"

I knew this was the echo of one of the tales of childhood's days about some one being smothered in a tavern by having the canopy lowered upon him while he slept, but seeing my poor wife was almost wild with nervous fright, I reasoned with her that there was no occasion for her nervousness, and having as I thought calmed her, dropped again into slumber, when a hand was placed over my mouth and a hoarse whisper sounded in my ear:

"Look at the light. It is being lowered; hear the creeping!"

Yes, it was so, and nearly out. I dashed into the outer room, nearly treading on a huge rat that scurried across the floor. All was quiet, and lighting a candle and looking at my watch, I found it was just one o'clock.

Suddenly the whole situation dawned upon me. There had been a ministerial dinner at the hotel that night, and everybody was up very late. This I had known, but had forgotten, and being in a remote part of the house, had heard nothing of it. The gas was just being turned off at the meter for the night. The remains of our luncheon on the table was an attraction for the rats and mice, while the noises were occasioned by their scampering over the polished floor. I explained all, and laughed it off, or tried to, but the tension had been too great; no more sleep visited her eyes and she arose with the first peep of day.

Coming from my room an hour later, I found her at the window drinking in the pure morning air.

The room presented a different appearance in the morning light from that formed in the darkness by her heated imagination, being a large, cool apartment with a most beautiful outlook.

A morning stroll, in the pure, bracing atmosphere by the bay, after our coffee, and a good breakfast at the hotel, served to dissipate the remembrance of the previous night, and we both thoroughly enjoyed our drive back to Rio.

CHAPTER XXVI
1868

BAHIA.—OUR LADY OF BOM FIM.—DINNER PARTIES ON SHIPBOARD.—CAPE CLEAR LIGHT.—LIVERPOOL

AFTER clearing at the Custom House, and a last shopping tour, we said good-by to our broker Machado, who kindly presented my wife, as a souvenir of her visit to Rio, a fine large book of photographic views in and about the city; a present she appreciated very highly, and from which a number of pictures are taken to illustrate this volume.

Early the following morning we went on board and took our departure in tow of a tug. Outside the islands sail was made, fasts cast off, and we were on our way to Bahia. Sighting the light at the entrance of the bay, on the morning of the sixth day out, we soon let go the anchor in front of the city. The harbor looked almost deserted, there were so few sail in port, viz., two English ships, three barques, an American brigantine, six or eight coasting schooners and two steamers.

Bahia, the second city in size in Brazil, has a population of about one hundred and seventy thousand. The harbor is spacious, the bay extending inland six or seven miles. Its industries are represented by several manufactories and a shipyard. Its chief exports are cotton, tobacco, and sugar. It is divided into two districts, called the upper and the lower town. The upper is the residential district, from which there is a fine view of the shipping and bay. Here is located the beautiful English church and cemetery, the latter laid out with great taste in spacious avenues, grand trees, almost every kind of flowering shrub, and a wealth of flowers, which greet the eye at every turn. The residences of Bahia's well-to-do citizens are marvels of comfort and elegance, well adapted to the climate, which is, at times, very hot. The streets leading to the upper town are very steep and winding, and, being smooth concrete, are very difficult to climb for those not accustomed to them, but the natives do not seem to mind. It is customary to ride up or down, or rather to be carried in caderas or sedan-chairs, borne on the shoulders of two or four porters, as the weight may be. It is certainly a much more comfortable mode of transit, especially for ladies, than attempting to risk a tumble by walking.

The lower town at the foot of the high hills is devoted to the business interests.

With the exception of a visit to the cozy home of Mr. Rogers, our ship-chandler, who with his charming daughter entertained us, we stayed on board ship while in port, where it was more comfortable.

On shore the heat was excessive. During our stay with Mr. Rogers, our host and I daily went down town to attend to business, while my wife was shown all the places of interest in the upper town, including drives to the English cemetery and out in the country,—the churches, beautiful residences, parks, etc.

At the expiration of a week, we bade adieu to our kind host and hostess, extending to them a cordial invitation to dine with us on board the "Keystone,"—an invitation which was as heartily accepted, and one of the most pleasant occasions while in port was that of the visit to our cozy quarters on the barque of Mr. Rogers and his daughter.

At the head of the bay stands the noted church of Our Lady of Bom Fim, very old, and held in great veneration. It was said to be a perfect museum in the number and diversity of the offerings that had been made to Our Lady on account of miraculous cures from all sorts of diseases, wonderful escapes from storms and shipwreck at sea and dangers of every kind, all attributed to the intercession of Our Good Lady at just the right moment.

Hearing so much regarding the phenomenon naturally increased our desire to become further acquainted with it, and my wife and another lady, the wife of the captain of an English barque, becoming interested, an excursion was planned to make it a visit by water, using the ship's boats, which were provided with awnings as a protection from the sun's rays. Anticipating an all day's stay, we had liberal luncheons put up for a party of seven in addition to our boats' crews, and set out quite early to avoid the heat as much as possible, with two boats, having on board: Captain Stone of the English barque, his wife and two children, Captain Hopkins of the brig "Trial," Mrs. Whidden and myself.

A pull of six miles brought us to a shingly beach but a short distance from the church, which stood on a point of land which afforded a fine view down the bay. We walked up from the landing.

At the entrance an old monk accosted us, and on learning our errand, called another to escort us and show us over the church and all contained therein. It was not a pretentious edifice, being very plain both outside and in, although substantially built of stone. A monastery adjoined, and services were continually going on. The most interesting thing was the quaint character and number of the offerings presented to Our Lady.

Accompanying each gift was an accurate, written account of the circumstances and conditions attending it. This was in fulfillment of a vow made at the time of sickness or danger.

In addition to jewelry of all kinds, testifying to the gratitude of the givers, there were crutches without number, and the mainsail of a brig. The account stated that it belonged to a vessel that in a great storm at sea was in imminent danger, and the crew made a solemn vow to dedicate the mainsail of the brig to Our Lady of Bom Fim, if she would intercede and save them. They were saved, and on their arrival in port, in fulfillment of their vow they marched in solemn procession to the church, carrying the mainsail with them. There it hung, conspicuous among the many other offerings of every kind and description: children's toys, clothing, and playthings from mothers, while in the rightly named "Chamber of Horrors "were models of limbs in every stage of different diseases that "flesh is heir to," from those who had been cured, with a full account of the circumstances.

The monks were very kind and courteous in showing and explaining to us everything that was interesting, and having seen all we cared to in a stay of between two and three hours, we bade them adieu, and sitting under the shade of a large spreading tree at some little distance from the church, we enjoyed our luncheon; after which we took up our march to the boats, and, finding the men awaiting our coming, embarked on our return trip.

The boats' crews leisurely pulled down the bay; the cool breeze swept across the water, and we watched the sun sink in its western quarter, and saw the shadows deepen and the stars appear, ere we reached home, well pleased with our outing to the church of Our Lady of Bom Fim.

At Bahia, also, there was great delay in loading. Uncertain whether it should be cotton or sugar, my consignees took advantage of my lay days to obtain advices, and every one was used up ere our lading was completed, and I congratulated myself that I had insisted on a third being abated from the charter-party. As it was, there was no use fretting, other vessels being delayed in like manner, and we tried to take it philosophically.

In the circle of acquaintances we had formed, social gatherings were frequent, and dinner parties were given by one and another captain to the others and their families. In connection with one of these a very funny incident occurred one day on board the American brig.

Captain Hopkins—whose cabin was small, though his heart was as large as any one's—resolved, notwithstanding his limited quarters, to give a dinner party on board the "Trial," in acknowledgment of his numerous invitations.

The brig, though having small accommodations below, had ample room on top of the cabin, the deck extending from side to side, with railings and cockpit aft, into which the after-cabin gangway opened; the slide of said companionway being level with the housetop on deck. On the top of the cabin, under the awnings, he would set his tables, with ample space to accommodate all his guests.

This settled, the Captain sent out his invitations and made preparations for a spread. He was a general favorite, well along in years, being upwards of sixty,—a small man, having a quaint, seamed, whiskerless face, hair—well, here was the captain's trouble; nothing so annoyed him as the thought of baldness. What hair he had was thin and of a grayish color, that which the Englishman designated as "mouldy." He had used all sorts of hair tonics, all to no purpose, but was now on a new tack. Some one had told him kerosene oil, well rubbed in, was the best thing for the hair, and would cause a healthy growth when everything else failed. He had firm faith in this, and applied it liberally several times a day, going around with his head glistening, and an odor distilling from him like a Pennsylvania oil derrick.

On the day of the party, his guests had arrived on board, one or two from shore in addition to the captains and their wives, and all were dispersed under the awnings, enjoying themselves, and awaiting the serving of dinner.

Captain Hopkins had gone below, presumably to put a few finishing touches to his appearance, and brush up his locks with a small application of his favorite kerosene. As he was alone in the cabin, no one knew just how it happened, but suddenly, every one was startled by a yell, and the next instant the head of old Hopkins appeared above the companionway, blazing like a giant candle! The ladies screamed, while one or two captains caught up buckets, and dipping up salt water over the brig's side, deluged the captain's head, extinguishing him in a moment, but leaving him as bald as an egg, although beyond a few blisters, he was not seriously hurt.

Few of those on board will ever forget his appearance as he emerged from the cabin resembling an animated torch.

The excitement over, Captain Hopkins made light of it, although it came near making light of him. He insisted on dinner being served as arranged, and going below, changed his apparel, but it is safe to say he did not monkey with any more kerosene experiments.

The occasion was a pronounced success, and a more jolly party never sat down together, and when the dinner was over, cigars were lighted, while the ladies enjoyed a social chat. This was our last dinner party, and one of the most pleasant. Captain Hopkins explained, in answer to inquiries, that he had lit a lamp, and in doing so had brought the lighted match in contact, some way, with his head, and the result that we had witnessed followed.

A few days after, we bade adieu to our many friends, and with anchors at the bow, and all canvas spread to a favoring breeze, we sailed from the harbor of Bahia, bound for Liverpool, England.

We crossed the equator and sailed through the trades, followed by a spell of light pleasant weather with variable winds, when taking a fine westerly, which carried us to Cape Clear, we made the light, a welcome sight, about two o'clock in the morning, the entire passage having been without incident of note.

Passing Queenstown, we picked up a pilot off Holyhead the following morning early.

Sailing craft and steamers were now all around us, presenting a most animated appearance, while old Holyhead stood out boldly in the morning light. Round the Skerries into the Irish Sea and past Point Lynas, we were hailed by the captain of a towboat, and engaging him after some dickering as to his charges, to tow the "Keystone" to Liverpool and dock her, we passed the hawser, and were soon spinning along at a lively clip, while sails were clewed up and furled for the last time this voyage, Jack working like a beaver, for Liverpool, his earthly paradise, was almost within touch.

A few hours more, and he would step on shore, a free man, with a good fat roll of Bank of England notes, or golden sovereigns to spend in having a good time, for nearly fifteen months' pay was due him, and with that amount in his pocket in Liverpool, he would not lack for friends, at least until he was again outward bound.

Coming to anchor in the stream to wait for the tide, all was made ready for docking. At high water, our tugboat took us in tow, and entering the basin, we were warped through the gates into the Georges Dock, where the "Keystone "was placed in berth for discharging her cargo. Engaging the stevedore, Mr. Robert Lovegrove, and consigning the barque to Messrs. Wm. Killey & Co., we took up our quarters at a boarding-house in St. Paul's Square, where two or three American captains, with their wives and families, were stopping. This we considered more pleasant than a hotel. Our hostess, Mrs. Lovegrove, the wife of our stevedore, was a most charming woman, bright and sunny in disposition, doing everything for the comfort of her guests, and with pleasant rooms, a cozy parlor and dining-room, a good table, and genial company, there was nothing left to be desired, and we settled down for a pleasant stay of a month or six weeks, for there were no freights in the market for a home port.

After telling Messrs. Killey & Co. to look out for a charter for the barque, there was nothing to do except to wait.

The time having expired that my crew shipped for, the American consul obliged me to pay them off, which involved three months' extra pay per man. It being in a foreign port, added about a thousand dollars to my payroll. The men were not desirous of being paid off until we arrived home, but the consul insisted, and I could only comply. Nearly all reshipped. The first officer leaving to get married, the second officer, Mr. Lovett, remained by the barque, taking his place. The cook and steward also reshipped for the next voyage, when we were again ready for sea.

CHAPTER XXVII
1868-1869

LIVERPOOL.—SPURGEON AND MYRTLE STREET CHAPEL.—AN IRISH JAUNTING CAR.—CAPTAINS' WIVES AT SEA

OUR stay in Liverpool was very pleasant, taking in all the places of interest. Across the River Mersey is Birkenhead, in Wales, with its beautiful park, which well repaid us for a visit.

A most delightful drive on a pleasant day was to Chidwell Abbey, some twenty miles distant from Liverpool, taking in the old town of Hale, where a visit to the old churchyard was found very interesting. Among the graves, covered by a slab of stone, we read a very curious inscription. It began with, "Here lies John the Child of Hale, who was nine feet eight inches tall." Then followed his dimensions, of limbs, also stating that he was a publican, that is, he kept a public house or tavern in the town, and died at the age of forty-six years. My wife took off the inscription verbatim, but it has been, unfortunately, lost.

All the drives around Liverpool into the country we found most charming, and the ladies were always planning some excursion, accompanied by our hostess, who entered into all their plans. Her servants were competent and reliable, so that she could do this without neglecting her household duties, and having a knowledge of the most interesting places, she was invaluable to her guests. Two or three evenings at concerts and the opera about covered the extent of our evening dissipation. The ladies, being fine musicians and possessed of good voices, could furnish such delightful music for impromptu concerts, the games and entertaining callers, of whom we had many, assisted so materially in making the cozy parlors attractive, that no one seemed desirous of going outside the house for amusement.

One evening, having had tickets of admission sent us, we went to the Myrtle Street Chapel, Rev. Hugh Stowell Brown, pastor, to hear the Rev. Charles H. Spurgeon, who preached a sermon in aid of the school then being built for his boys. As well as my wife, I had a great desire to hear the world-renowned preacher. We went early and obtained fine seats but a short distance from the pulpit. The church was crowded to excess, and uncomfortable from lack of ventilation, but I would not have missed the opportunity.

When Mr. Spurgeon entered the pulpit I felt rather disappointed. To me he did not have a clerical appearance. He was short and thick set, had a large, full face, and looked the typical, jolly Englishman. He glanced around the audience a moment, then commenced speaking, taking the unbelieving Thomas as his text, and after a few words, all thought of the clergyman's appearance had vanished. You recognized the fact that you were listening to the utterances of a master mind pleading the Master's cause. What impassioned language, driving home truths straight to the hearts of his hearers! How the audience hung upon his words, as he drew a picture of the youth growing up without care or a home, constantly subjected to evil communications and sin, and asked all to come forward and aid in rescuing him from moral degradation, and by placing him under good influences and teaching, to help prepare him for an upright Christian life, and to become a useful member of society!

He spoke for over an hour, but there was rapt attention, not the least sign of weariness.

Throughout the sermon I personally comprehended the magnetism of the man. I have heard him many times since, but he has never impressed me more than when I listened to him at the Myrtle Street Chapel.

The "Keystone" having finished discharging, Messrs. Wm. Killey & Co. offered me a round charter to take a cargo of salt out to Chittagong, British Burmah, situated at the head of the Bay of Bengal, with a return cargo of rice from Akyab to Falmouth for orders, telling me they considered it the best charter offered, and one that they had taken for one of their own ships lying at Bombay, and she would have to wait three months for it. As the rates were very good, I thought best to accept it, and taking in our outward salt cargo, we were very quickly again ready for sea.

As I was going aboard one day at the docks, a fellow having two dogs to sell accosted me alongside the barque, and importuned me to buy. One was a full-blooded Newfoundland, but a mere puppy, playful as a kitten, the other was a retriever, also very small, both thoroughbreds.

Striking a bargain, I had them placed on board, telling the second mate to have the carpenter knock up a house for them and to feed them daily, and soon Jube and Pincher, as they were named, became great favorites on board, both fore and aft.

309

Stores having been taken on, and new crew shipped, including nearly all my old hands, good-bys were said to all our friends, and we again embarked.

Hauling into the basin, with towboat ahead, we shot through the pier heads into the Mersey, the crowd on the pier to see us off giving a ringing cheer, which was heartily responded to by our men, and soon old Liverpool was again over our taffrail.

We passed the Rock Light, N. W. Lightship, Point Lynas, and had reached Holyhead ere the hawser was cast off, and our shore connection, with the leaving of our pilot, was severed.

The illustration shows the ship "Importer," Captain George T. Avery, passing Rock Light, bound in. She registered 1,400 tons, was built at Newburyport, Mass., especially for the Calcutta trade, and made many profitable voyages, paying for herself in less than four years. She was in later years sold to the Germans, and, altered to a barque rig, sailed under the German flag.

Being up with Tuskar Light, the following afternoon, the weather looking very threatening, with a rapidly falling barometer, we bore up and ran into Waterford Harbor, coming to anchor between Passage and Ballyhack. Before midnight it was blowing a tremendous gale, and I congratulated myself that we were in a good, safe harbor, with our anchors down, for outside we would have been obliged to heave to, and would probably have drifted or have been driven out of the North Channel, as the gale lasted without any abatement for nearly a week, to say nothing of the dangers of collision. So many vessels congregated together in a very limited space were more to be feared in blowing, thick weather, than anything else in the St. George's or the English Channel.

Going on shore at Passage the next day, and climbing the hill that affords a fine view seaward, we could see, with the glass, numerous ships, barques, and brigs, all under a mere rag of canvas, and buffeting the big seas, evidently making hard weather of it. The sky overhead was bright and clear, but the force of the wind was terrific.

We also improved the opportunity of visiting Waterford, and landing at Ballyhack with our own boat, and taking the steamer for the city, we arrived inside an hour's time.

After a good dinner at the hotel, I engaged an Irish jaunting-car, in which to ride around to see the city generally. This was a novel experience to my wife as well as myself. The passengers sit back to back, with their legs hanging over the sides of the vehicle, and until you get accustomed to it, there is a feeling as if you were going to fall off over the wheels, especially when rounding a corner at a high rate of speed; every one holding on for dear life, for these Irish Jehus do not spare the horse, being bound to give you your money's worth. After a while the pace becomes exhilarating, and you do not mind his driving. We certainly thoroughly enjoyed it.

Waterford is a thriving Irish city, prettily laid out, with many fine public buildings and private residences, good roads, and a population of upwards of twenty thousand. The country around produces great quantities of butter and cheese, so that Waterford has a large export trade of dairy products.

311

Sunday morning at daylight, with beautiful weather and a fair wind, our anchor was hove up, all sail made, and bidding adieu to old Ireland, we passed out into St. George's Channel.

Fortune now seemed to favor us. The wind continued fresh and fair, sometimes increasing to double-reef gales, until we crossed the parallel of 30 north, and again greeted our old friends, the trade winds.

About this time, my wife expressed a wish to learn navigation. She had always taken the time from the chronometer for my morning sights, and was much interested in the day's work, and pricking off the barque's position on the chart daily. She had always kept her private journal, noting down each day's special events as they occurred, descriptions of all places visited, persons that she met and their characteristics. At the time of writing these pages, it would have been specially valuable as a book of reference, had it not been unfortunately mislaid or lost.

Taking hold of the study of navigation in good earnest, she became quite proficient. She could take a sight and work it out as well as myself, and find the position on the chart without assistance. All this kept her mind employed, and with sewing, embroidery, fancy-work, reading and music, her time was well taken up, and she had very few idle moments.

This was the most enjoyable period of my sea experience.

Again we had the glorious nights on deck, as the "Keystone "sailed silently on under the soft rays of a tropical moon. All my old musicians had reshipped, and again in the evenings the strains of music, with song, came to our ears from forward.

The work of the ship went daily on, without friction. Mr. Lovett, former second officer, proved himself as efficient a first officer as Mr. Nelson, my former mate.

Let me here say a word as to the advisability of a captain taking his wife to sea with him.

A captain's position on shipboard at sea is a peculiar one. He is something like the mainspring of a watch. If that is all right, the works will do their duty, and all is well, but let the mainspring break, or anything happen to it, and everything goes wrong, or stops. So the captain, as the mainspring, in order to keep perfect discipline, which is so essential , to a well-regulated ship, must first discipline himself. He is thrown on his own resources. All on board, except himself, have companions; the crew have each other to talk with and confide their feelings to; the cook and steward fraternize; the first and second officers can confer, or even talk amicably together, although in this case, the first officer, if he knows his business, will preserve the line between the dignity of his position and undue familiarity, that in some instances is apt to be taken advantage of by the second. The captain, if he has no companion, stands alone, isolated, in a certain measure, from all on board. The old saying, "Familiarity breeds contempt," was never more truly applied than to these conditions on shipboard, and the master, no matter how socially inclined, although he may converse with his first officer on all matters pertaining to the ship, and even unbend and talk about side affairs, yet he must never forget his dignity or the claims of his position in any way that might be misinterpreted or taken advantage of; not that all officers would preserve the stiffness of demeanor, but to avoid trouble or unpleasantness, it is always best to be on the safe side.

So, I believe, if the captain is married, and his wife is in good health, enjoys travel, and is not afraid of the water, it were better she should accompany her husband on his voyages as one to whom he can always turn for companionship and confidences at sea.

Woman's influence on shipboard, if she is a true, good woman, is felt for good throughout the ship. She has a refining influence, and the sailors guard their words and actions more in her presence, for no sailor, old or young, would pain her by thought or deed. How often have I seen Jack's face brighten up, when "the old woman" spoke a few pleasant, kindly words to him! No matter how young the captain and his wife may be, they are always to the sailors on shipboard "the old man" and "the old woman." It is a habit they have, with no desire to be flippant or disrespectful.

The remark that I have heard so often, that a ship is no place for a woman, seems to my mind misapplied; if she loves the sea, and can have comfortable accommodations, I can see no reason why she should not accompany her husband on his voyages, and there is certainly no place where more respect and courtesy will be shown her than on shipboard. This is my judgment, and I believe many others will testify to the same experience.

Through the southeast trade belt, we are now bowling along, with fresh gales and bright sunshine, making good time towards the meridian of the Cape of Good Hope. Shoals of porpoises are daily seen, frisking and gambolling in the waves, playing leap-frog with each other, tumbling around the barque's bows as she drives the white foam far on either side, and one of their number often falls a victim to Jack's love for porpoise steak, fried liver or forcemeat balls. The porpoise is fine eating, and a good cook can get up most savory dishes, for both the cabin and forecastle.

Our feathered friends, the Cape pigeons and stormy petrels, begin to make their appearance, and as we draw into a higher latitude, an occasional albatross is seen hovering around, sailing in graceful curves about our quarter, ready to pounce upon anything in the food line thrown overboard by the cook. It is most interesting to watch them.

The weather has changed to cooler. No more stargazing and lingering on deck of nights. Our music is the whistling of the wind through the shrouds and rigging, although from our cozy after cabin, if not too rough, are heard the notes of Mrs. Whidden's piano, as they float up the companionway to mingle with the gale.

So we sail, day after day, occasionally sighting a vessel which we have overhauled, or being passed by some ship or barque whose sailing qualities are superior to our own.

CHAPTER XXVIII
1869

CHITTAGONG AND AKYAB.—AGAIN THE BURNING GHAUTS.—INTENSE HEAT DAY AND NIGHT.—REDUCING TEMPERATURE.—FROM AKYAB TO FALMOUTH, ENGLAND

WE are past the Cape of Good Hope, and now for the long stretch of five thousand miles ere we shall turn to the north'ard, and again breathe a warmer atmosphere, under a summer sky. The "Keystone "is now running down her easting in the "roaring forties," with strong gales bowling her along, part of the time under lower topsails in the furious squalls, which are accompanied with snow or driving, cutting hail, that causes one to turn his back to them, when the rattle against his stiff oilskins and sou'wester sounds like a discharge of small shot against some metallic substance.

The squall over, upper topsails are again mastheaded, with men standing by the halliards, ready to let go and clew down on the next order.

A big sea rolls after, the sun breaks forth and lights up the surges as they roll past, and perhaps in ten minutes:

"Let go the topsail halliards! Clew down!" comes the order.

"Aye, aye, sir," and the yards rattle down, as another squall bursts upon us, with a sky as black as night.

Oh, this, indeed, is glorious sailing! It is so pleasant to find at noon that you have covered from six to eight degrees of easting, for in this latitude the miles to the degree of longitude are much shorter than at the equator, and it is most satisfactory to see the long line covered on the chart, and reckon, at that rate, how many more days or weeks ere you can bear away for a warmer clime and more genial temperature, and it comes at last. We are nearing the equator, and eighty-five days from the Sabbath morning we sailed from Waterford Harbor, the "Keystone" crosses the line in the Indian Ocean.

Up to this time our passage had been good, but now we encountered a succession of calms and light, baffling airs, that was exasperating, being the last of the northeast monsoon, and it was thirty-five days more, ere we let go our anchor at midnight off the mouth of the Cawnpore River, on which lies the port of Chittagong.

The land about the river's mouth is very low, so that nothing could be seen, although the night was clear. The water was very shoal: from six to eight fathoms. We had run through a number of fishing stakes, but had seen no boats, and judging ourselves about off the bar, let go our anchor to wait for daylight.

Jube and Pincher, our dogs, who had now grown to good size, scented the land, and were highly excited.

I was a stranger to the port, and knowing nothing of the pilot service here, I ordered a few rockets and blue lights brought up from below, thinking I might be able to attract a pilot on board.

An empty beef barrel, containing a couple of pails of water, having been brought on top of the cabin, a rocket was placed therein, so that when the fuse was ignited the train of sparks would go into the water. In the meantime the dogs were very inquisitive, following me around

317

and nosing everything I touched. Placing a rocket in the barrel, I ordered Mr. Lovett to hand me a lighted roll of paper from the binnacle. As I applied it to the fuse, both dogs, one on each side, placed their forepaws against the sides of the barrel, with their noses within six inches of the fuse and directly under it, evidently wondering in their minds, what on earth I was trying to do. In less than thirty seconds, the fuse ignited, and a stream of fire rained down on the noses of two of the most astonished dogs that were ever seen, while the rocket shot skyward.

A simultaneous howl, and Pincher made a dive from the forward part of the house to the main deck, while Jube went over the after part, and neither took any more interest in the display of fireworks.

Having expended a few rockets, and a couple of blue lights, we awaited results, and instituted a search for the dogs, which were nowhere to be seen. Finally, Pincher was discovered crouched in the eyes of the hawse-pipe under the to'gallant fo'c'sle, scared and trembling. He was pulled out by one of the men, but all search for Jube was fruitless, and I at last came to the conclusion that he had not stopped after passing the break of the house, but had kept right on over the taffrail, and had found his end in the maw of some shark.

The night being fine, I retired for a short time, and dropping into a slumber, I was awakened by a whisper from my wife, that she could hear some one breathing, and listening, I could hear a sort of muffled sound. Procuring a light, I discovered Jube squeezed under the couch as far as he could get, sound asleep. From the housetop he had gone down the companionway, and through my after cabin into the stateroom, where he lay while all the search was going on, finally falling asleep and betraying his presence by his snoring. Routing him out, I turned him on deck, but he avoided the housetop and crept off forward.

Early in the morning a native pilot boarded us, bringing off fruit, and a quantity of fresh beef, which was hung up to the mainstay for the cook's convenience. Jack, in his kindness of heart, cut off large quantities and fed to the dogs, and they eagerly devoured the unaccustomed food, which, combined with the heat and excitement, set them into convulsions, from which Jube died just as we were crossing the bar, while Pincher barely recovered. Poor Jube! He was truly mourned by all, fore and aft. He was my wife's favorite, and she missed him greatly. Pincher, his playmate, also seemed to mourn for him, and was so disconsolate, going around the ship, looking into every nook and corner, that I finally gave him to a young Englishman, a clerk in the counting-house of the consignee, who had taken quite a fancy to him. Knowing he would be well treated, I let him go.

Working up the river, the wind being ahead, the "Keystone" was anchored off the town, dressed in all her bunting, having the honor of carrying the American flag on a merchant ship up the Cawnpore River to Chittagong for the first time.

Several vessels of different nationalities lay at anchor; among them an English barque. The weather was intensely hot, and exposing the men to the midday sun was out of the question, consequently, all the ship's work was done in the early morning hours, or late in the afternoon; all work on the cargo, caulking barque's bends, and whatever else was necessary, being done by coolies.

The house of our consignee was large and roomy, built with regard to the climate. There were not many frame buildings, but there was a very pretty church, built in a grove, that we attended one Sabbath morning, and listened to a very interesting discourse by an English missionary. There are several English, French and German mercantile houses, and considerable trade is carried on with the Mauritius or Isle of France.

Very little shore visiting was indulged in while there, the heat was so intense. It was much more comfortable on shipboard, and we remained afloat under double awnings, with hammocks swung beneath. Meanwhile our salt cargo was discharged and ballast taken in.

A few days before sailing, a long river steamer, bound from Calcutta to Rangoon, put into the river in distress, having met with an accident. One of her passengers had about five hundred head of sheep on board, that he was taking to Rangoon on speculation, sheep commanding a high price at any of the rice ports.

As the steamer would be a long time there, and having no market, he came on board and asked me to buy them, finally offering them to me at a rupee and a half a head, throwing in the feed. At this price I could see no risk, and bought the lot, putting them between decks and penning them in. A rupee is silver coin, value fifty cents.

Sailing from Chittagong, we dropped anchor at Akyab the third day after, and a native trader coming on board, I closed a bargain for all the sheep at seven rupees a head, putting them ashore at once. At this rate the sheep were a pretty good investment.

Calling upon my consignees, I found our cargo was ready for shipment, and the hold was at once put in readiness for taking in the rice.

The land surrounding this port, lying on the east side of the Bay of Bengal, like all this part of the coast, is low, and the atmosphere was intensely hot, the northeast monsoon being about finished, while the southwest had not yet set in. We were, so to speak, "between hay and grass."

We lay in Akyab, taking in our rice cargo, and for four weeks the thermometer ranged from 125 to 130 in the shade. It was almost a dead heat, with very little breeze stirring, except for a short time night and morning.

The cholera was raging among the native population, and the burning ghauts, consuming the bodies but a short distance from and in plain sight of the barque, were in full blast. The smoke, when wafted towards us with the faint air in the right direction, was so offensive that we were twice obliged to change our berth, but with no shore leave the men all continued in good health.

Mr. Whiting, our ship-chandler, who had the entire trade of the port, or nearly so, had arrived recently from England accompanied by his wife, and succeeded to the business of his uncle. There were three English captains in port, two of them having their families with them, and Mr. and Mrs. Whiting invited them, with Mrs. Whidden and myself, to take dinner with them at their bungalow.

On the day named we went ashore, late in the afternoon, and rode to their house, some little distance out. It was built on piles, or posts, about four feet above the earth. This was necessary, as in the wet season poisonous snakes and other vermin creep into the houses, and could do so more readily if they were not raised from the ground.

We were received by our hostess, who took charge of my wife, the others not having arrived, while I remained on the broad veranda that encircled the bungalow, to enjoy a cigar. Here were hammocks and reclining chairs in profusion, with punkas (swinging fans hung from the ceiling) everywhere. The building was but one story in height, but covered a large amount of space. On one side doors opened into Mrs. Whiting's apartments, while on the opposite were a number of apartments with doors opening on to the veranda. Hanging around the house, and sitting about the grounds and veranda, was a numerous retinue of servants, so indispensable to an East Indian household.

The other guests having arrived, dinner was served at seven,—a typical East Indian spread, comprising soups and curries, roasts, salads and fruit, wines and coffee. The dinner was heartily enjoyed despite the heat, as the punkas were kept steadily going over the dining-tables and throughout the great room, keeping a current of air in circulation that abated the heat and made it very pleasant.

Just as we arose from table, a squall that had been gathering burst upon us, accompanied by the most vivid lightning, with deafening peals of thunder. Taking the ladies to her rooms, our hostess called to her husband that she would show them her pretty things, while he, with his guests, smoked on the veranda.

Sitting on the lee side, we smoked and chatted, waiting for the squall to pass over, but instead of that, it settled into a fresh gale, necessitating our remaining on shore overnight.

Arrangements were soon made for the ladies to occupy the apartments of our hostess with her, while all the gentlemen remained by themselves in the rooms opening on the veranda.

Retiring between ten and eleven o'clock, we passed a rather restless night, for the native servants were constantly moving stealthily about the veranda, and arose early. The weather had cleared, and being a little cooler after the storm, was more endurable. We partook with Mr. Whiting of "chota-hazree" (little breakfast) and drove in town, leaving the ladies, who were not yet visible, to follow and meet us at the "godowns" or stores.

Shortly after, Mrs. Whidden having arrived with the ladies, we went on board the barque at once, before the sun got high. When we were alone she told me she had passed a sleepless night, for great lizards were crawling over the walls. Mrs. Whiting had told her that the lizards were harmless, that snakes were most to be feared, and some of the most venomous she had preserved in a jar, which she had exhibited and said they were captured in her own room during the wet season. It was always necessary, she said, to give your boots or shoes a shake before putting them on in the morning, for they would be likely to contain a centipede or scorpion.

"I never was so glad to see morning," my wife said, as she closed the review of the night; "I would not live there for a million a year!"

A cyclone of the previous year having ruined every piano in Akyab, Mr. Whiting was anxious to buy mine for his wife, and offered me three times the amount paid for it in Bordeaux, over two years before, and my wife saying that, as we were bound home, it did not matter, I reluctantly parted with it.

A few days more and our last bag of rice or "paddy" (rice with the husk on is called "paddy") was taken in, all business was closed, and we were to sail in the morning, only too anxious to get to sea.

Sleeping at night, owing to the intense heat, had for awhile been almost impossible, but I at last hit on a plan that lowered my temperature.

I had a bucket of salt water placed on each side of my hammock, and immersing my lower extremities nearly to the knee, one in each bucket, I lay back and slept like an infant.

All being in readiness, we awaited Mr. Locke, the pilot, and about six A. M. we saw his boat coming off. As soon as he came on deck, before he had time to tell us, I was sure by his appearance that he was the bearer of bad news.

Our hostess, Mrs. Whiting, had been taken with cholera the past night, had died before twelve o'clock, and was already buried. It was a terrible shock, and I was only too thankful we were outward bound.

324

Getting under way with a light breeze, we passed out to sea, and discharging our pilot, with a message of sympathy for Mr. Whiting, the "Keystone" was pointed down the bay.

CHAPTER XXIX
1869-1870

THE ISLE OF ST. HELENA.—LONGWOOD AND THE TOMB OF NAPOLEON.— FALMOUTH, ENGLAND.—ANTWERP, BELGIUM

As we drew off from the land, the breeze became a little fresher, and being well to the westward, we were enabled to lay our course clear of the Andaman and Nicobar Island, and passing Ceylon were soon in the belt of the S. E. trades, and with every inch of canvas spread, were rapidly speeding across the Indian Ocean, homeward bound.

Once again our delightful trades bear us towards the Cape of Good Hope, and as we inhale the draughts of pure air, our thoughts go back to Akyab with its broiling heat and pestilence-laden atmosphere, and I wonder how anybody escaped being stricken down. I am satisfied that only the great care exercised with the men in port kept them in good health.

Day after day the same steady breeze, sometimes varying a little in strength, but no calms or light airs to vex one. Jack, as usual, is well stocked up with pets, mostly from Chittagong, consisting of several fine monkeys and lots of the feathered tribe.

Mrs. Whidden had been presented by our stevedore with a large white cockatoo, having a bright yellow tuft or crest, which lay down along its neck from the crown of its head; a handsome bird, but wild. On the approach of any one it would ruffle up, and throw this crest forward, assuming an angry appearance, opening its beak, which was hawked and a most formidable weapon. The taming of the bird seemed to be an impossibility. He could not bear confinement, and would tear his bamboo cage to pieces when angry, but would sit all day on a line stretched across the deck just forward of the cabin, confining himself at first to those limits.

My wife, after many attempts to make friends with him, all to no purpose, finally gave him up as a most unsocial bird.

One morning, during the forenoon watch, Snip, as he was called, took a notion to go aloft. This he had never attempted before. Edging along until he reached the royal backstay, he grasped it and mounted aloft with all the ease in the world, and stepping from the backstay to the royal yard, sat there the picture of contentment. He had been aloft an hour or so, when Mr. Nicholas Petite, the second mate, coming on deck, spied him, and seeing me coming from the cabin, he stepped forward, saying:

"Mrs. Whidden's bird has gone on the royal yard, sir."

"Yes, I know it," I replied; "when he gets ready he'll come down."

"Sha'n't I go up and bring him down, sir?" he asked.

"Oh, no, it's not necessary, and more than likely he'd bite you if you touched him."

"Oh, no, sir," he said, "he would not bite me! Don't you think, sir, I'd better go? He may get overboard."

Seeing he was very anxious to go, I said, "All right, go if you wish to, but take good care you don't touch him with your bare hand," and after seeing Mr. Petite start aloft with a short stick in his hand for Snip to step on, I turned and went below, and was just on the point of coming up again, when I heard a great squawking, and emerged from the companionway just in time to see Mr. Petite jump from the rail and slap Snip angrily to the deck, his hand covered with blood, which was running freely.

"What's the matter, Mr. Petite, has he bitten you?" I inquired.

"It's nothing, sir," he replied with a sickly smile.

"Come here, sir, and let me look at it," I insisted, and finding it was a serious and most vicious bite through the fleshy part of the hand, between the thumb and forefinger, I dressed it with Fryer's Balsam and arnica, and bound it up, Mr. Petite all the time protesting that it was nothing, but the mate, Mr. Lovett, told me afterwards, that when I went below for the balsam, Mr. Petite walked up to Snip and, shaking his fist at him, hissed something uncomplimentary between his teeth.

It seems, that after getting to the royal yard, he held out his stick, which Snip alighted on, and Mr. Petite started to descend. In getting over the futtock-shrouds of the main top the stick came in contact with the craneline, and grabbing it, Snip started again for the backstay to go aloft, when, Mr. Petite being fearful he was going to lose him, forgot himself, and made a grab at him with his bare hand, with the result described.

Snip went aloft many times after that, but Mr. Petite was never anxious to go up and bring him down.

We sailed past Madagascar, and nearing the Cape, the trades were gone, but the wind held steady in the eastern quarter, and we were in hopes it would carry us round.

One morning the cry of "Land, ho!" came from aloft, and the high land between Cape Elizabeth and Cape Agulhas was dimly seen, and still farther on Cape Agulhas, the extreme tip of the great African continent came into view. Keeping the land well aboard, to take advantage of the current, which inshore sets past the Cape strong to the westward, we held our way, but later our wind died out, followed by a calm of short duration, when breezing up from west-nor'west and increasing, sail was reduced until midnight found the "Keystone "under lower topsails, heading to the south'ard with a stiff gale blowing and a high sea. We did not complain, however, for it had been fine so long, with smooth sailing, that this rather broke up the monotony, and shook everything up a little.

The following day, the wind hauling to S. S. W. gave us a slant of which we were not long in taking advantage, and in twenty-four hours more the Cape of Good Hope was astern, and we were in the south Atlantic again, heading for St. Helena with a rattling breeze, the "Keystone" shortening the distance rapidly. I intended to stop there and fill water, as our stock was getting low, having had no rain since leaving Akyab.

Ten days after passing the Cape, with the break of day "Land, ho!" again sounded through the ship, and the famous island of St. Helena was before us, rising from the waves like a great rock, which it is, nothing more nor less.

Getting anchors ready and chains on deck, we skirted the shore until, rounding the point, we came in full view of Jamestown Harbor or Roads, and running close in, we let go our anchor in twelve fathoms.

A number of foreign vessels lay at anchor, among them an English man-o'-war. Ordering the water-boat alongside, and instructing Mr. Lovett that we would leave that night, I went on shore with my wife, to pay our respects to our consul, and visit Longwood and Napoleon's tomb.

We had a pleasant call on our country's representative, and then took a carriage and drove—over a good road all the way, with a fine outlook—to the home, or prison, of the great general.

On arrival, we were given permission to look over the building and grounds, an old French soldier pointing out and explaining everything to us.

Since England handed Longwood over to the care of the French government, everything is kept with the utmost neatness, and as near the conditions that existed at the time Napoleon occupied it as possible. Previous to that we were told it had been very much neglected, but be that as it may, it was then in the most perfect condition.

His favorite walk and garden, and, in short, everything pertaining to the great soldier, came under our inspection. Every attention and courtesy was shown us, and on leaving, we found, to our surprise, that a gratuity or "tip," for services, was declined with thanks. The same custom prevailed at the tomb, which we visited after taking leave of Longwood. There, in a dell, enclosed within an iron railing, with weeping-willows bending over it, is still preserved the tomb where for years rested the remains of the world's greatest general; now reposing beneath the gilded dome of the Invalides, according to the wish expressed in his will dictated on this island: "I desire that my ashes may repose on the banks of the Seine, among that French people I so dearly loved."

We stood there, in silence, beneath the willows that grew above his untenanted grave, the setting sun tingeing the clouds with the glory of the departing day,—the one hundredth anniversary of his birth, August 15, 1869,—and as the shadows deepened, our consciousness of the present was lost in thought which harmonized with the poet's lines:

"Oh! Shade of the Mighty! Where now are thy legions?
     That rushed but to conquer, when thou led'st them on.
Alas! They have fallen, in far distant regions,
     And all but the name of their conquests are gone.
The lightnings may flash, and the loud cannon rattle,
     They stir not! They heed not! They're free from all pain!
They sleep their last sleep, they have fought their last battle,
     No sound can awake them to glory again."

Bidding good-by, and shaking the hand of the old soldier on guard, we entered our carriage, and were driven rapidly to Jamestown, where we found our boat awaiting us. Embarking, we were pulled on board, when, all being in readiness, the anchor was tripped, sail made, and we were speedily again on our way from St. Helena, having made a most pleasant break in our homeward voyage.

331

Before leaving the barque the day we went to Longwood, I had told a darkey boy to procure three or four cats and take them on board, and the mate, who had my instructions regarding the business, would give him half a crown apiece. There were a great many rats on board, and in case of damage to the rice cargo, I believed that the fact of my having cats on board, would clear the insurance all right.

Mr. Lovett now informed me that the boy had brought on board three cats, two wild, and one tame, and they had all taken refuge in the hold. That they were playing havoc with the rats we knew by the noise at night,—the squealing of the rodents and the scampering through the lazarette, distinctly heard in the after cabin, in the still watches of the night. After awhile the tame one formed the habit of coming into the cabin, being encouraged by the steward, who, secretly, as he knew I did not want him there, would take him into the pantry and feed him.

One night, some ten days after leaving St. Helena, he roused the sleepers in the after cabin by a wild, weird, discordant yell, and the steward's pet was found perched upon a trunk with his back arched at something—we did not stop to find out what, but took measures to effectually silence his music.

Past Ascension Island, our trades carried us across the line, when light, variable winds, with rain squalls, succeeded, and for nearly a week our progress was slow, but once through this belt of calms, we caught the N. E. trades in a squall, and from that time forward we made fair time north, the wind not being overstrong at any time.

Almost daily now we passed through great beds of gulfweed, sometimes extending for miles, and very thick. Mrs. Whidden amused herself by fishing up large quantities and shaking it over a tub of water.

Fishes—some of them an inch long—and crustacea (shell-fish) of every shape and kind were found, many so singular that we tried to preserve them, but having no alcohol, were unable to do so.

So far, we had seen but few sails, speaking none, although we had exchanged signals with two off the Cape. The "Keystone" now underwent the usual routine work of tarring, scraping and painting, preparatory to entering port after a long voyage, until the barque fairly shone. All hands, fore and aft, were now looking anxiously forward to the termination of the voyage, and each Sunday Jack could be seen overhauling his wardrobe, brushing and mending it, and examining the treasures he had laid in abroad for presents to his friends, and I am afraid many who were not friends, although he thought they were,—but this did not detract from his kindness of heart.

"Light, ho! Two points on the port bow, sir," came from the topsail yard in cheery tones, about six bells in the first watch, and in a short time, the Scilly Lights could be plainly seen from the deck. The night was fine and clear, and passing the Scillys, towards morning we made the Lizard, rounding which, and taking on board a pilot, the barque dropped anchor in Falmouth Harbor—once more in the waters of old England.

On shore I found orders awaiting me to proceed to Antwerp. Making inquiries as to a pilot, I was told I would get one off the Foreland, or

Ostend, and leaving Falmouth about dusk, the wind blowing a brisk gale, we fairly flew up the Channel, passing the Isle of Wight, and were under the forelands before daylight. It was still blowing very strong, and seeing nothing in the shape of a pilot, we kept her travelling across the North Sea, making sure of picking one up off Ostend. But no such luck. No boats were out. As we drew in with the mouth of the River Scheldt, there was no sign of any pilot. The sand-bars, which extend out a long distance, are well buoyed out and show the channels and fairway, and as long as daylight lasts and one can see, it is comparatively easy to avoid danger. In a dark night and blowing a gale, it becomes a ticklish spot without a pilot, but there was no help for it now. We kept her going until darkness made it impossible to see the buoys, and the water being quite shoal, we clewed up everything and rounded to, letting go the anchor, which held all right, for it was evidently good holding ground.

I sent up a rocket and burned a couple of blue lights in hopes of attracting the notice of a pilot.

I was hailed by a passing steamer, bound in, to know if I wanted anything.

"Yes," I replied, "a pilot."

"All right! I'll report you and send one out!"

In the meantime the night wore on, daylight appeared, and still no pilot. Getting under way we ran into the mouth of the river, where a river pilot boarded us. He asked for the pilot who took us in, and being told we came in without one, he expressed surprise, saying that it had been blowing so hard for a few days that no one had gone out, not expecting any vessel would run in until it moderated.

On our arrival at the city, we hauled into our berth for discharging, and took up our quarters at a hotel, for the barque had changed hands during my absence, and I now only awaited the discharging of our rice to turn her over, and after a short period of sightseeing, take the steamer for New York. I had now been absent thirty-four months— nearly three years—and I had about decided to give up the sea as a profession. Since the close of the war, the carrying trade had gone from bad to worse, and there was no money in it.

CHAPTER XXX
1870

THE DECADENCE OF THE SAILING SHIPS.—THE WAR TARIFF.—AMERICAN SHIPPING UNDER FOREIGN FLAGS.—THE AMERICAN MARINE THE SCHOOL OF RESERVE FOR THE NAVY.—FAREWELL TO THE "KEYSTONE" AT ANTWERP

IT cost so much to sail an American ship, that it was simply impossible to compete with foreign shipping in the freighting business. An English, German, or French ship could charter and make money at rates that would run an American in debt. Why should that be so? The reason is obvious. From 1850 to 1860, the United States had as fine a merchant marine as ever floated. The discovery of gold in California, and the consequent rush to that country, called for forwarding facilities, for provisions, and merchandise of every description, to be delivered in the shortest possible time, and without so much regard to rate of freight. There was then no Panama Railroad, or Union Pacific Railroad built, and transportation by wagons or mules across the plains of immense quantities of merchandise, was too slow, expensive, and hazardous. There was no route but those via Cape Horn or Straits of Magellan. The old-style sailing ships, big carriers, with their bluff bows and square sterns, were altogether too slow.

The emergency called for a class of ships whose carrying capacity was sacrificed to speed, the high rates of freight more than compensating for loss of cargo. As a result, the most magnificent class of clippers that ever swam the ocean were called into existence, challenging the admiration of the maritime world.

From '49 to '60, just before the outbreak of the Civil War, these beautiful vessels were turned out from our numerous shipyards, each increasing in tonnage and speed, and built on the most graceful lines. They resembled yachts rather than freighters, and sat the waters "a thing of beauty."

With fanciful names, they formed a class by themselves, their speed in transit being attested by such of their number as the "Flying Cloud," "Lightning," "Surprise," "Dreadnaught," "Eagle Wing," "Gray Eagle," "Trade Wind," and scores of others equally famous, which could truly be designated as "ocean flyers."

The routes of these ships were generally from an Atlantic port to San Francisco, thence to China or India in ballast, and either loading teas for homeward trip to the United States or England, or perhaps taking a freight in Calcutta for New York or Boston, or coolies from Macao to Havana, the latter a very lucrative trade, and one in which these clippers were much in demand. During this time, freighting was good, and shipping paid handsomely.

Then came the building of the Panama Railroad, and the Union Pacific Railroad, and the day of the clipper in the California trade, with its high rates of freight, was virtually over. Still, in foreign ports, with a freight in the market, in competition with shipping of other nations, such was their prestige, they always obtained the preference.

Then came the outbreak of our Civil War and as a war measure our tariff was increased on everything pertaining to shipping as well as everything else, which was a deathblow for the time to American ships,

337

the tariff being prohibitory to competition with foreign shipping. Not having a force to protect our merchant marine, the greater part were placed under a foreign flag, mostly English, for protection. Those that remained and still swung "Old Glory" from their peaks, became a prey to Southern privateers—the "Alabama," "Shenandoah," and others, while those that escaped capture were relegated to distant ports to pick up a precarious livelihood until the war was over.

With the close of the war our shipping was reduced to a minimum. Every ship that was placed under the English flag for protection "still remained an Englishman," as they could not again sail the seas under the folds of the "Star Spangled Banner." When they changed their flag, they changed for good.

With the ending of the war all hoped that the tariff, especially on shipping, would be reduced, to enable our shipyards to again resume building, and enter into competition for the world's carrying trade, where we had lost prestige, but it was not to be. The tariff was still kept on, the same as during the war, and no one, under these conditions, was insane enough to build. The carrying trade of the world that should have been in American bottoms was allowed to slip from us, and with it one of our finest New England industries—shipbuilding.

Not only this, but the nation suffered the loss of the nurseries and schools for American seamen, brought to perfection in our merchant marine, which stood ready as a reserve to be drawn upon in time of war, to man our war-ships and uphold the honor of the American flag.

Shipbuilding having ceased, men and boys no longer looked to the sea as a calling. With the decadence of the sailing ship the romance of the sea had departed; to the young there was no longer any incentive to become a sailor and their minds were diverted to other channels. American captains who still followed their profession hung on at reduced pay, or went to England, passed the examining board, and obtained command of English ships, sailing them for years. All these considerations combined caused me to make up my mind that I would give up the sea and go into business on shore.

Through the courtesy of Mr. Hambro, of Hambro Bros., bankers, who came over from London to attend to our rice cargo, we were enabled to visit many private galleries of paintings which otherwise would have been closed to us.

Stoddard, in his charming work, says of the fine old city of Antwerp or Anvers:

"Its name is said to be derived from the Flemish words meaning 'on the wharf,' and that indeed is the place where Antwerp's prosperity can be best estimated; it is a place of wonderful activity, and there its splendid quays, built by Napoleon when Antwerp formed a part of his colossal empire, are crowded now with ships and steamers. Yet, busy as it is to-day, it gives us but a hint of what its commerce was three hundred years ago. Then thousands of vessels floated in the river and more than five hundred were arriving and departing every day. Merchants came hither from all parts of Europe, and in addition to her own commercial houses, more than a thousand foreign firms contended here in friendly rivalry. Antwerp, however, has had much to contend with since that time. Again and again this region has been the cockpit of Europe, and for years, Antwerp's wealth and prosperity declined, but now she is rapidly recovering from her disasters."

A few days spent in Brussels, visiting objects of interest, completed our stay on the continent, when returning to the "Keystone," our cargo being out, I closed all business matters, turned over the command to Captain Berry, and taking the steamer for London, bade Antwerp a long farewell.

A night's run brought us to the pier just below London Bridge. We remained in London a few weeks, visiting our old friends and the many places we had not seen, among them the Tower, Hampton, Windsor, Chelsea and Kew Gardens, Virginia Water, Eton College, Epping Forest and Greenwich.

We went by train to Liverpool, having secured passage on the Cunarder "Palmyra," Captain Watson, remaining there a couple of days, picking up what few things we wanted for the trip home, and on a raw, chilly morning, took our departure from the Prince's Landing Stage for the "Palmyra," lying at anchor in the Mersey.

"All aboard!" The anchor was weighed, and the steamer was pointed down river. The saloon passenger list was very small, not exceeding fifteen, with about one hundred and fifty in the steerage.

Although the passage to Boston was exceedingly rough, the steamer encountering very heavy westerly and nor'westerly gales, with violent snow and hail squalls and high seas, yet no accident occurred, and the passengers, both in saloon and steerage were comparatively comfortable. It was too rough for pleasure on deck and amusements for the steerage were being constantly improvised. A mock trial held the boards every evening for over half the passage, and was participated in by the passengers and members of the ship's company; stewards, sailors, petty officers, representing plaintiff and defendant, lawyers, judge, jury and witnesses, crier, constables or police, and court officers generally.

The case was a very difficult one to decide. The arguments on both sides were spicy and witty, showing a good knowledge of legal acumen, and it became such a feature, and so interesting that nightly the male portion of the saloon passengers would steal forward into the steerage to listen to the debates. It finally ended in a verdict for the female defendant, to everybody's satisfaction.

Fifteen days from the Mersey, the "Palmyra" passed Boston Light, steamed up the harbor, and docked at her pier at East Boston, our long passage ended, and with it my quarter-century's sea experience, from a boy in a ship's forecastle to the quarter-deck as captain and part owner.

FINIS.

Made in the USA
Charleston, SC
20 October 2016